THE WESLEY LIBRARY

The Nature of the Kingdom

Wesley's Messages on the Sermon on the Mount
Edited and Updated by Clare George Weakley, Jr.

JOHN WESLEY

BETHANY HOUSE PUBLISHERS
MINNEAPOLIS, MINNESOTA 55438
A Division of Bethany Fellowship, Inc.

Formerly entitled *Happiness Unlimited* by Logos International

All Scripture references, unless otherwise noted, are taken from the King James Version.

Copyright © 1979
Clare Weakley, Jr.
All Rights Reserved

Published by Bethany House Publishers
A Division of Bethany Fellowship, Inc.
6820 Auto Club Road, Minneapolis, MN 55438

Printed in the United States of America

Library of Congress Cataloging in Publication Data

Weakley, Clare G.
    The nature of the Kingdom.

    A paraphrase of 13 selections from: Sermons on several
occasions / John Wesley.
    Previously published under title: Happiness unlimited. This
ed. slightly abridged.
    Includes bibliographical references.
    1. Sermon on the mount—Early works to 1800.
I. Wesley, John, 1703-1791. Sermons on several occasions.
Selections. II. Title.
BT380.W35   1986   226'.906   85-28622
ISBN 0-87123-875-6

---

*This book is gratefully dedicated to
Jean:
wife, friend, companion, sister in the Lord,
as well as editor and typist!*

JOHN WESLEY (1703–1791) was the founder of Methodism. Although raised in a godly home and trained for the ministry at Oxford, Wesley's failure as a missionary to the colonists and Indians in Georgia (1735–1738) revealed his unsaved condition. Strongly influenced upon his return to England by the Moravian Peter Boehler, Wesley was converted (May 1738) to genuine faith in Christ while reading Luther's preface to Romans.

Shortly after his conversion, Wesley visited the Moravian settlement at Herrnhut and met Count Zinzendorf. He returned to England and embarked on his lifework. His objective was "to reform the nation, particularly the Church, and to spread Scriptural holiness over the land." He declared that he had only "one point of view—to promote so far as I am able vital, practical religion; and by the grace of God to beget, preserve, and increase the life of God in the souls of men." Some have viewed him as the eighteenth-century apostle commissioned to evangelize Great Britain.

Wesley discovered the most effective medium for reaching the masses was open-air preaching and his life became one of an itinerant preacher. Facing the Church's resistance to his evangelical doctrine, Wesley formed societies in the wake of his mission. The organization of Methodism was thus a direct outcome of his success in preaching the gospel. Wesley's writings include his now classic *Journals*, sermons, letters, expositions, tracts, histories, and abridgments.

CLARE WEAKLEY, JR. is a businessman, lecturer, and chaplain-at-large in his community. He received a B.A. from Southern Methodist University, and an M.A. from Perkins Seminary. He is married and he and his family make their home in Dallas.

CONTENTS

Introduction

Three small chapters, five, six and seven, of the Gospel of Matthew are commonly known as the Sermon on the Mount. There is little question about this sermon being one of the most important and significant parts of the New Testament. Its impact changed the moral direction of the history of the world.

Christians and non-Christians alike recognize the importance of these teachings of Jesus. They speak to the heart of all men as truth, and provide an example for all men to follow for a perfect life. This small collection of teachings supplies the truth about the relationships between God and man, and man to man. Those who take them seriously will find that their lives are changed. They will come to know themselves, meet God, and enter into the kingdom of heaven while still on earth.

John Wesley, the eighteenth-century apostle to the English-speaking world, took the sermon very seriously. Thirty percent of his doctrinal sermons, thirteen of forty-four, are on the Sermon on the Mount. Wesley began to work on his commentary sermons, which explain the Sermon on the Mount, in 1735. By 1750 he had written and published all thirteen. In those fifteen years, he was born again, and began the field preaching which offered the rebirth with the Holy Spirit to thousands of unconverted English laborers. These thirteen discourses on the sermon were tested in that difficult situation. Their validity and effectiveness are attested to by the results of Wesley's ministry. At the same time that Wesley's results affirm the Sermon on the Mount, they affirm the One who preached it. Jesus, the Nazarene, has been understood in many different ways, by many different people, over the years. He has been called myth, fraud, blasphemer, revolutionary, teacher, master, Lord, Son of God, and God. No matter what He is called, or how He is understood, the Sermon on the Mount gives proof of His unique knowledge of both God and man. Even His greatest doubters must admit to the genius of the sermon. It is undeniable that Jesus knew more about God than anyone, either before or since His time. The evidence of this is plain. No man before Jesus ever explained the God-man relationship in such simple, clear, and complete terms. No man who has followed Jesus has been able to improve upon His understandings of this God-man relationship. None have been able to show a better or more complete understanding of the nature of the brotherhood of man which comes out of the sermon, though many have tried.

Because the results of Jesus' teaching give their own evidence about His nature, there is no need to make a statement here in regard to it. This book is not intended to be either a christological statement or a Christian apology. It is simply to present Wesley's commentary on the Sermon on the Mount. In order to do this most effectively, two chapters are utilized to lead into the thirteen discourses. Chapters one and two, from Wesley's "Standard Sermons," present Wesley's understandings of man and faith in a sort of summary fashion. Thus, I utilize them as a portal which leads into the thirteen discourses.

The fifteen chapters of this book are sermons from Wesley's "Standard Sermons." This means that they are recognized doctrines for all who call themselves "Wesleyan Christians." This is especially true for members of any Methodist church. Every Christian who affirms a denominational affiliation to any Methodist or Wesleyan denomination should approach these sermons, these chapters in this book, with vigor and renewed interest. This is a great part of what those churches say they believe.

Finally, it is necessary to restate the principles and the rationale of this "modern language translation" of Wesley's works.

According to Wesley's published introduction to his "Sermons on Several Occasions," he attempted to speak in the language of the common man. He claimed to both write and speak, *ad populum*, "to the bulk of mankind, to those who neither relish nor understand the art of speaking; but who, notwithstanding, are competent judges of those truths which are necessary to present and future happiness. I mention this, that curious readers may spare themselves the labor of seeking for what they will not find."

While Wesley wished to present "plain truth to plain people," his plain truths were lost to the average man over the years. This loss occurred as a result of changes in the English language. Wesley's style and vocabulary simply became out of date and unreadable to the average person. Consequently Wesley's writings were read by fewer and fewer people. When this happened, Wesley's works became almost the exclusive property of scholars and theologians. While he is still one of the most often quoted theologians in the Protestant church, he is rarely read by the laity of that church.

This problem can now be solved. In recent years, new modern language translations of the Bible have appeared. Public acceptance of these translations has been overwhelming. The result is that the Bible has been opened to many who could not or would not read the King James Version.

Public acceptance of this technique of translation of the Bible has made it possible to translate Wesley's works in the same manner. Thus, he can again speak *ad populum*. Now every person who is seeking a fresh understanding of the living Christian faith may read Wesley's works. It is no longer necessary to be satisfied with secondhand statements about him and his "new living faith."

It should be emphasized that Wesley's writings are only presented here as a means to a better end. There is no intention of simply presenting what he wrote as some type of academic exercise. The purpose is to use his writings to lead the reader into a fresher, deeper, clearer, and more meaningful relationship with the One who preached the Sermon on the Mount. Jesus came to give us life, and give it more abundantly. The purpose of His sermon was to lead us as children of God into this abundant life. Unless this great treasure is gained and magnified through the use of this book, reading it has been in vain.

1

Who Are You?[1]

There are three basic types of people in the world. Each one of us is one of the three. The first type is one in a state of mind without fear of God or love of others. In the Scripture this is termed "a natural man." Next is one who is under the spirit of bondage and fear. This state is sometimes called "being under the law." In religious history, it frequently signified one who was under the Jewish dispensation. It was one who thought himself obliged to observe all of the rites and ceremonies of the Jewish law in order to please God. In our times, all who attempt to please God by their good works or right actions are under a law of their own. The last is the one who has exchanged the spirit of fear for the Spirit of love. That person is properly said to be under grace.

The Apostle Paul spoke of this in his letter to the Romans, when he said, "Ye have not received the spirit of bondage again to fear; but ye have received the Spirit of adoption, whereby we cry, Abba, Father."[2]

Paul here speaks to those who are the children of God by faith. Those who are indeed God's children have received God's Spirit. "You have not received the spirit of bondage again to fear." Now he says, "Because you are sons of God, God has sent forth this Spirit of his Son into your hearts." The result of this is, "You have received the Spirit of adoption whereby you can cry, 'Abba, Father.'"

The spirit of bondage and fear is contrary to this loving Spirit of adoption. Those who are influenced only by slavish fear cannot be called "sons of God." Some of them may be called God's servants, and they are not far from the kingdom of heaven.

But it is feared that most of mankind, even that which is called the Christian world, have not attained even this. Most are still far off and God is not in their thoughts. A few can be found who love God. There are a few more who fear him. But the greater part of mankind have neither the fear of God before their eyes nor the love of Him in their hearts.

Perhaps some of you, by the mercy of God, now have a better spirit. You may remember the time when you were just as they are. You were under the same condemnation. At first you did not know it. You were wallowing daily in your sins and separation. Then in due time, you received the spirit of fear. You received, for this fear is also the gift of God. Afterwards, that fear vanished away. The Spirit of love filled your heart.

It is very important for us to know what spirit we have in us. Because of this, we shall attempt to clearly define each state.

First is the state of natural man. The Scripture represents this state as one of sleep. God cries out to that person, "Awake."[3] The soul of this person is in a deep sleep. His spiritual senses are not awake. They cannot discern either good or evil. The eyes of his understanding are closed. They are sealed together and cannot see.

Clouds and darkness continually rest upon him. He lies in
the valley of the shadow of death. He has no inlets for the
knowledge of spiritual things. All the avenues of his soul
are shut up. He is ignorant of all that he needs most to
know. He is utterly ignorant of God. He knows nothing
concerning God and cares to know nothing. He is totally a
stranger to the law of God. The law's true, inward,
spiritual meaning is lost to him. He has no concept of that
evangelical holiness which leads one to the Lord. He is
missing that happiness which is found only through a life
which is hid with Christ in God.[4]

For this very reason, because he is fast asleep, he is in
some sense, at rest. Because he is blind, he is also secure.
He says, "There shall no harm happen to me." The
darkness which covers him on every side keeps him in a
kind of peace. This is only a kind of peace which comes
from the work of the devil, and from an earthly, devilish
mind. He does not see that he stands on the edge of
disaster. Therefore, He cannot fear the disaster. He
cannot tremble at the danger he does not know. He does
not have enough understanding to fear. Why is it that he
has no concept of God? It is because he is totally ignorant
of Him.

Natural man can be either atheistic, agnostic or deistic.
If he is atheistic, he says, "There is no God." If he is
agnostic, he says, "It is impossible to know anything
about God." If he is deistic, he says, "God sits outside of
those things which are done on earth." The deist will
satisfy himself as well by saying, "God is merciful." In this
one idea of mercy he confounds and ignores all of God's
essential hatred of sin. By stressing God's holiness alone,
he ignores God's justice, wisdom and truth. Natural man
has no dread of the retribution that will come on all of
those who do not obey God's law. He lacks this dread
because he does not understand the law. He imagines that

the main point of the law is to do it, in order to be outwardly blameless. He does not see that it extends to every temper, desire, thought, and emotion of the heart. Often he imagines that his obligation to the law has ended. He will say that Christ came to destroy the law and the prophets. Thus he believes that Jesus came to save people in their sins, but not from their sins. He preaches that God will give heaven without holiness. He ignores Jesus' own words, "One jot or one tittle shall in no wise pass from the law, till all be fulfilled."⁵ He would like to forget that Jesus also said, "Not every one that saith unto me, Lord, Lord, shall enter into the kingdom of heaven; but he that doeth the will of my Father which is in heaven."⁶

He is secure because he is utterly ignorant of himself. Therefore, he talks of repenting in the future. He does not indeed know exactly when. He believes that he shall repent some time or other before he dies. He takes it for granted that this is quite within his own power. What should hinder his doing it, if he wills it? If he does but once set a resolution, he has no fear of making it good!

But this ignorance never so strongly shows as it does in those who are called men of learning. If a natural man be one of these, he can talk grandly of his rational faculties. He speaks extensively of his freedom of will. He argues for the absolute necessity of such freedom, in order to constitute man a moral agent. He reads, and argues, and proves, through a demonstration, that every man may do as he chooses. He claims that any may dispose his own heart, either to evil or good, as it seems best in his own eyes. Thus, Satan spreads a double veil of blindness over his heart. He does this to prevent, by any means, the entrance of the light of the glorious gospel of Christ to shine upon it.

From the same ignorance of himself in God, there may

sometimes arise in the natural man a kind of joy. He experiences a kind of joy in congratulating himself upon his own wisdom and goodness. He may often possess this worldly type of joy. He may have pleasure of various kinds. He may receive pleasure in gratifying the desires of the flesh, or the desire of the eye, or the pride of life. Particularly if he has many possessions and enjoys affluence, he may then have pleasure in clothing and eating well every day. And so long as he does this well, the world will doubtless speak good of him. Men will say, "He is a happy man." Indeed, this is the sum of worldly happiness. Worldly happiness is to dress, and visit, and talk, and eat, and drink, and rise up to play.

It is not surprising if one in such circumstances as these, dosed with the drugs of flattery and sin, should imagine that he walks in great liberty. In this dream, he may easily persuade himself that he is at liberty from all common errors. He believes himself to be free from prejudices, always judging exactly right and keeping clear of all extremes. He may say, "I am free from all the religious extremes of weak and narrow souls. I am void of superstition, the disease of fools and cowards who are always too righteous. I am free from that bigotry which continually follows those who do not have a free and generous way of thinking." And too sure it is, that he is altogether free from the wisdom which comes from God. Natural man is free from holiness, from the religion of the heart, and from the whole mind which was in Christ.

All of this time, he is the servant of sin. He commits sin, more or less, day by day. Yet he is not troubled in his condition. He is in no bondage, as some speak. He feels no condemnation. He contents himself with the idea, "Man is frail. We are all weak. Every man has his infirmity."

Sometimes he misquotes Scripture. He might say,

"Why does Solomon say the righteous man falls into sin seven times a day?"[7] He charges, "Doubtless they are all hypocrites or fanatics who pretend to be better than their neighbors." If at any time a serious thought fixes in his mind, he stifles it as soon as possible. He says to himself, "Why should I fear, since God is merciful and Christ died for sinners?" Thus, he remains a willing servant of sin, content with the bondage of corruption. He is inwardly and outwardly unholy, and he is satisfied with his condition. He is satisfied in not only not conquering sin, but in not striving to conquer it. He particularly ignores those sins which beset him.

Such is the state of every natural man. It is his state whether he be a gross, scandalous transgressor, or a more reputable and decent sinner. It is his state even if he has the form of godliness. But how can such a person be convinced of sin? How is he brought to repent, to be under the law, and to receive the spirit of bondage unto fear? This is the next point to be considered.

God, in His own way, can touch the heart of natural man that lies asleep in darkness and in the shadow of death. He does this by some awesome providence or by His Word applied with a demonstration of the Holy Spirit. Natural man is terribly shaken out of his sleep. He awakes into a consciousness of his danger. Perhaps in a moment, perhaps by degrees, the eyes of his understanding are opened. Now the veil which clouded his understanding is partly removed. He can discern the real state he is in. Horrid light breaks in upon his soul. By this light, he catches a glimpse of the bottomless pit into which he is about to fall.

At last he sees that the loving, merciful God can also be a consuming fire. He sees that God is just and punitive, rendering to every man according to his works. God renders a judgment with the ungodly for every idle word. Man is accountable even for the imaginations of his heart. He now clearly perceives that the great and holy God has eyes too pure to behold iniquity. At last he realizes that God is an avenger of every one who rebels against Him. God repays the wicked to his face. It is a fearful thing to fall into the hands of the living God.

The inward, spiritual meaning of the law of God now begins to dawn upon him. He perceives that God's commandments are exceedingly broad. There is nothing hidden from God's eyes. He is now convinced that every part of God's law relates to his every act. It relates not barely to outward sin or obedience, but even to that which occurs in the secret recesses of the soul. It applies to that which no eyes but God's can penetrate. Now if he hears, "You shall not kill," God speaks in thunder, "Whosoever hateth his brother is a murderer."[8] "Whosoever shall say, Thou fool, shall be in danger of hell fire."[9] If the law says, "Thou shall not commit adultery," the voice of the Lord sounds in his ears, "Whosoever looketh on a woman to lust after her hath committed adultery with her already in his heart."[10]

So it is in every point he feels the Word of God to be quick, and powerful and sharper than a two-edged sword. It pierces even to the dividing of his soul and spirit, his joints and marrow. And so much the more painful it is, because he is conscious of having neglected God for so long. He is aware of having trodden Jesus under foot, who would have saved him from his sin. He is guilty of having counted the blood of the New Covenant as unholy, a common, unsanctifying thing.

Now he knows that all things are naked and open to the eyes of God, with whom he must deal. So he sees himself naked, stripped of all the fig leaves which he has sewn together. He has lost all of his poor pretenses to religion or virtue. His weak excuses for sinning against God are worthless. Now he sees himself like the ancient sacrifices, split in two, as it were, from the neck downward, so that all within stands open to public view. His heart is bare, and he sees it is all sin. He knows he is deceitful above all things, and desperately wicked. He is aware that his heart is altogether corrupt and abominable, more than it is possible for words to express. He knows that no good thing dwells in it. There is only unrighteousness and ungodliness. His every notion, every temper and thought, is only evil continually.

He not only sees, but feels in himself, by an emotion of the soul which he cannot describe, that he deserves to be punished by God. He perceives this is so, even if his outward acts were without blame. He feels that the just punishment of his sins is death.

His pleasing dream ends here. His delusive rest, his false peace, his vain security, is ended. His joy now vanishes as a cloud. Pleasures once loved delight no more. They pall upon the taste. He loathes their nauseating flavor. He is weary of bearing them. The shadows of happiness flee away and sink into oblivion. He is stripped of all. He wanders to and fro, seeking rest and peace. He finds none.

He finds that sin let loose upon the soul is perfect misery. He feels the anguish of a wounded spirit in his pride, anger, evil desire, self-will, malice, envy, revenge, and other inward sins. He feels sorrow of heart for the blessings he has lost. He knows a curse is on him. He has remorse for having thus destroyed himself, and despises his own mercies. Now the lively sense of the wrath of God, and of the consequences of His wrath, hangs over his head. He sees this as justly deserved punishment.

Fear of death, as being to him the gate of hell, the entrance of death eternal, is ever present. Now he fears the devil, the executioner of the wrath and righteous vengeance of God. He has a fear of men, who, if they were able to kill his body, would thereby plunge both body and soul into hell. His fear sometimes arises to such a height that the poor, sinful, guilty soul is terrified with everything and with nothing. He trembles like a leaf shaken of the wind. Sometimes this fear may even border upon distraction, making a man drunk, though not with wine. It can suspend his exercise of memory, of understanding, and of all the natural faculties. Sometimes this fear may lead into the very brink of despair. In those times, he who trembles at the name of death, may be ready to plunge into it every moment, just to be loosed from life. Well may such a man roar, like him of old, for the very disquietness of his heart. He may cry out, "The spirit of a man will sustain his infirmity; but a wounded spirit who can bear?"[11]

Such a person desires to break loose from sin and begins to struggle with it. But though he strives with all his might, he cannot conquer. Sin is mightier than he. He would escape, but he is fast in prison. He cannot get loose. He resolves against sin, and sins on. He sees the snare, and abhors, and runs into it. His boasted reason avails only to increase his guilt. Now it increases his misery. Such is the freedom of will. It is free only to envy. It is free to drink in iniquity. It is free to wander farther and farther from the living God, and to do so despite the spirit of grace.

The more he strives, wishes and labors to be free, the more he feels his chains, those grievous chains of sin with which Satan binds and leads him captive in his free will.

He is Satan's servant. Though he rebels, he cannot overcome. He is still in bondage and fear by reason of sin. This is generally some outward sin to which he is particularly disposed, either by nature, custom, or outward circumstances. He is always in bondage to some inward sin, such as evil temper or unholy affection. And the more he frets against it, the more it prevails. He may bite the chain, but he cannot break his chain.

Thus he toils without end, repenting and sinning, and repenting and sinning again. Finally, at length, the poor, sinful, helpless wretch is even at his wit's end. He can barely groan, "Oh wretched man that I am! who shall deliver me from the body of this death?"[12]

This whole struggle of one who is under the law, under the spirit of bondage and fear, is beautifully described by Paul in the seventh chapter of the Book of Romans. There he spoke in the person of an awakened man. He said, "I was alive without the law once: [I had such a life, wisdom, strength and virtue. So I thought.] but when the commandment came, sin revived, and I died."[13] The commandment, in its spiritual meaning, came into Paul's heart with the power of God. Then his inbred sin was stirred up, fretted, inflamed, and all his virtue died away. The commandment, which was ordained to life, he found to be death. Sin, taking occasion by the commandment, deceived him, and slew him by it. It came upon him unawares, and slew all his hopes. It plainly showed that in the midst of life, he was in death. "Wherefore the law is holy, and the commandment holy, and just and good."[14] Then he no longer lay the blame on this, but on the corruption of his own heart. He acknowledged that the law is spiritual but he was carnal, sold under sin. He could then see the spiritual nature of the law. For the first time he could understand his own carnal, devilish heart, which was sold under sin. He was totally enslaved to it, like slaves bought with money were absolutely at their masters' disposal. He could only cry out, "That which I do I allow not: for what I would, that do I not; but what I hate, that do I."[15] He groaned under this bondage, this tyranny of his hard master of sin. He could continually will to do better, but did not know how to perform what he willed. For the good that he wanted to do, he could not. The evil which he wished to avoid, that he did. He found it to be a law, an inward constraining power, that when he would do good, evil was present with him. He could consent to the law of God in his mind, but he could see his body doing the other things. There was some other power causing a war against the law of his mind or inward man. It kept him in captivity to the law, under the power of sin. It dragged him along, as it were, at his conqueror's chariot wheels, into all the things which his soul wished to avoid. It caused him to cry out, "O wretched man that I am! Who shall deliver me from the body of this death?" Who could deliver him from that helpless, dying life, from that bondage of sin and misery? Till that was done, he served the law of God with his mind and conscience, but served the law of sin with his body. He was hurried along by a force which he could not resist.

How clear a picture is this of one who is under the law. It describes the man who pants after liberty, power and love, but is in fear and bondage still! Here he will remain until the time that God answers his prayers. Then that bondage will end and he will no longer be under the law, but come under grace. He will be delivered from this bondage of sin and the body of death. He will be delivered by the grace of God through Jesus Christ the Lord.

Then it is that this miserable bondage ends. He is no more under the law, but under grace. This is the third state to be considered. It is the state of one who has found grace, or favor, in the sight of God. It is the state of one who has the grace and power of the Holy Spirit reigning in his heart, given by God the Father. It is the state of one who has received, in the language of Paul, the Spirit of adoption. Now he knows God, and can cry out to Him, "Abba, Father."

The man under law cried out to God in his trouble. God delivered him out of his distress. His eyes were opened in quite another manner than ever before. Now he can see God as a loving, gracious person. While he is calling, "I beseech you, show me your glory!" he hears a voice in his inmost soul.

God says to him, "I will make all my goodness pass before thee, and I will proclaim the name of the Lord before thee; and will be gracious to whom I will be gracious, and will show mercy on whom I will show mercy."[16]

Then it is not long before the Lord descends in the clouds and proclaims the name of the Lord. Then the sinner sees, but not with eyes of flesh and blood. Through his spirit, he sees the law of God as merciful, gracious, long-suffering, and abundant in goodness and mercy. He knows that God keeps mercy for thousands, forgives iniquities, and transgressions, and sin.

Heavenly, healing light now breaks in upon his soul. God looks upon him. The God who commanded light to shine out of darkness now shines in his heart. He sees the light of the glorious love of God in the face of Jesus Christ. He has a divine evidence of things not seen. He has by an inward sense an awareness of the deep things of God. More particularly, he experiences the pardoning love of God to him that believes in Jesus. Overpowered with the sight, his whole soul cries out, "My Lord and my God!"

Now he sees all of his iniquities laid upon Jesus, who bore them in His own body on the cross. He beholds the "Lamb of God," taking away his sins. Now he is able to clearly discern that God was in Christ, reconciling the world to himself. God made Him who knew no sin to be sin for us, so that we might be made the righteousness of God through Him. Now we can understand that He himself reconciled us to God by that blood of the covenant.

Now both guilt and the power of sin come to an end. The new man can say, "I am crucified with Christ: nevertheless I live; yet not I, but Christ liveth in me: and the life which I now live in the flesh I live by the faith of the Son of God, who loved me, and gave himself for me."[17] Remorse, sorrow of heart, and the anguish of a wounded spirit come to an end. God turns this heaviness into joy. He had made us sore with the law, and now His hands heal us. Here ends also that bondage to fear. Now the heart stands fast believing in the Lord. Then we can no longer be in fear of the wrath of God. That wrath is now turned away from those who look upon Him no more as an angry judge, but as a loving father. The fear of the devil is erased, through the knowledge that he has no power except what is given to him from above. The fear of hell is gone, for the new person in Christ is an heir of the kingdom of heaven. Consequently there is no longer a fear of death. Now he knows that when this life ends, he has a house with God. That house is not made with hands, but eternal in the heavens. He earnestly desires to be clothed upon with that house which is in heaven. He groans to shake off this house of earth, so that mortality may be swallowed up in eternal life. He knows that God has wrought him for this very thing. He also knows that God has given him the reward of the Holy Spirit.

Where the Spirit of the Lord is, there is liberty. There

is liberty, not only from guilt and fear, but from sin. There is liberty from that heaviest of all yokes, that basest of all bondage. Spiritual labor is no longer in vain. The snare is broken and he is delivered. He not only strives, but now prevails. He not only fights, but conquers also. From this point on he does not serve sin. He is dead to sin and alive to God. Sin no longer reigns even in his mortal body. He no longer obeys sin, or the desires of the flesh. He does not yield his body as an instrument of unrighteousness for sin. His body is now an instrument of righteousness unto God. Now being made free from sin, he has become the servant of righteousness.

Now having peace with God through the gift of the Holy Spirit, he rejoices in the hope and glory of God. Having power over all sin, over all evil desire, and temper, and word and work, he is a living witness of the glorious liberty given to all of the sons of God. Along with all other partakers of this precious faith, he bears record with them, "We have received the Spirit of adoption, whereby we cry, 'Abba, Father!' "

It is the Spirit who continually works in him the ability both to will and to do God's will. It is the Holy Spirit that sheds the love of God abroad in his heart. It is that Spirit which gives him love for all mankind. Through the power of the Holy Spirit, his heart is purified from the love of the world, from the lust of the flesh, the lust of the eye, and the pride of life. It is by that Spirit that he is delivered from anger and pride, and from all vile and inordinate affections. The result is that he is delivered from evil words and works, and from all unholiness of conversation. He can no longer do evil to any person and he is always zealous in doing all good works.

The summary of all of this is apparent. The natural man neither fears nor loves God. Man under the law fears God.

Man under grace loves God. The first has no light in the things of God and walks in utter darkness. The second sees the painful picture of hell. The third sees and enjoys the joyous light of heaven. He that sleeps in death has a false peace. He that is awakened has no peace at all. He that believes has true peace—the peace of God filling and ruling his heart. The heathen, baptized or unbaptized, has a fancied liberty which is only licentiousness. Man operating only under the laws of God is in heavy, grievous bondage. He who is filled with the Holy Spirit enjoys the true, glorious liberty of the sons of God. An unawakened child of the devil sins willingly. One that is awakened sins unwillingly. A child of God through the Holy Spirit does not sin, and Satan does not touch him. The conclusion is that a natural man neither conquers nor fights sin. The man under law fights with sin, but cannot conquer it. The man under grace fights and conquers and is more than a conqueror through God who loves him.

From this account of the threefold state of man, the natural, the legal, and the spiritual, it appears that it is not sufficient to divide mankind into the categories of sincere or insincere. A man may be sincere in any of these states. Man may be sincere not only when he has the Holy Spirit, but when he has the spirit of bondage and fear. He may be sincere while he has neither this fear nor God's love. Undoubtedly, there may be sincere heathens as well as sincere Jews or Christians. This circumstance, then, does not prove that a man is in a state of acceptance with God.

The essential question is, "What is the ruling principle of one's soul?" This question should be examined closely, for it is essential to everyone. Is the ruling principle of your soul the love of God? Is it the fear of God? Is it neither one nor the other? Is it the love of the world, the love of pleasure and financial gain? Is your motivation that of ease in living and reputation with men? If so, you have not come as far as the man under the law. You are a heathen still.

Do you have heaven in your heart? Have you the Holy Spirit, so that you can cry out, "Abba, Father"? Or do you cry out to God overwhelmed with sorrow and fear? Are you a stranger to this whole affair and cannot imagine what is meant by it? Stand bare-faced and look up to heaven! Admit to God the state of your heart and life.

Do you commit sin or do you not? If you do, is it willingly or unwillingly? In either case, God has told you who you are. "He that committeth sin is of the devil."[18] If you commit sin willingly you are his faithful servant. He will not fail to reward your efforts. If you commit sin unwillingly, you are still his servant. Only God can deliver you out of Satan's hands.

Are you fighting daily against all sin? Are you able to conquer it? If so, you are a child of God in the power of the Holy Spirit. Now stand fast in that glorious liberty.

Are you fighting sin, but not conquering it? Are you striving for mastery over it, but unable to attain that mastery? Then you are still not a believer in your spiritual salvation. Continue on steadfastly and you shall come to know your salvation.

Are you not fighting sin at all? Are you engaged in leading an easy, indolent, and fashionable life? Have you, in this condition, dared to claim yourself to be a Christian? Do you do this when your life is only a reproach to Him, and His teachings? If so, awake from your sleep. Call upon God before hell swallows you up.

Perhaps one reason why so many think of themselves more highly than they ought to think, why they do not understand what state they are in, is because these several states of the soul are often mingled together. Quite often, they meet together in some measure in the same person. Common experience shows that the legal state, or state of fear, is frequently mixed with the natural state. Few men are so fast asleep in sin that they cannot sometimes be more or less awakened. The Holy Spirit of God does not wait for the call of man. Sometimes He forces us to hear Him. On occasion He puts even natural man into fear, so that for a while, at least, he recognizes his own state and limitations. Then he can feel the burden of sin and earnestly desire to flee from God's judgment. But this does not last very long. He seldom allows this conviction to go deep into his soul. He quickly stifles this grace of God in order to return to wallowing in his sin.

In the same manner, the evangelical state of love and grace is frequently mixed with the legal. Only a few of those who are in the spirit of bondage and fear continually remain without hope. Our wise and gracious God rarely allows this. He always remembers that we are but "dust." He does not will that we should forever fail before Him. It is not His choice that we should never know His Spirit. Therefore, at times of His choosing, He gives a dawning of light to all of us who sit in darkness. He causes a part of His goodness to pass before us, and shows that He is a God that hears the prayers of a sinner. Then we see that this promise of His Spirit, which is attained by faith, is available to us. Through this we are encouraged to continue with patience the race which is set before us.

Another reason why some deceive themselves is because they do not consider how far a man may go and still be in a natural or legal state. A man may be of a compassionate or a benevolent temper. He may be affable, courteous, generous and friendly. He may have some degree of meekness, patience, temperance, and many other moral virtues. He may feel many desires of shaking off all vice, and of attaining the highest degrees of virtue. He may abstain from evil. He may abstain from all of that which is contrary to justice, mercy or truth. He may do much good, may feed the hungry, clothe the naked, relieve the widow and fatherless. He may attend regular worship. He may use prayer in private and read books of devotion. Yet, for all of this, he may be a mere natural man, knowing neither himself nor God. In this state he can also be a stranger to the spirit of fear and that of love. For having neither repented nor believed the gospel, he remains without the Holy Spirit and power.

Be careful then, you who are called by the name of Christ. Be careful that you do not fall short of the mark of your high calling. Beware that you do not rest in the natural state with too many who are counted "good Christians." Do not be content to live and die in the legal state receiving only the esteem of men. God has prepared better things for you. Follow on until you attain these things. You are not called to fear and tremble in anxiety. You are called to rejoice and love like the angels of God. "Thou shalt love the Lord thy God with all thy heart, and with all thy soul, and with all thy mind."[19] You shall come to rejoice forever. You shall know what it is to pray without ceasing. You will be able to give thanks in all things. You can do the will of God on earth as it is done in heaven. You will be able to prove what is the good and acceptable and perfect will of God. You will be able to present yourself as a living sacrifice, holy, and acceptable to God. Hold fast to those spiritual gains that you have already attained. Reach forth to greater gains which are still before you. The God of peace can make you perfect in every good work. He can work in you all that is pleasing in His sight. This will be done through the teachings and work of Jesus, and the gift of the Holy Spirit.

2

Hindrances to Holiness[1]

"We are not ignorant of his devices" (2 Cor. 2:11). Satan, the subtle god of his world, labors to destroy God's children, and to keep them from achieving the holiness which is set before them. He tries to perplex, hinder and torment all those that he cannot destroy. One of his numberless plans is to divide the Bible against itself, and by one part of it contradict and overthrow the other part.

The inward kingdom of heaven is set up in the hearts of all who repent and believe the gospel. That kingdom is none other than righteousness, and peace, and joy in the Holy Spirit.[2] Every babe in Christian faith knows that we are made partakers of these blessings the moment we believe in Jesus. However, these are but the first fruits of His Spirit. The final harvest is still to come. Although these blessings are inconceivably great, yet we hope to see a greater blessing than these. We hope to love the Lord our God, not only as we do now, with a weak though sincere affection, but with all our hearts, all our minds, all our souls, and with all our strength.[3] We look for power to rejoice evermore, to pray without ceasing and in

29

everything to give thanks, always knowing that this is the will of God in Christ Jesus concerning us.[4]

We expect to be made perfect in love.[5] Such perfection casts out all painful fear. It casts out all desires except that of glorifying God whom we love, and of loving and serving Him more and more. We look for such an increase in our experiences of knowledge and love of God our Savior that we can always walk in the light as He is in the light.[6] We believe the whole mind that Jesus had will be in us, so that we shall love every man enough to be ready to lay down our life for his sake. By this love we expect to be freed from anger, pride, and every unkind attitude. We expect to be cleansed from all of our idols, and from all filthiness, whether of flesh or of spirit.[7] We will be saved from all of our uncleannesses, inward or outward, and purified as He is pure,[8] and be made holy.

We believe in His promise that the time will surely come when, in every word and work we shall do His will on earth as it is done in heaven.[9] Then, all our conversation will be properly seasoned, serving to minister grace to hearers. Then whatever we do shall be done to the glory of God. All our words and deeds shall be in the name of the Lord Jesus, giving thanks unto God, the Father, through Him.[10]

Now, the prime scheme of Satan is to destroy this first work of God in the soul, or at least to hinder its increase. Therefore, my purpose is first, to point out the several ways by which Satan endeavors to do this. Secondly, it is to observe how we may overcome his schemes, and how we may rise spiritually through what he intends to be the cause of our failing.

First, here are the several ways by which he endeavors to destroy our expectation of greater perfection. He attempts to dampen our joy in the Lord by causing us to consider our own sinfulness and unworthiness. Satan reminds us that there must be a far greater change than has yet occurred in us or we cannot see the Lord. If we believe that we must remain as we are, even to the day of our death, we might possibly draw a kind of poor comfort from it. But we know we need not remain in this state, because we are assured that there is a greater change still to come. Unless sin is all done away with in this life, we know we cannot see God in glory. On this point Satan often dampens the joy we should feel in what we have already attained by his perverse representation of what we have not yet attained, along with our knowledge of the absolute necessity of total attainment. Therefore, we cannot rejoice in what we have, because there is so much more which we do not yet have. We do not rightly enjoy the goodness of God, who has done such great things for us, because there are so many greater things which He has not yet done. Likewise, the deeper the conviction God works in us about our present unholiness, the more vehement the desire for the entire holiness which He has promised. Then, we are even more tempted to think lightly of our present gifts from God, and to undervalue what we have already received, because of what we have not yet received. If Satan can prevail this far, if he can dampen our joy in the Lord, he will soon attack our peace also.

Satan will suggest, "Are you fit to see God? He is of purer eyes than to behold iniquity. How then can you flatter yourself, imagining that He beholds you with approval? God is holy and you are unholy. What communion has light with darkness?[11] How is it possible that you, sinful as you are, could be accepted by God? You see the mark, the prize of your high calling, but do you not see it is a far distance from you?[12] How can you presume, then, to think that all your sins are already blotted out?[13] How can this be, until you are brought nearer to God, until you bear more resemblance to Him?"

Thus, Satan will try not only to shake your peace, but even to overcome the very foundation of it. He tries to return you, by insensible degrees, to the point where you first set out, seeking forgiveness by your own good works. He tries to make you think that there is something in you which is the basis for your acceptance by God, or is at least necessary for it.

Even when we hold fast to "Other foundation can no man lay than that is laid, which is Jesus Christ,"[14] and "Being justified freely by his grace through the redemption that is in Christ Jesus,"[15] Satan will not cease.

He urges, "But the tree is known by its fruits.[16] Have you the fruits of salvation? Is that mind in you which was in Christ Jesus?[17] Are you dead unto sin and alive unto righteousness?[18] Are you made conformable to the death of Christ? Do you know the power of His resurrection?"[19]

And then, comparing the small fruits we feel in our souls with the fullness of the promises, we are ready to conclude, "Surely God has not said that my sins are forgiven me! Surely I have not received the remission of my sins. What place have I among them, those saints who are pure and holy?"

More especially in times of sickness and pain, Satan will press this with all his might. "Is it not the word of him who cannot lie, 'Without holiness no man shall see the Lord'?[20] But you are not holy. You know that very well. You know holiness is the full image of God. This is far above and out of your reach. You cannot attain it at all. Therefore, all your efforts have been in vain. All these things you have suffered in vain. You have spent all your strength for nothing. You are still in your sin, and therefore must perish in the end."

And so, if your eye is not steadily fixed on Jesus, who has borne all your sins, Satan will bring you again under that fear of death whereby you were so long under bondage.[21] By this means he will impair, if not wholly destroy, your peace, as well as your joy in the Lord.

But Satan's masterpiece of subtlety is still to come. Not content to strike at your peace and joy, he will carry his attempts even further. He will level his assaults against your righteousness. He will endeavor to shake, and if possible to destroy, that holiness which you have already received, by your very expectations of receiving more of the image of God.

The manner by which he attempts this partly appears from what we have already seen. First, by striking at our joy, he strikes likewise at our holiness, because joy in the Holy Spirit is the most precious means of promoting every holy disposition. Joy is a choice instrument of God by which He carries on much of His work in a believing soul. Joy is a considerable help, not only to inward, but to outward holiness. It strengthens our hands to go on working in faith and in the labor of love, and to "fight the good fight of faith, [and] to lay hold on eternal life."[22] Joy is peculiarly designed by God to be a balance both against inward and outward sufferings. It is to "lift up the hands which hang down and confirm the feeble knees."[23] Consequently, whatever dampens our joy in the Lord proportionally obstructs our holiness. As far as Satan shakes our joy, he hinders our holiness.

The same effect results if our peace is either destroyed or shaken, for the peace of God is another precious means of advancing the image of God in us. There is no greater help to holiness than this, a continual tranquility of spirit, the evenness of a mind stayed upon God, and a calm repose in the blood of Jesus. Without this, it is hardly possible to grow in grace and the vital knowledge of the Lord Jesus Christ. All fear, except tender filial fear, freezes and benumbs the soul. It binds up all the springs of spiritual life, and stops all motion of the heart of God. Doubt mires the soul so that it sticks fast in the mud. Therefore, in the same proportion as either of these prevail, our growth in holiness is hindered.

At the same time that Satan tries to make our belief in the necessity of perfect love an occasion for shaking our peace by doubts and fears, he endeavors to weaken, if not destroy, our faith. All of these are inseparably connected, so that they must stand or fall together. So long as our faith exists, we remain in peace. Our heart stands fast while it believes in the Lord. But, if we let go of our faith and confidence in a loving, pardoning God, our peace is at an end. The very foundation on which it stood is now overthrown, and faith is the only foundation of holiness as well as of peace. Whatever strikes at faith strikes at the very root of all holiness. Without this faith, without an abiding sense that Christ loved me and gave himself for me, without a continuing conviction that God, for Christ's sake is merciful to me, a sinner, it is impossible for me to love God. "We love him, because he first loved us."[24] We love God in proportion to the strength and clearness of our conviction that He has loved us and accepted us in His Son. Unless we love God, it is not possible to love our neighbor as ourselves. Neither can we have any right affections either toward God or man. It evidently follows that whatever weakens our faith must, in the same degree, obstruct our holiness. This is not only the most effectual, but also the quickest way of destroying our holiness. This does not affect any one Christian temper or any single fruit or grace of the Spirit, but so far as it succeeds, tears out the very root of the whole work of God.

Therefore, it is no wonder that Satan, the ruler of the darkness of this world,[25] should put forth all his strength at this point. By experience we will see that this is true. It is far easier to conceive than it is to express the violence with which this temptation is often urged on all those who truly hunger and thirst after righteousness. We clearly see on one hand the desperate wickedness of our own hearts, and on the other hand the unspotted holiness to which we are called in Jesus Christ. On one hand is the depth of our own corruption, our total alienation from God. On the other is the height of the glory of God, that image of the holy one, to which we are to be renewed. Many times there is almost no spirit left in us. We could almost cry out, "Even with God, this is impossible!" We are ready to give up both faith and hope, and cast away that very confidence through which we are to overcome all things through Christ strengthening us, forgetting that "after [we] have done the will of God," we are to receive the promise.[26]

If we hold fast the beginning of our confidence to the end,[27] we shall undoubtedly receive the promises of God, reaching through both time and eternity. However, here is another snare laid before our feet. While we are earnestly seeking that part of the promise which is to be accomplished in our liberty as children of God,[28] we may be led away from considering the glory which shall yet be revealed. Our eye may be turned aside from that crown which God has promised to give to all who love His appearing.[29] We still may be drawn away from the view of that incorruptible inheritance which is reserved in heaven for us. This also would be a loss to our souls, and an obstruction to our holiness. To walk in the continual light of the goal of holiness is a necessary help in our running of the race which is set before us.

It is said of Jesus that, "For the joy that was set before him, [He] endured the cross, despising the shame, and is set down at the right hand of the throne of God."[30] From this example, we may easily see how much more necessary is the view of a joy yet to come, so that we may endure whatever the wisdom of God lays upon us, pressing on through holiness to glory.

While we are reaching this, as well as the glorious liberty which is preparatory to it, we may be in danger of falling into another snare of the devil. We take too much thought about tomorrow, neglecting the improvements we may make today. We may so expect perfection as not to use that love which is already shed into our hearts. There have been instances of those who have greatly suffered because of this. They were so taken up with what they were yet to receive that they neglected what they had already received. In expectation of having five talents more, they buried their one talent in the earth. At least they did not improve it as they might have done to the glory of God and the good of their own souls.

The subtle adversary of God and man, Satan, continues his endeavors to negate the Word of God by dividing the gospel against itself, using one part of it to overthrow the other. So, the first work of God in the soul is destroyed by the expectation of His final, perfect work. We have seen several of his attempts to cut off the springs of holiness. He does this even more directly by making our hope an occasion for unholy attitudes.

Thus, when we are thirsting eagerly for all of God's great and precious promises, our soul breaks out with the fervent desire, "Why is He so long in coming?" Immediately Satan uses this opportunity to tempt us to murmur against God. He uses all his wisdom and all his strength to influence us to complain about Jesus for delaying His coming. At least Satan will try to cause us some degree of fretfulness and impatience, along with envy of those who appear to have already achieved the prize of holiness. He knows that by giving way to any of these attitudes, we are pulling down the very thing we wish to build up. By thus following after perfect holiness, we can become more unholy than before, with the great danger that our last state will be worse than our first. We can become like those of old, of whom the apostle spoke when he said, "It had been better for them not to have known the way of righteousness, than, after they have known it, to turn from the holy commandment delivered unto them."[31]

From this, Satan hopes to reap another advantage. He wants to bring up a bad report about perfection and holiness. He is aware of how few are able to distinguish, or even try to distinguish, between accidental abuse and the natural tendency of a doctrine. Therefore, regarding the doctrine of Christian perfection, he continually blends them together, in order to prejudice the unwary against the glorious promises of God. How frequently and generally he prevails in this!

Who observes any of these accidental ill effects of the holiness doctrine and does not immediately conclude that this is its natural tendency? They readily cry out, "See, these are the fruits, the normal end results of this doctrine."

Not so! They are fruits which may accidentally spring from a great and important truth. But, the abuse of this, or any other scriptural doctrine, does by no means destroy its use. Neither does the unfaithfulness of man, perverting his right way, make the promises of God of no effect. No, God is true and men are liars.[32] The word of the Lord shall stand. "Faithful is he that calleth you, who also will do it."[33] Let us not be removed from the hope of the gospel.[34] Rather, let us observe what is the second thing proposed, how we may resist Satan and rise higher through what he intends to be an occasion for our failing.

Satan tries to dampen our joy in the Lord by making us consider our own sinfulness. Added to this problem is the charge that without entire universal holiness no man can see the Lord. You may thrust this back at him, because through the grace of God, the more you feel of your own sinfulness, the more you should rejoice in the confident hope that all of this shall be removed from you. While you hold fast to this hope, every evil temper you feel, though you hate it with a perfect hatred, may be the means of increasing your humble joy, rather than decreasing it.

This fault of mine, you may say, shall likewise perish in the presence of the Lord. Like the wax melts at the fire, so shall this melt before his face.[35]

By this means, the greater that change is which remains to be done in your life, the more you triumph in the Lord, and the more you may rejoice in the God of your salvation, who has done so great things in you already. You can know He will do even greater things for you.

The more vehemently Satan assaults your peace, the more earnestly you need to hold fast to what you have. Satan accuses, "God is holy and you are unholy. You are far away from that holiness without which you cannot see God. You cannot be in the favor of God. There is no way you can imagine that you are forgiven."

Remember, that not by works of righteousness which I have done am I found in Him. I am accepted in the beloved not because of my own righteousness as the cause, either in whole or in part, of my salvation before God. I am saved by faith in Christ, the righteousness which is of God by faith.[36]

Wear this about your neck, write it upon your heart, keep this as you would a bracelet on your arm, always before your eyes. I am "justified freely by his grace through the redemption that is in Christ Jesus."[37] Value and esteem, more and more, that spiritual truth, by grace we are saved through faith.

Admire, more and more, the free grace of God in so loving the world as to give His only begotten son, that whosoever believes in Him shall not perish, but have everlasting life.[38] Then, the sense of the sinfulness you feel, on one hand, and the holiness you expect on the other hand shall contribute to establish your peace and make it flow like a river. That peace shall flow on with an even stream, in spite of all those mountains of ungodliness which shall disappear when the Lord comes to take full possession of your heart.

Sickness, pain, or the approach of death will not occasion any doubt or fear. A day, an hour, a moment with God, is as a thousand years. He will not change the time of the work which remains to be done in your soul. God's time is always the best time. Therefore, do not worry about this. Only make your requests known to God, not with doubt or fear, but with thanksgiving.[39] We have been previously assured that God will not withhold anything that is good from you. The more you are tempted to cast away your faith and confidence in love, so much the more take care to hold fast to that which you have attained.[40] Labor much more to stir up the gift of God which is in you.[41] Never let that slip away. Remember that we have an advocate with the Father, Jesus Christ the righteous.[42] "The life which I now live in the flesh I live by the faith of the Son of God, who loved me, and gave himself for me."[43]

Let this be your glory and crown of rejoicing. See that no one takes away your crown. Hold fast to, "I know that my redeemer liveth, and that he shall stand at the latter day up on the earth."[44] Remember always that we have redemption in His blood and the forgiveness of our sins.[45]

Thus, being filled with all peace and joy in believing, press on in peace and joy in faith to the renewal of your whole soul, in the image of God who created you. Call continually to God that you may see the prize of your high calling,[46] not as Satan represents it as a horrible and dreadful shape, but in its genuine and native beauty. See it not as something which must be or you will go to hell, but as what may be to lead you into heaven. Look upon perfection and holiness as the most desirable gift which is in all of the stores of the rich mercies of God. Seeing it in this true point of light will cause you to hunger after it more and more. Your whole soul will be athirst for God and for this conformity to His likeness. Having received a good hope of this and a strong consolation through grace, you will no more be weary and faint in mind, but will continue on until it is attained.

In this power of faith, press on to glory. God has joined from the beginning pardon, holiness and heaven. Then why should man put them asunder? Beware of this and let not one link of this golden chain be broken.

God, for Christ's sake, has forgiven me. He is now renewing me in His own image. Shortly He will make me fit for himself, and take me to stand before His face. I, whom He has forgiven through the blood of His son, being thoroughly sanctified by His Holy Spirit, shall quickly ascend into the new Jerusalem, the city of the living God.[47] In a little while I shall come to the general assembly of the church of the first born, and to God, the judge of all, and to Jesus, the mediator of the New Covenant.

How soon will all shadows flee away and the day of eternity draw upon me. I shall soon drink of the river of the water of life going out of the throne of God and of the Lamb. There all His servants shall praise Him and shall see His face and His name shall be upon their foreheads. No night shall be there, and they have no need of a candle or of the light of the sun, for the Lord God enlightens them and they shall reign forever and ever.[48]

If you would taste the good word and the powers of the world to come, you will not murmur against God simply because you are not ready for the inheritance of the saints of light.[49] Instead of complaining that you are not wholly delivered, praise God for delivering you this far. Magnify God for what He has done and take it as evidence of what He will do. Do not fret against God because you are not yet perfectly holy, but bless Him because you shall be. Now, your salvation from all sin is nearer than when you first believed. Instead of uselessly tormenting yourself because that time has not yet come, calmly and quietly wait for it, knowing that it will come and will not tarry.[50] You may therefore more cheerfully endure the burden of sin that still remains in you, knowing it will not always remain. In a little while it will be completely gone. Wait on the Lord's timing. Be strong, and He shall comfort your heart, if you put your trust in Him.[51]

If you see any who appear to be partakers of this great hope and are already made perfect in love and holiness, do not envy the grace of God that is in them. Let it rejoice and comfort you, and glorify God for their sakes. If one member is honored, all the members should rejoice.[52] Instead of jealousy or evil thoughts, praise God for them. Rejoice in having a fresh proof of the faithfulness of God in fulfilling all His promises. Stir yourself up the more to take hold of that for which you were also taken hold of by Jesus Christ.[53]

In order to do this, redeem the present. Improve the present moment, and use up every opportunity of growing in grace and doing good. Do not let the thought of receiving more grace tomorrow make you negligent about today. You have one talent now. If you expect five more, improve that which you have. The more you expect to receive hereafter, the more you should labor for God now. Sufficient to the day is the grace of it. God is now pouring His benefits upon you. Prove yourself to be a faithful steward of the present grace of God. Whatever may be tomorrow, be diligent to add to your faith, courage, temperance, patience, brotherly kindness and the fear of God, until you attain that pure and perfect holiness and love.[54] Let these things abound in you now. Do not be slothful or unfruitful. "So an entrance shall be ministered unto you abundantly into the everlasting kingdom of our Lord and Savior Jesus Christ."[55]

If in the past you have abused this blessed hope of being holy as God is holy, do not cast it away yet. Let the abuse cease and the use remain. Use it now to the more abundant glory of God and profit of your own soul. In steadfast love, in calm tranquility of spirit, in full assurance of hope, rejoicing evermore for what God has done, press on into perfect holiness. Daily growing in the knowledge of our Lord Jesus Christ, and going on from strength to strength, in resignation, in patience, in humble thanksgiving for what you have attained, and what you shall attain, run the race set before you. Look unto Jesus, until through perfect love, you enter into His glory.

3

Being Blessed[1]

"And seeing the multitudes, he went up into a mountain: and when he was set, his disciples came unto him: And he opened his mouth, and taught them, saying, Blessed are the poor in spirit: for theirs is the kingdom of heaven. Blessed are they that mourn: for they shall be comforted" (Matt. 5:1-4).

Jesus had now gone about all Galilee, starting at the time when John was cast into prison.[2] He taught in the synagogues and preached the gospel of the kingdom of heaven. Also, He healed all kinds of sickness and all kinds of disease among the people. A natural result of this was that many followed Him from Galilee, Decapolis, Jerusalem, and from all Judea and the regions beyond the Jordan.[3] There was such a multitude following Him that no synagogue could contain them. He went up into a mountain where there was room for all that came to Him from every quarter. When He had sat down, His disciples came to Him. He then opened His mouth (an expression denoting the beginning of a solemn discourse), and began to teach them.

It is important to observe who it is that is here speaking. In observing this, we may take heed as to how we hear Him. Jesus was the representative of the Lord of heaven and earth, the Creator of all. As such, He had a right to dispose of all God's creatures. The Lord, our governor, rules over all. His kingdom is from everlasting. He is the great lawgiver who can well enforce all His laws. He is able to save and to destroy. He can punish with everlasting separation from His presence and from the glory of His power. It is the eternal wisdom of God the Father, who knows of what we are made. He understands our innermost being. He knows how we stand related to Him, to each other, and to every creature He has made. Consequently, He knows how to adapt every law He prescribes to all the circumstances in which He has placed us. It is He who loves every man. He has mercy over all His works. It was the God of love who gave us Jesus on earth, to declare His will to all men. When this work was done, Jesus was to return to God the Father. Jesus was sent from God to open the eyes of the blind, and to give light to them that still sit in spiritual darkness. He is the great prophet of the Lord. God had solemnly declared of Him long ago, "Whosoever will not hearken unto my words which he shall speak in my name, I will require it of him."[4] Or, as this was later expressed, "Every soul which will not hear that prophet, shall be destroyed from among the people."[5]

And what is it Jesus is teaching here on the mountain? Jesus, who was sent from heaven, is here showing us the way to heaven. He is showing us the place God has prepared for us. He is showing us the glory He had before the world began. He is teaching us the true way to life everlasting. This is the royal way which leads to the kingdom of God. It is the only true way, for there is none other. All other paths lead to destruction. From the character of the speaker, we are assured He has declared the full and perfect will of God. He has not uttered one bit too much. He has not said anything more than what He received from God. Nor has He said too little. He has not neglected to declare the whole counsel of God. He has not uttered anything wrong, anything contrary to the will of God who sent Him. All His words are true and right concerning all spiritual things. These words would stand fast forever and ever, being tested by both time and men.

He took care to refute the mistakes of the scribes and Pharisees. They were the false teachers in that age, who had perverted the word of God. Their false teaching and practical mistakes were inconsistent with salvation. Those same mistakes would later arise in the Christian church. Their false comments and teachings on the law showed in advance how Christian teachers of all ages and nations could pervert the Word of God. Wary souls following those teachings would be only seeking death in the error of their life.

Now it is necessary to observe who He was teaching. He was not teaching the apostles alone. If He were teaching only the apostles, He had no need to go up into the mountain. A room in the house of any of the apostles would have contained all of them. In addition, it does not appear that the disciples who were with Him were the twelve only. The Scripture may be understood to include all of those who desired to learn from Him. This fact can be put out of all question and made undeniably plain. Where it is written, "He opened his mouth and taught them," the word "them" includes all of the multitudes who went up with Him into the mountain. This is affirmed by the concluding verses of the seventh chapter. There it was written that the multitudes were astonished by His teachings. He taught them, the multitudes, as one having authority and not as the scribes.[6]

It was not only those multitudes who were with Him on the mountain, to whom He taught the way of salvation. Jesus was teaching all of us. He was teaching all men, the whole race of mankind. Jesus was teaching for the children who were yet unborn, and all the generations to come. He was teaching to everyone who should ever hear the words of life in this life.

Most people, regardless of their other beliefs, will agree with at least some part of Jesus' discourse. All can agree that what Jesus said about poverty of spirit relates to all mankind. In spite of this, many have supposed that other parts of it concern only the apostles, or the first Christians, as ministers of Jesus. They argue that these teachings were never designed for other men. Consequently, they will have nothing at all to do with them.

How did they come to this conclusion? Why do they say that some parts of this discourse concern only the apostles, or the Christians of the apostolic age? Bare assertions from unknown teachers are not a sufficient proof to establish a point of so great importance. Jesus did not teach us that some parts of His discourse did not concern all mankind. Had it been so, he would have told us. He would not have omitted such necessary information. There is no place where Jesus implied His teachings were for limited dissemination. There is not the least inclination of it. He said no such thing elsewhere, not in any of His other discourses. Neither Jesus nor any of the apostles, or other inspired writers, left any such instruction on record. No assertion of this kind is to be found in the whole Bible. Why is it then, that some men consider themselves wiser than even God? Why is it that those who consider themselves so wise take it upon themselves to change the meaning of this discourse?

Perhaps some will say that the reason of the thing requires that a restriction be made. If it does, it must be upon one of two accounts. A restriction could be if either the text were apparently absurd, or if it contradicted some other Scripture. But this is not the case. It will plainly appear by examination that there is no absurdity at all. All that Jesus has said here can be applied and delivered to all mankind. Neither will it infer any contradiction of anything else He taught. It will not contradict any other Scripture whatever. All of these Scriptures are connected together and joined as the stones of an arch. You cannot take away one without destroying the whole structure. Therefore, it is apparent that all the parts of this discourse are to be applied to all men in general. If this is not so, then all men everywhere are exempt from the teachings.

Last, we may observe how Jesus teaches here. Surely Jesus always spoke as man never spoke before. He particularly so spoke here. He spoke not as the holy men of old, even though they spoke under the anointing of the Holy Spirit. He spoke not as the apostles, even though they were wise master builders of the church. He did not speak here as He did at any other time, or on any other occasion. It does not appear that it was ever Jesus' intent at any other time or place to lay down at once the whole plan of a new religion. In the Sermon on the Mount, He gave us a full prospect of true religion. He described at large the nature of holiness, without which no man shall see God. Jesus described particular parts of this on a thousand different occasions. But never, besides here, did He give a general review of the whole. There is nothing else of this kind in all of the Bible.

Above all, one can see the amazing love with which Jesus revealed God's will to man. He did not call us back to a mountain burned with fire, or into blackness, darkness and tempest. He does not thunder out of heaven with hailstones and coals of fire. Jesus now addresses us with His still, small voice. "Blessed [or happy] are the poor in spirit." Happy are the mourners; the meek; those that hunger after righteousness; the merciful; the pure in heart; happy in the end, and along the way. Happy are they in this life and in the life everlasting. It is as if He says to us, "Who is it that lusts to live a good life and wants to have good days? Behold, I will give you the thing for which your soul longs. Here is the way you have so long sought in vain. Here is the way of pleasantness. Here is the path to calm, joyous peace, to heaven below and heaven above."

Now notice the authority with which Jesus teaches. Well might they say that He taught "not as the scribes." Notice His manner, which cannot be expressed in words. Notice the air with which He speaks. He speaks not as Moses, the servant of God. He speaks not as Abraham, God's friend. He speaks not as any of the prophets, or as any son of man. Here is something more than human. Jesus displays more than that of any other created being. He speaks as Creator of all. He speaks the Word of God with the authority of God. He delivers this Word as the self-existent, the supreme, the God who is over all, blessed forever.

This divine discourse was delivered in the most excellent method. It is divided into three principal branches. The first is contained in chapter five of the Book of Matthew, the second in chapter six and the third in chapter seven. In the first, the sum of all true religion is laid down in eight particulars, which are explained and guarded against any changes by men. In the second are rules for that right intention which we are to preserve in all of our outward actions, unmixed with worldly desires, or anxious cares for the necessities of life. In the third are cautions against the main hindrances of true religion, closing with an application of the whole.

In the fifth chapter, Jesus first set forth eight examples of all true religion. Then He explained them, to guard against a false interpretation of men.

Some have imagined that Jesus designed to point out the several stages of true spiritual life. They have thought that Jesus was showing the steps which a Christian successively takes in his journey into the kingdom of God. Others suppose that all of the particulars here given belong at times to all spiritual people. Should we allow both of these interpretations? Is there inconsistency between them? It is undoubtedly true that every temper which Jesus mentioned here is at all times in a greater or lesser degree in every truly religious person. It is equally true, that real Christianity always begins in poverty of spirit. It then moves on in the order Jesus used here, until the man of God is made perfect. We began at the lowest of these gifts of God. We do not give up these gifts when we are called by God to move up higher. We hold fast to that which is already attained, while we press on to that which is yet to come. We always press on to the highest blessings of God as revealed in Jesus.

The foundation of all of this is poverty of spirit. Therefore, Jesus began this discourse with the teaching, "Blessed are the poor in spirit: for theirs is the kingdom of heaven."

Visualize those to whom Jesus was speaking. It is supposed that those gathered around Him were mostly the poor of the world, with few of the rich being there.

From this circumstance, He made a transition from temporal to spiritual things. "Blessed," said He, or happy as the word can be translated, in this and the following verses. "Blessed are the poor in spirit." Jesus did not say they were poor as to their outward circumstances. It is possible that some of the rich may be as far from happiness as a monarch upon his throne. Jesus said the "poor in spirit." He was speaking of those, regardless of their material possessions, who have that disposition of the heart. He was speaking of those who are poor in spirit, which is the first step to all real and substantial happiness. Without this quality, there is no happiness in this world or that which is to come.

Some have believed, that by the poor in spirit, He here meant those who loved to be in poverty. They believe that Jesus was speaking of those who were free from covetousness, and the love of money. They imagined that it was desirable to fear, rather than to seek, riches. Perhaps they had been induced to judge so by wholly confining their thoughts to the exact term. Perhaps they were motivated by the teaching of the Apostle Paul that "the love of money is the root of all evil."[7] The result of those beliefs was that they sought poverty. They divested themselves, not only of riches, but of all worldly goods. Hence, the vows of voluntary poverty have arisen among spiritual people. They supposed that a large degree of poverty would be a long step toward the kingdom of heaven.

Concerning this idea, much more needs to be said. The expression of Paul must be understood with some restrictions, otherwise it is not true. The love of money is not the sole root of all evil. There are a thousand other roots of evil in the world, as sad experience daily shows. His meaning was, it is the root of many evils. It is perhaps the root of more evils than any other single vice. This definition of poor in spirit, will by no means suit Jesus' purpose in this discourse. Jesus is laying a general foundation on which the whole fabric of true religion may be built. This intention could in no way be fulfilled by guarding against only one particular vice. So, even if Jesus were warning against the love of money as one part of His meaning, it could not possibly be the whole of His meaning. If poverty of spirit were only freedom from covetousness and the love of money, or the desire of riches, it would be only a branch of purity of heart.

Who then are the poor in spirit? Without question, to Jesus the poor in spirit are the humble. The poor in spirit are those who know themselves. It is they who are convinced of their own sins. The poor in spirit are those to whom God has given that first repentance. This must first be given before there can be that faith which is in Jesus.

He who is poor in spirit no longer depends upon his material possessions. He can no longer say, "I am rich and increasing in goods, and need nothing." The poor in spirit knows that he is wretched, poor, miserable, blind, and naked. He is convinced that he is spiritually poor indeed. He knows that he has no spiritual good abiding in him. He says, "In me dwells no good thing, but only that which is evil and abominable." He has a deep sense of the loathsome sin which has been surrounding him since his birth. He knows that sin overspreads his own soul and totally corrupts every power and faculty of it. He sees, more and more, the bad tempers which spring from that bad root. He is aware of his pride and haughtiness of spirit. He knows of his constant bias to think more of himself than he ought to think. He is convicted of his vanity and thirst after the esteem and honor that comes from men. He knows that he has hatred, envy, jealousy, revenge, anger, malice, and bitterness. He admits to an inbred enmity both against God and against man, which appears in thousands of shapes. He admits to loving the world rather than loving God. He confesses to the self-will, the foolish and harmful desires, which cleave to his inmost soul. He is aware of how deeply he has offended God and man with his words. If he is not guilty of profane, immodest, untrue or unkind words, he is guilty of conversation which does not edify and does not glorify God. He knows that his speech has not been useful to administer grace to his hearers. It has corrupted them, and therefore grieved God's Holy Spirit. His evil past is now always in his sight. If he were to tell his faults, they would be more than he would be able to express. He may as well try to number the drops of the rain, the sands of the sea, or the days of eternity, as to number his many mistakes. The poor in spirit is now fully aware of his guilt.

He knows the punishment which he deserves. He knows he could be punished for his carnal mind and the universal corruption of his nature. However, he is much more aware of the punishment he deserves for all his evil desires, thoughts, sinful words, and actions. He does not doubt, even for a moment, that the least of these deserves damnation. Above all, he knows he is guilty of not believing Jesus. He wonders how he can escape being punished for having neglected the salvation which is in Jesus. Intuitively, he knows that those who do not believe the words and works of Jesus are condemned already. He knows that he has been separated from God by this neglect. The wrath of God properly abides upon him.

How can he make up for this past? What can he trade to God in exchange for his soul? What can he do to stop the vengeance of God? How shall he come before Him? How shall he pay that which he owes? If he were, from this very moment, to perform perfect obedience to every command of God, this would make no amends for the past. He already owes God all the service he is able to perform, from this moment to the end of eternity. If he could pay this, it would make no manner of amends for what he should have done before. Therefore, he sees himself utterly helpless with regard to atoning for his past sins. He is unable to make any amends to God. He cannot pay any ransom for his own soul.

He knows he cannot even make a deal with God. He cannot promise to sin no more in return for God's forgiveness. He cannot agree constantly to obey all of God's commands. He knows such a condition is beyond his ability to perform. He knows and feels he is not able to obey even the outward commandments of God. He knows he cannot obey the outward commandments while his heart remains in sinfulness and corruption. He is wise enough to know that an evil tree cannot bring forth good fruits. He also knows he cannot cleanse his own sinful heart and purify his personality. He knows this is impossible for men. He has tried it before and failed. So, he is utterly at a loss, even to know how to begin to walk the path of God's commandments. He does not know how to go forward one step in the way. Surrounded with sin, sorrow, fear and finding no way through the gate, he can only cry, "God, save me or I perish."

Poverty of spirit, then, is a just sense of both inward and outward sin. It is a sense of our true guilt and helplessness. It becomes the first step we take in running the spiritual race which is set before us. Some have perverted this into a pride of their guilt. They would teach us to be proud of knowing we deserve to be damned. But Jesus' expression is of an entirely different nature. He teaches us of our total lack. He teaches us of our naked sin and helpless guilt and misery.

Paul, where he attempts to bring sinners to God, speaks in a like manner. "The wrath of God is revealed from heaven against all ungodliness and unrighteousness of men," says he in the Letter to the Romans.⁸ With this statement to all the unrighteous, he proves they are under the wrath and condemnation of God. He next showed that the Jews were no better, and were under the same condemnation. He wrote this so that all excuses might be stopped. He showed that all the world was guilty before God.

Paul proceeded to show that all were helpless as well as guilty. This is the plain purpose of all of the following expressions. "Therefore, by the deeds of the law, there shall no flesh be justified." "But now the righteousness of God, which is by our faith in Jesus, without the law is manifested." "We conclude, that a man is justified by faith, without the deeds of the law." These expressions all lead to the same point. They are to hide pride from man. They are to humble him to the earth, without teaching him to reflect upon his humility as a virtue. They are to inspire him with a full, piercing conviction of his utter sinfulness, guilt, and helplessness. When this is done, it casts the sinner, stripped of all and lost and undone, on the mercy of God.

Thus it is that true spirituality begins just where heathen morality ends. It begins with poverty of spirit and conviction of sin. It begins by the renouncing of ourselves. It begins with the awareness that we do not have our own righteousness. This is the very first point of the religion which Jesus taught. This point leaves all pagan religions behind. This point was always hidden from the wise men of the world. The whole Roman language, with all the improvements of the Augustine age, does not have one word to describe humility. Neither was the word found in all of the copious language of Greece, until it was invented by Paul.

We must come to feel what the heathen could not even express. We must awake to the fact of our sins. We must come to know our true spiritual state. We must know and feel that we are the sons of disobedience, children of wrath, having lived in the passions of our flesh. Throughout our life, we have been heaping sin upon sin, ever since we could tell the difference between good and evil. We must become willing to come under the mighty hand of God, knowing we are guilty of death everlasting. To be poor in spirit, we must cast off, renounce and abhor, all imaginations of ever being able to help ourselves. We must come to know that we can be purified and forgiven only through the grace of God which was given in Jesus. When this is done, we can then receive the promise. We then can witness, "Happy are the poor in spirit, for theirs is the kingdom of heaven."

The kingdom of heaven, then, is in us. This is what the kingdom of heaven, or kingdom of God, is. It is righteousness and peace and joy in the Holy Spirit. Righteousness is the life of God in the soul. It is having that same mind which was in Jesus. It is the image of God stamped upon the heart. It is the being renewed in the likeness of God who created us. It is the personal experiencing of the love of God. It is the loving of all mankind for God's sake, because He first loved us. And this peace is the peace of God. It is a calm serenity of soul. It is a sweet belief in Jesus which leaves no doubt of our acceptance of Him. It is a peace which excludes all fear except the loving fear of offending God who has given us this grace and forgiveness. This inward kingdom of God includes joy in the Holy Spirit. That Spirit convinces us in our hearts that we have received the redemption which came through Jesus. It is a joy of having the righteousness, which was in Jesus, imputed to us. It is a joy of knowing that all of the sins of the past are forgiven and remitted. It is a joy of knowing that we have received our inheritance and are at one with God. It is the joy of knowing that we are His children and that we will be with Him always. This kingdom of heaven is heaven already opened up into the soul here on earth. It is the springing up of those rivers of pleasure which flow from God and His grace.

You, whom God has caused to be poor in spirit, are the inheritor of this kingdom of heaven. When you feel yourself lost, you know that you have a right to the kingdom of heaven. The gracious promises and teachings of Jesus are true. This kingdom was purchased for you by Him. It is very near. You are on the brink of heaven. One more step, and you will enter into the kingdom of righteousness and peace and joy. Do you believe you are all sin? Look to Jesus, who promised to take away all of the sins of the world. Are you all unholy? See in Jesus the righteousness which He has promised you. Are you unable to make up for the least of your sins? He has taken all of your sins upon himself. If you can but believe this, all of your sins are forgiven. Do you know yourself to be totally unclean in soul and in body? The grace of God will cleanse you and make you sinless. Dare to believe this. You need stagger no more in unbelief. Arise, and believe these promises. Then you will be able to give glory to God and cry out in thanksgiving from the ground of your heart.

From this, you learn from God to be lowly in heart. This is the true, genuine, spiritual humility, which flows from the sense of the love of God. It is the being reconciled to God through the word and work of Jesus. Poverty of spirit, in this meaning of the word, begins where a sense of guilt and the wrath of God ends. It is a continual sense of our total dependence upon Him for every good thought, word or work. Poverty of spirit makes us aware of our utter inability to all good, unless God be with us every moment. This includes an abhorrence of the praise of men, knowing that all praise is due God only. With this is joined a loving shame, a tender humiliation before God, even for the sins which we know He has forgiven. There remains a tender humiliation for the sins which still remain in our hearts, although we know they bring us no condemnation. Nevertheless, the conviction we feel of this inbred sin is deeper and deeper every day. The more we grow in grace, the more we become aware of the wickedness in our heart. The more we advance in the knowledge and love of God through Jesus, the more we discern our alienation from Him. Through the words and works of Jesus, we become aware of the enmity that is in our carnal mind. We see the necessity of our being entirely renewed in righteousness and holiness.

Those who are early in this kingdom of heaven have little conception of this. They are full of excitement and joy in their new relationship with God. They feel they can never be removed from this new relationship. God, they believe, has made them totally strong. Sin is so far beneath their feet that they can scarcely believe it remains in them. Even temptation is silenced. It does not come at them again. Temptation cannot approach them, but must remain far off. Thus, they are borne aloft in love and joy. They soar as on the wings of the eagle. But Jesus well knew that this triumphant state does not often continue long. Jesus therefore immediately taught, "Blessed are they that mourn, for they shall be comforted."

We cannot imagine that this promise is for those who mourn because of some earthly circumstance. It is not for those who are in sorrow or heaviness, merely on account of some worldly trouble or disappointment. It does not apply to those who have suffered the loss of their reputations, friends, or fortunes. Neither do those who are intentionally afflicting themselves have any claim on this comfort. Those who fear some temporal evil and pine away with anxious care for earthly things, will remain sick of heart. They will not receive these blessings from God. This is because God is not in their thoughts at all. Therefore, they walk in a shadow and worry themselves in vain. All they will receive from the Lord is what they are receiving from the world.

The mourners of whom Jesus speaks are those who mourn on another account. He speaks of those who mourn after God. It is those who have lost that spiritual joy which they once had been given. They have lost the pardoning power of His Word and a taste of the good world which is yet to come. Now God seems to hide His face from them and they are troubled. They cannot see Him through the dark cloud. Now they see temptation and sin which they had supposed to be gone, never to return. Temptation and sin arise again, following after them, and holding them on every side. It is not strange that their soul is now upset with them. Trouble and heaviness take hold upon them. At this time, Satan comes to attack even more. It is he who asks, "Now where is your God? Now where is the blessedness you once had? Where is the beginning of the kingdom of heaven on earth? You claimed God had forgiven your sins. Surely God did not say that. That was only a dream, a mere delusion, a figment of your own imagination. If your sins are forgiven, why are you feeling this way? Can a pardoned sinner be this unholy?"

This attack brings on heaviness, sorrow of heart, and inexpressible anguish. Satan is wiser than men. If they attempt to reason with him, instead of immediately crying out to God, the state will continue. Even when God comes back into the soul and takes away all doubt of His mercy, the weak in faith may still be tempted. They may be tempted and troubled on account of what is to come. This is especially so when inward sin is revived. This inward sin thrusts hard at him and he may fall. He cries out in fear that he may perish and lose his eternal salvation. He fears that he will make a wreck of his faith and sink into everlasting hell.

It is sure that this present affliction is not joyous. It is grievous. Nevertheless, it can bring forth peaceable fruit to them who are attacked by it. Blessed, therefore, are they that thus mourn. If they wait upon the Lord, and do not allow themselves to be turned away from Him, they will be comforted. They cannot afford to accept the miserable comforts and comforters of the world. They must resolutely reject all the comforts of men, folly and vanity. They must avoid all of the idle diversions and amusements of the world. Those are pleasures which perish in the using and only tend to benumb and stupefy the soul. The result is the soul is neither aware of itself or of God. Blessed are they who continue on to know God and steadfastly refuse all other comfort. They shall be comforted by the consolations of His Holy Spirit. They will receive a fresh manifestation of His love. They will receive a fresh witness of His acceptance which shall never again be taken from them. This full assurance of faith swallows up all doubt as well as all tormenting fear. God now gives them sure hope of an enduring substance and strong consolation through grace. It is not necessary to dispute if it is possible for anyone to fall away who was once enlightened and made partakers of the Holy Spirit. It suffices them to say, by the power now resting in them, "Who shall separate us from the love of Christ? . . . I am persuaded, that neither death, nor life, nor angels, nor principalities, nor powers, nor things present, nor things to come, Nor height, nor depth, nor any other creature, shall be able to separate us from the love of God, which is in Christ Jesus our Lord."[9]

This process of both mourning for the absent God and recovering the joy of His presence seems to be repeated in what Jesus said the night before His death. "Do you enquire among yourselves of that I said, A little while, and ye shall not see me: and again, a little while, and ye shall see me? Verily, verily, I say unto you, That ye shall weep and lament."[10] Namely, when you do not see Jesus, the world shall rejoice and triumph over you. It will be as though your hopes were now at an end. In those times you will be sorrowful through doubt, fear, temptation, and vehement desire. But then your sorrow shall be turned into joy by the returning of Him whom your soul loves. It is as Jesus said, "A woman when she is in travail, hath sorrow, because her hour is come: but as soon as she is delivered of the child, she remembereth no more the anguish, for joy that a man is born into the world. And ye now therefore have sorrow: but I will see you again, and your heart shall rejoice, and your joy no man taketh from you."[11]

This mourning, then, comes to an end and is lost in holy joy by the return of God's presence. There is still another blessed mourning which comes upon God's children. They still mourn for the sins and miseries of mankind. They weep with those that weep. They weep for them that weep not for themselves, for those who sin against their

own souls. They mourn over the weakness and
unfaithfulness of those who are in some measure saved
from their sins. They are grieved for the dishonor
continually heaped upon God. At all times, they have an
awesome sense of this. This brings a deep seriousness
upon their spirits. This mourning is greatly increased
since the eyes of their spiritual understanding were
opened. It is increased by their continually seeing the vast
ocean of eternity which has swallowed up millions and
millions of people. They mourn that it is gaping to devour
them that yet remain in hopelessness. They see here the
availability of God and His kingdom; there they see hell
and destruction without a covering. The result is they feel
the importance of every moment which appears quickly,
and is then gone forever.

All of this wisdom of God is foolishness to the world.
The whole affair of mourning and poverty of spirit is
stupidity and dullness to the world. Seldom does the
world even pass as favorable a judgment as this on it.
Usually the world calls it mere moping and melancholy.
Occasionally it is branded as downright lunacy and
distraction. It is no wonder at all that those who do not
know God are under this judgment. Suppose, as two
persons are walking together, one should suddenly stop.
Then with strong signs of fear and amazement, he would
cry out, "We are standing on the edge of a precipice! See,
we are on the point of falling to our deaths! One more step,
and we shall fall into death! Stop! I will not go on for all of
the world!"

The other, who believes himself to be equally
sharp-sighted, would look forward and see nothing. What
would he think of his companion, but that he was out of his
mind? He would say that his head was out of order. Much
religion has surely made him mad!

Do not let yourself be moved by the blindness of the world. Children of God need not be troubled by those who still walk in darkness. Your eyes are enlightened and you do not walk in vain shadows. God and eternity are real things. Heaven and hell are indeed open before you. You are on the edge of the great gulf. It has already swallowed more than words can express. It has swallowed up nations, and kindreds, and peoples and tongues. It longs to devour even more, whether they see it or not. It reaches out for those who are giddy and miserable. Come, and cry out to be spared. Everyone can lift up their voices to God, who grasps both time and eternity. Both you and your family can be counted worthy to escape the destruction which comes as a whirlwind. Seek His salvation, so you may be brought safely through all of the waves and storms of life into the haven where God would have you be. Seek Him now in poverty of spirit, until God wipes away the tears from your eyes. Then weep for the misery which has come upon the earth. Weep for the world, until the God of all will put an end to misery, sin, and suffering. The time will come when He will wipe away the tears from all faces. There will be that day when the knowledge of God shall cover the earth as the waters cover the sea.

4

Inheriting the Earth[1]

"Blessed are the meek: for they shall inherit the earth. Blessed are they which do hunger and thirst after righteousness: for they shall be filled. Blessed are the merciful: for they shall obtain mercy" (Matt. 5:5-7).

When winter is past, the time of singing comes. The voice of the dove is then heard in the land. God, who comforts the mourners, is now returned to them so He may abide with them forever. At the brightness of His presence, dark clouds of doubt and uncertainty disperse. Storms of fear flee away. The waves of sorrow subside. The spirit again rejoices in God, the Savior. It is then that this Scripture is fulfilled. Then those whom God has comforted bear witness: happy and blessed are the meek. Truly, they shall inherit the earth.

But, who are the meek? They are not those who grieve at nothing, because they know nothing. The meek are not those who have no concern about the evils which occur, because they do not know evil from good. The meek are not those who are sheltered from the shocks of life by stupid insensibility. Neither are the meek those who by nature or art resent nothing, because they feel nothing. Apathy is as far from meekness as it is from humanity. Too many Christians in the past have confused these two. The result of this is to mistake one of the worst errors of heathenism for a branch of true Christianity. Neither does Christian meekness imply being without zeal for God. It does not imply this any more than it implies ignorance or insensibility. Meekness keeps clear of every extreme, either of too much or too little. It does not destroy affections, but balances them. God never planned for our affections to be rooted out by grace. They are only to be brought under control and kept under His direction through His grace. His grace directs the mind correctly. It holds an even balance with regard to anger, sorrow, and fear. It preserves the midline in every circumstance of life. It does not lean to the right hand or to the left. Meekness, therefore, seeks to relate to ourselves. However, it may be used in reference to both God and our neighbor. When this composure of mind has reference to God, it is usually termed resignation. It is defined as a calm acquiescence in whatever is His will concerning us, even if that is not pleasing to us by nature. Meekness continually says, "It is the Lord. Let Him do whatever seems good to Him." When we consider this more exactly with regard to ourselves, we understand it as contentment or patience. When it is exerted toward other men, it is called mildness. We call it mildness if it is a good quality and weakness if it is seen as a bad quality.

Those who are truly meek can clearly discern what is evil. The meek can also suffer from evil. They are aware of everything that is evil, but still remain meek. They are extremely zealous for God. Their zeal is always guided by knowledge. It is tempered in every thought, word and work, with the love of man, as well as the love of God.

They do not want to extinguish any of the passions which God has implanted in their nature for His wise ends. They have the mastery of all of their passions. They hold them all in subjection and employ them only in subservience to God's ends. Thus, even the more harsh and unpleasing passions can be applied to the greatest purposes. As a result, anger, hatred, and fear can be engaged against sin, and regulated by faith and love. When this is accomplished, they are as walls and bulwarks to the soul. Thus, they protect the soul from any harm by the wicked one, Satan. It is evident that this divine temper is not only to abide, but also to increase in us each day. Occasions for exercising and increasing it will continually arise while we remain on earth.

We have a great need for patience, so that we may suffer and do the will of God. Afterwards, we know that we will receive God's promises. We have a need of resignation. We must, in all circumstances, say, "Not my will, but thine, be done."[2] We have a need for gentleness toward all men. We need gentleness especially toward the evil and unthankful. Otherwise, we will be overcome by evil, instead of overcoming evil with good.

Meekness does not only restrain the outward act, as the scribes and Pharisees taught. Miserable teachers, untaught by God, continue in this error in all ages. Jesus guards against this. He shows the true extent of it. In His words, "Ye have heard that it was said by them of old time, Thou shalt not kill; and whosoever shall kill shall be in danger of judgment: But I say unto you, That whosoever is angry with his brother without a cause shall be in danger of the judgment: and whosoever shall say to his brother, Raca, shall be in danger of the council: but whosoever shall say, Thou fool, shall be in danger of hell fire."[3]

Jesus here ranks with murder that anger which goes no farther than the heart. This can be an anger which does not show itself with even so much as a passionate word. "Whoever is angry with his brother"—with any man living, seeing we are all brothers—is in violation of this teaching. Whoever feels any unkindness in his heart, or any temper contrary to love, is sinning inwardly. Whoever is angry without a cause, without a sufficient cause, or more angry than that cause requires, shall be in danger of judgment. He is at that moment offensive in the eyes of God.

Is it not preferable to stress a reading of the phrase, "without a cause"? Is that clause not entirely superfluous? If anger at a person is a temper contrary to love, how can there be a cause, a sufficient cause, that will justify it in the sight of God?

Anger at sin is allowed. In this sense, we may be angry and not be in sin. In this sense, Jesus himself was once reported to have been angry. It is written, "And when he had looked round about on them with anger, being grieved for the hardness of their hearts."[4] He grieved at the sinners, while being angry at the sin. This is undoubtedly a correct reaction in the sight of God.

"Whosoever shall say to his brother, Raca," and give way to anger in uttering any contemptuous word, is in danger of judgment. It has been observed that raca is a Syriac word. It signifies empty, vain, and foolish. It is as inoffensive a word as can be used toward anyone with whom we are displeased. And yet, Jesus reminds us that whoever uses this word shall be in danger of the council. He shall be liable to a more severe sentence from God.

Whoever says, "You fool," giving place to an outbreak of reviling, is liable to higher condemnation. The falling into reviling, with intentionally reproachful and contemptuous language, makes one liable to hell fire.

It should be observed that Jesus described all of these as subject to capital punishment. The first of these punishments was strangling, which was usually inflicted upon one who was convicted by a lower court. The second was death by stoning, frequently inflicted on those who were condemned by the great Council at Jerusalem. The third was burning alive, inflicted only upon the highest offenders, in the valley of the sons of Hinnom. The word which we translate as "hell" is evidently taken from the name of that place.

Men naturally imagine that God will excuse some of their defects in repayment for their conformity to other duties. Jesus takes care to cut off that vain, though common, imagination. Jesus shows that it is impossible for anyone to trade with God. God will not accept one duty for another. He will not accept part obedience for total obedience. Jesus warns us that performing our duty to God will not excuse us from our duty to our neighbor. Works of piety, as they are called, will not commend us to God if we lack charity. On the contrary, the lack of charity will make all of our religious works an abomination to God.

"Therefore if thou bring thy gift to the altar, and there rememberest that thy brother hath ought against thee," because of your unkind behavior toward him, perhaps because you called him raca, or fool, do not think that your gift will atone for your anger. There will be no acceptance of it with God so long as your conscience is defiled with guilt from unrepented sin. "Leave there thy gift before the altar, and go thy way; first be reconciled to thy brother, and then come and offer thy gift."[5] At least, do all you can toward being reconciled with him.

Let there be no delay in what so completely concerns the health of your soul. Agree with your adversary quickly. Do it now, on the spot. Do it while you are with him, if it is possible. Do it before he gets out of your sight, lest at any time he deliver you to the judge, lest he appeal to God, the judge of all. Then the judge will deliver you to the officer, Satan, the executioner of the wrath of God. Then you will be cast into the prison of hell, there to be reserved until the judgment of the great day. "Verily I say unto thee, Thou shalt by no means come out thence, till thou hast paid the uttermost farthing."[6] But it is impossible for you to ever do, seeing you have nothing to pay. Therefore, if you are once in that prison, you must remain there for ever and ever.

Still, it is the meek who shall inherit the earth. Such is foolishness to the worldly and wise. The wise of this world have warned against this again and again. They taught that those who tamely allow themselves to be abused will be unable to earn a living on earth. They taught that the meek will never be able to procure the common necessities of life. They predicted that the meek would be unable to keep even what they had. They warned that the meek could expect no peace, no quiet possession, no enjoyment of anything.

Such teachings would be true if there were no God in the world. Those predictions would come true if God did not concern himself with His children. However, when God rises to judgment, it is to help all of the meek on earth. God scornfully laughs at all heathen wisdom, and turns the fierceness of man to His praise. God takes particular care to provide the meek with all things necessary for life and goodness. He secures for the meek the provisions they need despite force, fraud, or malice of men. God secures for the meek and gives them much to enjoy. Whatever they receive is sweet to them, be it little or be it much. As in patience they possess their souls, they truly possess whatever God has given them. They are always content. They are always pleased with what they have. Their circumstance pleases them because it pleases God. Their heart, their desire, their joy, is in heaven. In this circumstance and state of soul, they may truly be said to have inherited the earth.

Jesus has been teaching about removing the hindrances of true religion. Among these is pride, the great hindrance of all religion. Pride is taken away by poverty of spirit. Other hindrances are levity and thoughtlessness, which prevent any religion from taking root in the soul, until these are removed by mourning. Also, anger, impatience and discontent hinder true religion, until they are healed by Christian meekness. When these hindrances are once removed, the native appetite of the heaven-born spirit returns. That spirit then hungers and thirsts after righteousness. Jesus promises that those who hunger and thirst after righteousness would be blessed. They would be made happy. Their quest would be filled.

Righteousness, as was observed before, is the image of God. It is the mind which was in Jesus. It is every heavenly and holy temper in one. It springs from and terminates in the love of God, as our Father and Redeemer. It fulfills itself in the love of all men for God's sake.

Blessed are they who do hunger and thirst after this. To thoroughly understand this expression, we should understand that hunger and thirst are the strongest of all our bodily appetites. In like manner, this hunger in the soul, this thirst after the image of God, is the strongest of all our spiritual appetites, once it is awakened in the heart. It swallows up all the rest of our desires in that one great desire. We hunger and thirst to be renewed in the likeness of God, who created us. Next, we should observe that from the time we begin to hunger and thirst, those appetites do not cease. They become more and more craving and demanding until we eat or drink, or die. And so it is from the time we begin to hunger and thirst after the whole mind which was in Jesus. These spiritual appetites do not cease. They cry after their food with more and more importunity. They cannot possibly cease until they are satisfied, while there is any spiritual life remaining. Thirdly, we may observe that hunger and thirst are satisfied with nothing but food and drink. He who needs these seeks nothing else. He has no interest in apparel, position, treasure upon earth, money or honor. All of these things are of no value to him. He would still say, "These are not the things I want. Give me food or else I die." The very same is the case with every soul who truly hungers or thirsts after righteousness. He can find no comfort in anything but this. He can be satisfied with nothing else. Whatever you offer besides, it is only lightly esteemed. He seeks no honor, riches or pleasure. He still says, "This is not the thing I want! Give me love, or else I will perish!"

It is impossible to satisfy a soul which is athirst for God with what the world calls religion. Worldly happiness cannot satisfy that soul either. The religion of the world implies three things: (1) Doing no harm, abstaining from outward sin; at least from that which is scandalous, such as robbery, theft, swearing, and drunkenness; (2) Doing good, relieving the poor; being charitable as it is called; (3) Using the means of grace, at least going to church and using the Lord's Supper. He in whom these three marks are found is termed a religious man by the world. But this will not satisfy him who hungers after God. This is not food for his soul. He wants a religion of a better kind. He seeks a religion higher and deeper than this. He can no more feed on this poor, shallow, formal thing than he can fill his stomach with the east wind. It is true that he is careful to abstain from any appearance of evil. He is also zealous of doing good works. He attends to all of the ordinances of God. But all of this is not what he longs for. Those are only the outside of the religion for which he insatiably hungers.

The knowledge of God as given in Jesus is what he seeks. He wants the life which is his with Jesus, in God. He yearns to be joined to the Lord in one spirit. He needs to have fellowship with the Father. He desires to walk in the light, as God is in the light. He needs to be purified, even as God is pure. This is the religion, the righteousness after which he thirsts. He cannot rest until he thus rests in God. "Blessed are they who hunger and thirst after righteousness, for they shall be filled." They shall be filled with the things for which they long. They shall be filled with righteousness and true holiness. God shall satisfy them with the blessings of His goodness. He shall fill them with the bread of heaven, with the manna of His love. He shall give them a drink of His pleasures as out of the river. Those who drink of His Spirit shall never thirst, except for more and more of that water of life. That thirst, for more of His Spirit, shall endure forever. If God has caused you to hunger and thirst after His righteousness, ask Him to keep you from ever losing that estimable gift. Pray that this divine appetite may never cease. If any criticize you, and tell you to hold your peace, disregard them. Pray even more, "God have mercy on me. Let me not live except to be holy as you are holy." Cease laboring for that which will not satisfy the soul. Can you hope to dig happiness out of the earth or to find it in the things of the world? Trample underfoot all of its pleasures. Despise all its honors. Count all its riches as worthless. Look only to the excellency of the knowledge of Jesus for the entire renewal of your soul in the image of God. It is for this the world was originally created. Beware of quenching that hunger and thirst by what the world calls religion. Religion of form, of outside show, leaves the heart as earthly and sensual as ever. Let nothing satisfy you but the power of godliness. Seek a religion that is Spirit and life. Seek to dwell in God and have God dwell in you. In doing this, you become an inhabitant of eternity. You enter into the kingdom of heaven by the blood of the sprinkling. You then sit in heavenly places with Jesus.

The more we are filled with the life of God, the more tenderly we become concerned for those who are still without God in the world. We are concerned because we know they are still dead in trespasses and sin. This concern for others will not lose its reward. Blessed are the merciful, for they shall obtain mercy.

The word merciful, which Jesus uses, implies the compassionate, the tenderhearted. The immediate result is that the merciful earnestly grieve for those who do not hunger after God. The eminent part of brotherly love is here. Mercy, in the full sense of the term, is to love your neighbor as yourself. There is a great importance in this love. For this reason, the Apostle Paul said that nothing availed if it were done without this love. God has given us, through the Apostle Paul, a full and particular account of love. Considering that account, we clearly see who are the merciful that shall obtain mercy. Paul wrote, "Though I speak with the tongues of men and of angels . . . though I have the gift of prophecy, and understand all mysteries, and all knowledge; and though I have all faith, so that I could remove mountains, . . . and though I bestow all my goods to feed the poor, and though I give my body to be burned, . . . it profiteth me nothing."[7]

Love, or charity, is the love of our neighbor as God loves us. Love is patient and long-suffering. It accepts all the weakness, temptation, error, infirmities, and all littleness of faith in the children of God. Love absorbs the wickedness and malice of the men who are in, and of, the world. Love is patient, not only for a short time, but as long as necessary. Love continues to feed an enemy when he hungers. If he thirsts, love will still give him a drink. Thus love continually heaps coals of fire, of melting love, upon his head.

In every step toward this desirable end, overcoming evil with good, love is kind. Love is soft, mild, and benign. It stands at the uttermost distance from moroseness. It lacks any harshness or sourness of spirit. Love inspires the sufferer at once with the most amiable sweetness, and the most fervent and tender affection.

Consequently, there is no envy through love. It is impossible to be merciful and to be envious. Love is directly opposite to that undesirable attitude. He who has this tender affection for all, and wishes all blessings to others, cannot envy. He seeks all good things in this world, and the world to come, to every person whom God has made. Therefore, he can never be pained at God's bestowing any good gift on anyone. If he has received the same, he does not grieve, but rejoices that another person gets the same benefit. If he does not have such gifts, he thanks God that at least his brother has them. If in true love, he is then happier for his brother than for himself. The greater his love, the more he rejoices in the blessings of all mankind. Through this holy love, he is greatly removed from every kind and degree of envy toward any creature.

Love is not rash or hasty in judging. It will not hastily condemn anyone. It does not pass a severe sentence, a slight or sudden opinion of things. It first weighs all the evidence, particularly that which is not in favor of the accused. A true lover of his neighbor is not like most men. Most men, even in cases of the nicest nature, see a little and presume a great deal. They jump to conclusions, but not he. No, he proceeds with a wariness and circumspection, taking heed at every step. He willingly subscribes to that rule of the ancient heathen, "I am so far from lightly believing what one man says against another, that I will not easily believe what a man says against himself. I will always allow him second thoughts, and many times will counsel him to do so."[8] Oh, how I wish the modern Christian could measure up to this.

It follows that love is not puffed up. It does not allow any man to think more highly of himself than he ought to think. Love requires us to think soberly. It humbles the soul and keeps it down to earth. It destroys all high conceits which engender pride. It makes us rejoice to be little, and as nothing, the lowest of all and the servant to all. Those who have kind affections for one another with brotherly love will prefer the company of one another. Those having this same love are of one accord. In this lowliness of mind, each esteems the other as better than himself.

Love does not behave itself in an unseemly way. It is not rude or willingly offensive to any. It renders to all their due. It gives respect to whom respect is due, and honor to whom honor is due. Love produces courtesy, civility, and humanity to all the world. The honoring of all men is simply a matter of good breeding. In the highest degree of politeness, it is a continual desire to please, which appears in all behavior. Therefore, there is none so well bred as a child of God, who is a lover of all mankind. He desires to please all men for their good and edification.

This desire cannot be hidden. It will necessarily appear in all of his relations with other men. His love is without dissimulation. It will appear in all of his actions and conversations. It will cause him, though without guile, to become all things to all men, if by any means he may save some.

In becoming all things to all men, love seeks not its own. In striving to please all men, the lover of mankind has no concern at all for his own advantage. He covets no one's money or belongings. He desires nothing but the salvation of their souls. In some sense, he may be said not to seek his own spiritual advantage any more than his temporal advantage. While he is in the full effort to save men's souls from death, he forgets himself. He does not think of himself, so long as a zeal for the glory of God swallows him up. At some times, he may almost seem, through an excess of love, to give up himself. He seems to ignore both his body and his soul. He cries out with Moses that God will forgive their sins. If not, he wishes to be blotted out of the book of life himself.[9] He can say with Paul, "I could wish that myself were accursed from Christ for my brethren, my kinsmen according to the flesh."[10]

It is no wonder that such love is not "easily provoked." Let it be observed that the word easily, strangely inserted in the translation, is not in the original. Paul's original words are absolute. Love is not provoked. It is not provoked to unkindness to anyone. Occasions will frequently occur which produce provocations of various kinds. However, love does not yield to provocation. It triumphs over all. In all trials, it looks to Jesus as the example for strength. Then it is more than conqueror in His love.

It is not improbable that our translators inserted the word easily to excuse Paul. They may have supposed that

Paul was lacking in the love which he so beautifully described. They may have supposed this from a phrase in the Book of Acts which is also inaccurately translated. Paul and Barnabas disagreed concerning John Mark. The translation states this, "And the contention was so sharp between them, that they departed asunder."[11] This naturally induces the reader to suppose that they were equally sharp. On the surface, it appears that Paul, who seemed to be right in this occasion, was as much provoked as was Barnabas. Barnabas had given proof of his anger by leaving the work to which he had been appointed by God. The Greek phrasing shows no such thing. It does not infer that Paul was provoked at all. Those Greek manuscripts simply state, "And there was a sharpness," a display of anger. The result of this is that Barnabas left Paul, took John Mark, and went his own way. Paul then chose Silas, and departed for Syria and Cilicia, as he had proposed.

Love prevents a thousand provocations which would otherwise arise. It prevents these because it "thinks" evil of no man. Indeed, the merciful man cannot avoid knowing many things that are evil. He cannot help but see them with his own eyes and hear them with his own ears. Love does not put out his eyes. It is not possible for him to miss seeing what things go on in the world. Neither does love take away his understanding any more than his other senses. He cannot but know there is evil around him. For instance, when he sees one man strike another, or hears one blaspheme God, he cannot question what has been done, or the words spoken. He cannot doubt that what was done was evil. The word "thinks" does not refer to either our seeing or hearing. It does not refer to the first and involuntary act of our understanding. It refers to our willingly thinking about those things which we need not think. It refers to our inferring evil where evil does not readily appear. It has to do with our reasoning about things which we do not see and supposing what we have neither seen nor heard. This is what true love absolutely destroys. It tears up, root and branch, all imaginings of what we have not actually experienced. It casts out all jealousies, all evil surmisings, all readiness to believe evil. It is frank, open and unsuspicious. It cannot design evil, so neither does it fear evil.

Love does not rejoice in injustice. Unfortunately, it is common among some Christians to rejoice over their enemy when he has fallen into affliction, error or sin. Indeed, they can hardly avoid this when they are zealously supporting a party or group. How difficult it is for them not to be happy with any fault which they discover in those of opposite views and persuasions. They enjoy any real or supposed blemish, either in their principles or practices. Few strong defenders of any cause are clear of these faults. Who is he who is so calm as to be altogether free of these faults? Who does not rejoice when his adversary makes a false step, which he thinks will be an advantage to his own cause? Only a man of love can avoid this. He alone weeps over the sin and folly of his enemy. He gets no pleasure in hearing or repeating those things. Rather, he desires this may be forgotten forever.

The man of merciful love rejoices in the truth, wherever it is found. He rejoices in the truth which is of godliness. He rejoices in this truth, for it brings forth its proper fruit. It brings forth holiness of heart and holiness of conversation. He rejoices to find truth in even those who oppose him. He knows there are lovers of God who can oppose his opinions on some points of practice. He is glad to hear good of them and speaks all he can consistent with truth and justice. Indeed, good in general is his glory and joy. He rejoices in good wherever it is found in the race of mankind. As a citizen of the world, he claims a share in the happiness of all its inhabitants. Because he is a man, he is concerned in the welfare of any man. He rejoices in whatever will bring glory to God, and promote peace and goodwill among men.

This love covers all things, because the merciful man does not rejoice in iniquity. He does not willingly discuss iniquity. Whatever evil he hears, sees, or knows, he conceals as much as he can. He does this if he can avoid making himself a part of other men's sins. If he sees another person in sin, it does not go out of his lips, unless to the person concerned. He discusses it then only if he may gain his brother. He is far from making the failings or faults of others a matter of any of his conversation. He never speaks of those who are absent at all, unless he can speak well. A tale-bearer, a back-biter, a whisperer, an evil-thinker, is the same to him as a murderer. He would just as soon cut a neighbor's throat as to murder his reputation. He would just as soon think of diverting himself by setting fire to his neighbor's house, as of thus scattering abroad words of criticism, while saying, "Am I not right?"

He makes only one exception. Sometimes he is convinced that it is necessary for the glory of God. If he feels it is for the good of his neighbor, through the will of God, that an evil should not be covered, he will speak. In this case, for the benefit of the innocent, he is required to declare the guilty. But even here, he will not speak at all until superior love requires him to do so. He cannot do it from a general confused view of doing good, or promoting the glory of God. He does this only from a clear view of some particular end, some determined good which he pursues. Still, he cannot speak until he is thoroughly convinced that this very means is necessary to that end. He must believe that the end cannot be reached, at least not as effectively, by any other way. Then he does it as the last and worst choice, a desperate remedy in a desperate case. He sees it as a kind of poison, never to be used except to expel another poison. Consequently, he uses it as sparingly as possible. He does this with fear and trembling. He fears he might transgress the laws of love by speaking too much. He knows that speaking more than he should is worse than not speaking at all.

Love believes all things. It is always willing to think the best. It seeks to put the most favorable construction on everything. It is always ready to believe anything which speaks well of another person's character. It is easily convinced of the innocence and integrity of any person. It believes in the sincerity of his repentance if he had once erred from the way. It is glad to excuse whatever is wrong. It always seeks to avoid condemning an offender if possible. It attempts to make all the allowance for human weakness which can be made without betraying the truth of God.

And when it can no longer believe, then love hopes all things. Is any evil related of any man? Love hopes that which is related is not true. Love hopes the thing related was never done. Is it certain that it was? Love hopes it was not done with such bad circumstances as are related. In allowing the fact, love believes there is room to hope it was not as bad as represented. Was the action apparently undeniably evil? Perhaps the intention was not so. Is it clear the intention was evil also? Love hopes it did not spring from a settled nature of the heart, but from a quick passion or some vehement temptation which moved the man beyond his reason. When it cannot be doubted that all the actions, designs, and tempers are equally evil, still love hopes that God will at last gain a victory over the circumstances. Love believes that there will ultimately be more joy in heaven over this one sinner who at last repents than over ninety-nine just persons who need no repentance.

Lastly, this love, mercy and charity endures all things. It completes the character of him who is truly merciful. He endures not some, not many, not most, but absolutely all things. Whatever the injustice, the malice, the cruelty of man can inflict, he is able to endure it. He calls nothing intolerable. He never says of anything, "This cannot be borne." No, he cannot only do, but suffers all things through the Holy Spirit who is in him. All which he suffers does not destroy his love, nor impair it in the least. It is proof against all. It is a flame that burns even in the midst of the great deep. Many waters cannot quench his love. Floods cannot drown it. It triumphs over all. It never fails, either in time or in eternity.

Jesus says that the merciful shall obtain mercy. They obtain mercy by God's repayment of the love they bear to their brethren a thousand-fold in their own heart. This is given to them now, in this world. Likewise, it will be given in the kingdom prepared for them from the beginning of the world.

For a little while, you may lament the conditions under which you are required to live. You may pour out your own soul bemoaning the loss of pure, common, genuine love in the world. It is lost, indeed. You may shake your head in wonder at the lack of love even among Christians. You may say, "See how these 'Christians' love one another!" These "Christian" countries even go to war with one another. These "Christian" armies send thousands into a fast hell. The "Christian" nations are on fire with brawls, party against party, faction against faction. These "Christians" have deceit and fraud, oppression and wrong, robbery and murder, in their streets. The "Christian" families are torn asunder with envy, jealousy, anger, domestic trials, without number and without end. And what is most dreadful, most to be lamented of all, are those "Christian" churches. Those churches that bear the name of Christ, the Prince of Peace, wage continual war with each other. How can this be hidden either from the Jews, Moslems or pagans?

This church has attempted to convert sinners by burning them alive. It has been drunk with the blood of the saints. It has brought praise only to Satan. It deserves the abominations of the earth. This charge is laid not only at the early church, but the Protestant churches know how to persecute also. When they have power in their hands, it can end in the shedding of blood. And meanwhile, how they do also ostracize each other. They condemn each other to the nethermost hell. What wrath, what contention, what malice, what bitterness is found everywhere among them. Even where they agree in essentials, and only differ in opinions, or in the circumstances of religion, they cannot cooperate.

Who follows only after the things which make for peace and the things with which one may edify another? O God! How long? Shall your promises fail?

Fear not. Have hope. Believe in hope! It is God's good pleasure to yet renew the face of the earth. Surely all these things shall come to an end. All of the inhabitants of earth shall learn righteousness. Nation shall not lift up sword against nation, nor shall they know war any more. The mountain of God's house shall be established on the top of the mountains. All the kingdoms of the world shall become the kingdom of God. Then they shall not hurt or destroy His holy place. They shall all be without spot or blemish, loving one another, even as Jesus has loved us. You are called to be part of the first fruits, even if the total harvest has not yet come. You are to love your neighbor as yourself. Ask God to fill your heart with a love to every soul so you will be ready to lay down your life for His sake. Ask that your soul will continually overflow with love, a love which swallows up every kind and every degree of unholy temper. Receive this merciful love now, until He calls you up into the heaven of love, to reign with Him through eternity.

5

The Kingdom of Heaven¹

"Blessed are the pure in heart: for they shall see God. Blessed are the peacemakers: for they shall be called the children of God. Blessed are they which are persecuted for righteousness' sake: for theirs is the kingdom of heaven. Blessed are ye, when men revile you, and persecute you, and shall say all manner of evil against you falsely, for my sake. Rejoice, and be exceeding glad: for great is your reward in heaven: for so persecuted they the prophets which were before you" (Matt. 5:8-12).

Excellent things are spoken about the love of our neighbor. It is called the fulfilling of the law. It is the end of the great commandment. Without this, all we have, all we do, all we suffer, is of no value in the sight of God. This love of our neighbor must be that which springs from the love of God. Othewise, in itself, it is worth nothing. It behooves us, therefore, to examine upon what foundation our love of our neighbor stands. Is it freely built upon the love of God? Do we love because He first loved us? Are we pure in heart? This is the foundation which shall never be moved. "Blessed are the pure in heart, for they shall see

God."

The pure in heart are those whose hearts have been purified even as He is pure. These are they who are purified through faith in Jesus from every unholy affection. These are they who have been cleansed from all sinfulness of flesh and spirit. They are in perfect holiness and in the love and fear of God. They are, through the power of His grace, purified from pride by the deepest poverty of spirit. They are purified from anger and from every unkind or turbulent passion, by meekness and gentleness. They have been cleansed from every desire other than to please and enjoy God. They seek to know and love Him more and more. Their hunger and thirst after righteousness now engrosses their whole soul. They now love the Lord their God with all their heart, and with all their soul, and mind, and strength.

This purity of heart has been ignored by the false teachers of all ages. They have taught men only to abstain from the outward impurities which God has forbidden by name. They did not strike at the heart of the matter. By not guarding against an impure heart, they countenanced, in effect, inward corruptions.

Jesus showed us a remarkable instance of this. He taught, "Ye have heard that it was said by them of old time, Thou shalt not commit adultery."[2] In explaining this, those blind teachers of the blind only insisted upon man's abstaining from the outward act. "But I say unto you, That whosoever looketh on a woman to lust after her hath committed adultery with her already in his heart."[3] God requires truth in the inward parts. He searches the heart and tries the soul. If you are inclined to iniquity in your heart; God will not hear you.

God allows no excuse for the retaining of anything which is a cause of impurity. Therefore, Jesus taught, "If thy right eye offend thee, pluck it out, and cast it from thee: for it is profitable for thee that one of thy members should perish, and not that thy whole body should be cast into hell."[4] If persons as dear to you as your right eye are a cause of offending God, a means of exciting unholy desire in your soul, do not delay, and forcibly separate from them. "And if thy right hand offend thee, cut it off, and cast it from thee: for it is profitable for thee that one of thy members should perish, and not that thy whole body should be cast into hell."[5] If any person, who seems as necessary to you as your right hand, is an occasion of sin, of impure desire, even though it were never to go beyond the heart, to never break out in a word or action, submit yourself to an entire and final parting. Cut him off in a stroke. Give him up to God. Any loss, whether of pleasure or substance or friends, is preferable to the loss of your soul.

Two simple steps may cure the problem before such an absolute and final separation is necessary. First, try to drive the unclean spirit out by fasting and prayer, and by carefully abstaining from every action, and word, and look which you have found to be an occasion of evil. Then, if you are not delivered by this means, ask counsel of God, who watches over your soul. Ask Him the time and manner of that separation. Do not confer with any man, lest you be given up to a strong delusion to believe a lie, and follow bad advice.

Not even marriage, holy and honorable as it is, may be used as a pretense for giving way to our desires. Indeed, it has been said, "Whosoever shall put away his wife, let him give her a writing of divorcement." Then, all was well. No offense needed to be alleged. No cause was necessary, but that he did not like her, or liked another better. Yet Jesus taught, "But I say unto you, That whosoever shall put away his wife, saving for the cause of fornication, causeth her to commit adultery."[6]

All polygamy is clearly forbidden in these words. Jesus expressly declares, that for any woman who has a husband alive, to marry again is adultery. By parity of reason, it is adultery for any man to marry again, so long as he has a wife alive, even though they were divorced. In the case of adultery, many scholars feel there is no Scripture which forbids remarriage.

This is the purity of heart which God requires. He works it through His grace in those who believe in Jesus. And so, blessed are they who are thus pure in heart. They shall see God. He will manifest himself. He will bless them with the clearest communications of His Spirit. He will award them the most intimate fellowship with the Father and the Son. He will cause His presence to be continually before them. The light of His countenance will shine upon them. It is the ceaseless prayer of their heart, "I beseech you, God, show me your glory." They receive the gift they ask of Him. They now see Him by faith. Even in His lowest works, He is in all that surrounds them. They are aware of Him in all that He has created and made. They see Him in the height above, and in the depth beneath. They see Him filling all in all. The pure in heart see all things full of God. They see Him in the firmament of heaven, and in the moon, walking in brightness. They see Him in the sun, where He rejoices as a giant to run His course. They see Him making the clouds His chariots and walking upon the wings of the wind. They see Him preparing rain for the earth, and blessing the increase of it. They see Him giving grass for the cattle, and green herb for the use of men. They see the Creator of all, wisely governing all, and upholding all things by the Word of His power. They cry out, "O Lord, our governor, how excellent is your name in all the world."

For all His providences relating to themselves, to their souls or bodies, the pure in heart do more particularly see God. They see His hand ever over them for good, giving them all things by His weight and measure, even numbering the hairs on their head. They see Him making a wall around them and all that they have, disposing of all the circumstances of their life. They understand that He does this according to the depth of His wisdom and mercy.

But in a more special manner, they see God in His ordinances. They see Him when they meet together in congregations to pay honor to His name, and worship Him in the beauty of holiness. He is with them when they enter into their closets and there pour out their souls before Him. They see Him whether they search the oracles of God, or hear the ambassadors of Christ proclaiming glad tidings of salvation, or by eating of that bread and drinking of that cup, which shows forth His death till He comes in the clouds of heaven. In all of these, His appointed ways, they experience such a near approach to Him that it cannot be expressed. They see Him, as it were, face to face. They talk with Him as a man talks with his friend. This is a fit preparation for the mansions in heaven above, where they shall see Him as He truly is.

Not seeing God were those teachers who taught that oaths were permissible. The Pharisees taught this. They allowed all manner of swearing in common conversation. Even forswearing is a small thing. They simply prohibited swearing by the particular name of God.

Jesus, however, absolutely forbids all common swearing, as well as all false swearing. He shows the ugliness of both. In consideration, He shows that every creature is God's creature. God is everywhere present in all and over all. "I say unto you, Swear not at all; neither by heaven; for it is God's throne: Nor by the earth; for it is his footstool: neither by Jerusalem; for it is the city of the great King. Neither shalt thou swear by thy head, because thou canst not make one hair white or black. But let your communication be, Yea, yea; Nay, nay: for whatsoever is more than these cometh of evil."[7] To swear by heaven is the same as swearing by God, since God sits in the heaven. Since He is present everywhere, He is in earth as in heaven, so swearing by earth is again swearing by God. Jerusalem was God's holy city. Therefore, to swear by Jerusalem was to swear by God. It is plain that nothing is ours. All is God's. He is the sole disposer of all in heaven and earth. Therefore, swearing proceeds from the devil, is of the evil one, and is a mark of Satan's children. The pure in heart limit themselves to a bare, serious, affirming of the facts.

Jesus does not here forbid the swearing in judgment and in truth, when we are required to do so by the law. This is apparent from the occasion of this part of His teaching. He is reproving abuse. He is reproving all swearing as common swearing. Swearing before a magistrate is quite a different question. From the very words wherein He forms His general conclusion, "Let your communication be yes, yes; no, no," indicates that honest answers may be given. From His own example, we see that He answered himself upon oath when required by a magistrate. When the high priest said to Him, "I adjure thee by the living God, that thou tell us whether thou be the Christ, the Son of God," Jesus immediately answered in the affirmative. "Thou hast said," which meant, that is the truth.[8] God the Father confirmed by oath His willingness to show the heirs of promise, the immutability of His counsel.[9] Also, Paul, who we think had the Spirit of God and understood the mind of Jesus, gave us an example. "God is my witness," he said to the Romans, "that without ceasing I make mention of you always in my prayers."[10] To the Corinthians he said, "I call God for a record upon my soul, that to spare you I came not as yet unto Corinth."[11] And to the Philippians, he said, "God is my record, how greatly I long after you all . . . in Jesus Christ."[12] Therefore, it undeniably appears, that if Paul knew the meaning of Jesus' words, they do not forbid swearing on important occasions even to one another. How much less do they forbid swearing for a magistrate. At least, from that assertion of Paul's, some swearing in general was approved. In Hebrews he taught, "Men verily swear by the greater," by one greater than themselves, "and an oath for confirmation is to them an end of all strife."[13]

There is a great lesson which Jesus is teaching here. He illustrates it by this example. God is in all things. We are to see the Creator mirrored in every creature. We should use, and look upon, nothing as separate from God. With true magnificence of thought, we should understand that heaven and earth, and all that is in it, is contained by God in the hollow of His hand. By His intimate presence, He holds all things in His being. He pervades and actuates the whole created frame of things. He is, in a true sense, the soul of the universe. To think otherwise is to practice a form of atheism.

Up to this point, Jesus has been more directly employed in teaching the religion of the heart. He has shown what Christians are to be. He proceeds to show what they are to do also. He shows how inward holiness is to exert itself in our outward conversation. He says, "Blessed are the peacemakers, for they shall be called the children of God." It is well known that the word "peace" in the Scriptures implies all manner of good. It implies every blessing which relates to either the soul or the body, or to time or eternity. Accordingly, when Paul, in the titles of his epistles, wishes grace and peace to the readers, it is as if he had said, "As a fruit of the free, undeserved love and favor of God, may you enjoy all blessings, spiritual and temporal. May you enjoy all the good things which God has prepared for them who love Him."

From this, we easily learn in how wide a sense the term peacemakers is to be understood. In its literal meaning, it implies those lovers of God and man who utterly detest and abhor all strife and debate. It includes those who avoid all variance and contention. It is those who labor with all of their might, either to prevent this occurring, or when it does occur, from breaking out. When strife has broken out, they prevent it from spreading any farther. They endeavor to calm the stormy spirits of men. They seek to quiet turbulent passions. They yearn to soften the minds of contending parties, and if possible, reconcile them to each other. They use all innocent arts and employ all their strength in doing this. They use all the talents God has given them to preserve peace where it is, and to restore it where it is not. It is the joy of their hearts to promote, confirm, and increase, mutual goodwill among men. They do this more especially among the children of God, however distinguished they are by differences of small importance. They all have one Lord and one faith, and are all called in one hope of their calling, so they may all walk worthy of this calling. With all lowliness, meekness and long-suffering, they are forbearing to each other in love. They endeavor to keep unity of the Spirit in the bond of peace.

But in the full extent of the word, a peacemaker is one who, as he has opportunity, does good to all men. He is one who is filled with the love of God and all mankind. He

cannot confine the expression of that love to his own
family, friends, acquaintances, party or those of his own
opinions. He does not limit this to those of his own religious
faith. His doing good steps over all of these narrow
bounds. He seeks to do good to every man. He hopes that
he may, in some way or the other, manifest his love to
neighbors and strangers, friends and enemies. He does
good to them all as he has opportunity. He does this on
every possible occasion. He redeems the time in order to
do it. He buys up every opportunity, improving every
hour, losing no moment where he may help another. He
does good, not of one particular kind, but good in general,
in every possible way. He employs all of his talents of
every kind in this. He uses all of his powers and faculties
of body and soul, all of his fortune, interest and
reputation. He desires only that when Jesus comes, He
may say, "Well done, good and faithful servant."

He does good to the uttermost of his power. He does
this good to the bodies of all men. He rejoices to offer his
bread to the hungry, and cover the naked with his
clothing. Is any a stranger? He takes him in and relieves
him according to his necessities. Are any sick or in prison?
He visits them and administers such help as they most
need. And all of this he does, not as unto man. He
remembers that Jesus said, "Inasmuch as you have done
it unto one of the least of these my brethren, you have
done it unto me."

How much more does he rejoice if he can do any good for
the soul of any man. Indeed, this power belongs to God. It
is God only who changes the heart. Without His grace,
every other change is lighter than vanity. Nevertheless,
it pleases God, who works in all, to help man, chiefly
through another man. Through man He conveys His own
power and blessing and love from one to another.
Therefore, although it is certain that the help which is

done on earth is done by God himself, no man should stand idle on this account. The peacemaker cannot. He is ever laboring as an instrument in God's hand, preparing the ground for his master's use. He is ever sowing the seed of the kingdom of God, or watering whatever he has already sown. He always hopes God will give an increase from this work. According to the measure of grace which he has received, he uses all diligence to reprove the gross sinner. He reclaims those who run headlong in the broad way of destruction. He gives light to them who sit in darkness, ready to perish for lack of knowledge. He supports the weak and lifts up the hands which hang down. He seeks to bring back and heal those who were lame and turned out of the way. He is equally zealous in comforting those who have already entered in the straight gate. He tries to strengthen those who now stand, so they may run with patience the race which lies before them. He attempts to build up in the most holy faith all those who believe in God. He exhorts them to stir up the gifts of God which are within them. Thus, they daily grow in grace. An entrance is ministered abundantly unto them into the everlasting kingdom of our Lord and Savior.

Blessed are they who are continually employed in the work of faith, and the labor of love, for they shall be called the children of God. God shall continue giving them the Holy Spirit. He shall pour Him more abundantly in their hearts. He shall bless them with all the blessings of His children. He shall acknowledge them as sons before angels and men. If they are sons, then they are heirs. They are heirs of God, and joint heirs with Jesus.

Such is a person full of genuine humility. He is unaffectedly serious. He is mild, and gentle, and free from selfish design. He is devoted to God, and an active lover of men. One might imagine that such a person should be the darling of all mankind. But Jesus knew human nature better in its present state. He therefore closes His teachings about the character of this man of God by showing him the treatment he is to expect in the world. He says, "Blessed are they which are persecuted for righteousness' sake, for theirs is the kingdom of heaven."

It is important to fully understand this warning. First, let us inquire who are they who are persecuted? We may easily learn this from the writings of Paul. He said, "But as then, he that was born after the flesh persecuted him that was born after the Spirit, even so it is now."[14] On another occasion Paul wrote, "Yea, and all that will live godly in Christ Jesus shall suffer persecution."[15] The Apostle John thought the same, for he wrote, "Marvel not, my brethren, if the world hate you. We know that we have passed from death unto life, because we love the brethren."[16] It is as if he had said Christians cannot be loved except by those who have passed from spiritual death into this new spiritual life. And almost expressly, Jesus said, "If the world hate you, ye know that it hated me before it hated you. If ye were of the world, the world would love his own: but because ye are not of the world, . . . the world hateth you. Remember the word that I said unto you, The servant is not greater than his lord. If they have persecuted me, they will also persecute you."[17]

By all these Scriptures, it clearly appears who they are that are persecuted. The righteous are persecuted. He that is reborn by the Spirit is persecuted. All that attempt to live godly lives according to Jesus will be persecuted. Those who have passed from death in this world to spiritual life can expect the same treatment. Those who are meek and lowly in heart, and not of the world, will be rejected by the world. Those who mourn after God and hunger to be in His likeness, will be seen as fools. Those who love God and their neighbor, and, as they have opportunity, do good to all men, will be reviled for their goodness.

It is then to be asked why they are persecuted. The answer is equally plain and obvious. It is for righteousness' sake. It is because they are righteous, because they are born of the Spirit. It is because they want to live godly in Jesus. They are persecuted because they are not of the world. Whatever else may be pretended, this is the real cause. What other faults they might have, if it were not for this, the world would put up with them. The world loves its own. They are persecuted because they are poor in spirit. The world accuses them of being poor spirited, mean, dastardly souls, good for nothing, not fit to live in the world. They are charged with this because they are in holy mourning. They are accused of being dull, heavy, lumpish creatures, giving gloom to anyone who sees them. They are accused of killing innocent mirth and spoiling company wherever they are. Because they are meek, they are accused of being tame, passive fools, fit only to be trampled upon. Because they hunger and thirst after righteousness, they are said to be a parcel of hot-brained fanatics, gasping after they know not what, not content with usual religion. They are said to be running madly after raptures and inward feelings. Because they are merciful, and lovers of all—even the evil and ungrateful—they are accused of encouraging all manner of wickedness. They are said to be tempting people to do mischief by impunity. For their forgiveness, they are accused of tempting others to be very loose in their principles. Because they are pure in heart, they are uncharitable creatures that damn all the world but those who are of their own sort. They are said to be blasphemous wretches that make God a liar, for they pretend to live without sin. Above all this, they are persecuted because they are peacemakers who attempt to take all opportunities for doing all good to all men. This is the grand reason why they have been persecuted in all ages. This is why they will be persecuted to the restitution of all things.

The world says, "If they would but keep their religion to themselves, they would be tolerable, but it is this spreading of their errors, this infecting of others, which is not to be endured. They do so much mischief in the world, they ought not to be tolerated any longer. It is true that they do some things well enough. They relieve some of the poor. This too, however, is done only to gain more to their cause. The effect is that they do more damage."

The men of the world sincerely believe this when they speak it. The more the kingdom of God prevails, the more the peacemakers are able to propagate lowliness, meekness, and all other divine tempers. The more this is accomplished, the more persecutions they receive. As true Christianity grows, the more the world is enraged against the authors of it, and the more vehemently will they persecute them.

Then we should understand who are the persecutors. Paul again answers this for us. He said, "He that is born after the flesh" cannot love those who are born of the Spirit. Those who are born of the Spirit, or desire to be, are all those who at least labor after a godly life, according to Jesus. Those who are not in this group are of the world, and cannot love the spiritual man. That is, according to Jesus, they who do not know Him and God who sent Him. They do not know God, the pardoning, loving God, through the teaching of His own Holy Spirit.

The reason for this is plain. The spirit which is in the

world is directly opposite to the Holy Spirit, which is of God. It must, therefore, be that those who are of the world will be opposite to those who are of God. There is the utmost difference between them. They differ in their opinions, their desires, designs and tempers. We know that they cannot be in peace together. The proud, because he is proud, will persecute the lowly. The light and airy will persecute those who seriously mourn for their sins. And it is so to every other kind. The unlikeness of disposition is a perpetual ground of enmity. Therefore, all the servants of the devil will contrive to persecute the children of God.

We can also discover how they will be persecuted. This may be answered in general. It will be in whatever way that best tends to the Christian's growth in grace, and the enlargement of God's own kingdom. There is one branch of God's government of the world which is always in His control. His ear is never deaf to the threatenings of the persecutors, or the cry of the persecuted. His eye is ever open. His hand is stretched to direct even the minutest circumstance. He directs when the strife shall begin, how high it shall rise, the direction of its course, when and how it shall end. By his unerring wisdom, he controls the persecutors. When the ends of his grace are answered, the persecutors are saved. Such was the case of Saul, who became the Apostle Paul.

At some rare times in the past, as when Christianity was first planted, the storm was permitted to rise high. At that time Christians were called even to the martyr's death. There seems to be a particular reason why God allowed this to happen even to the apostles. It was so their testimony might be even more authentic.

From the history of the church we learn an additional and far different reason. It was because of the monstrous corruptions which reigned even in the early church. It seems that God allowed those who were part of heresy to be purged from the church. He chastened, but at the same time, strove to heal.

Perhaps the same observation may be made with regard to persecutions in our time. God has dealt very graciously with our nation. He poured out various blessings upon us. He had given us peace abroad and at home. He had given us wise leadership. Above all, He had allowed the good news of Jesus' teachings to rise and shine among us. But what has He received in return? He looked for righteousness. He received oppression, wrong, ambition, injustice, malice, fraud and covetousness. Then God rose to maintain His own cause against those who held His truth in contempt. He allowed many of them to be persecuted, by a judgment mixed with mercy. He allows affliction to punish, while offering a medicine to heal the backsliding of His people.

But God seldom allows the storm of persecution to rise so high as torture, or death, or imprisonment. Christians are frequently called to endure only lighter kinds of persecutions. Often they suffer estrangement of family, and loss of friends. In this, they find the truth of Jesus' teaching. "Suppose ye that I am come to give peace on earth? I tell you, Nay, but rather division."[18] And so, the zealous witness for Jesus can naturally expect the loss of some business or employment. Prosperity may decrease rather than increase. However, these circumstances are always under the wise direction of God. He allows to everyone only that which is best for them.

Not all receive the persecutions described above. There is, however, a persecution which follows all of the true children of God. It is that which Jesus describes in the following words. "Blessed are you when men shall revile you and persecute you, and say all manner of evil against you falsely for my sake." This cannot fail. It is the very badge of discipleship. It is one of the seals of God's calling. It is a sureness of reviling which will fall on all the children of God. If we have not been reviled for our new living faith, we are not true sons of God. The children of God are of good report among their own brothers. They are known as being meek, serious, humble and zealous lovers of God and man. This way of living brings evil reports from the world. In spite of righteousness, the world continues to count and treat them as filth, and the refuse of the world, because they are different.

Who ever imagined that this scandal and mistreatment will cease before the times of this world end? Some hope that God will cause Christians to be esteemed and loved by those who are still sinners. Yes, and sure it is that even now, God at some times stays the contempt as well as the fierceness of worldly men. Setting aside these exceptions, the scandal of Christianity is not yet over. So a man must say still, "If I please men, I am not the servant of Jesus." Let no man therefore believe that pleasing suggestion that bad men only pretend to hate and despise good men. They do not indeed love and esteem good men in their hearts. They may use them on occasion, but it is only for their own profit. They may put confidence in them, for they know a Christian's way is not like those of other men. But they still do not love them. They will accept them only so far as the Holy Spirit is striving with them. Jesus' words are clear. "If you were of the world, the world would love its own. Because you are not of the world, the world hates you." The serious follower of Jesus can expect to be hated by the world as cordially and sincerely as it hated Jesus himself.

Only one question remains. How are spiritual followers

of Jesus to behave under persecutions? First, they ought not do anything to bring it on themselves. That is contrary to both the example and advice of Jesus and all of His apostles. They taught us not only to not seek, but to avoid it. We are to avoid it as far as we can without injuring our conscience. We cannot give up any part of that righteousness which we are to prefer before life itself. So, Jesus expressly said, "When they persecute you in this city, flee to another." When this can be done, it is the best way of avoiding persecution.

Do not think that you can always avoid it, either by this or any other means. If ever that imagination comes into your mind, put it away at once. "Remember the word that I said unto you, the servant is not greater than his lord. If they have persecuted me, they will also persecute you." "Be wise as serpents and harmless as doves." But will this behavior screen you from persecutions? Not unless you have more wisdom than Jesus. Not unless you are more innocent than He.

So you should neither desire to avoid it, nor to completely escape it. If you do, you are not a follower of Jesus. If you escape the persecutions, you will miss the blessings. There is a blessing for all of those who are persecuted for righteousness' sake. If you are not persecuted for righteousness' sake, you cannot enter into the kingdom of heaven. "If we suffer, we shall also reign with him: if we deny him, he also will deny us."[19]

Then, rejoice and be glad when you are persecuted for His sake. When they persecute you by reviling you and saying all manner of evil against you falsely, be glad. They will blacken you to excuse themselves. Therefore, they will not fail to mix in with their reviling every kind of persecution. "For so persecuted they the prophets which were before you." They persecuted those who were most eminently holy in heart and life. Yes, they persecuted all the righteous who have been since the beginning of the world. Rejoice, because by this mark, you know to whom you belong. Great will be your reward in heaven. It is a reward purchased by the blood of the covenant. It is freely bestowed in proportion to your sufferings, as well as to your holiness in heart and in life. Be glad, knowing these light afflictions, which are but for a little while, work out for you a far more eternal weight of glory.

Meantime, let no persecution turn you out of the way of lowliness and meekness. Continue in love and beneficence. "Ye have heard that it hath been said, An eye for an eye, and a tooth for a tooth: But I say unto you, That you resist not evil."[20] Do not retaliate in kind. Rather than that, do this. When someone hits you on your right cheek, turn to him the other also. If any man will sue you at law, and take away your coat, let him have your cloak also. And whenever one compels you to go with him a mile, go with him two.

Let your meekness be invincible. Your love is to be suitable to your faith. Give to him that asks of you, and to him that would borrow of you. Only give not that which is another man's. That is not yours to give. Therefore, take care to owe no man anything, for what you owe is not your own, but another's. Provide for those in your own household. God has required you to do this. You are to provide what is necessary to sustain them in life and godliness. Then, give or lend all that remains, from day to day, or from year to year. Knowing that you cannot give to all, first remember your spiritual brothers.

Jesus described the meekness and love we are to feel. He told of the kindness we are to show to them who persecute us for righteousness' sake. "Ye have heard that it hath been said, Thou shalt love thy neighbor, and hate

thine enemy. But I say unto you, Love your enemies."
Love them that curse you. Pray for them who hate you.
Do not be overcome by evil, but overcome evil with good.
Pray for those who despitefully use and persecute you.
    Let your actions show that you are as real in love as
they are in hatred. Return good for evil. If you can do
nothing more, at least pray for those who despitefully use
and persecute you. You can never be prevented from
doing this. None of their malice and violence can hinder
you from doing it. Pour out your soul to God. Pray not only
for those who do this once and now repent. Pray for,
wrestle with God for those who do not repent, those who
still despitefully use and persecute you. Forgive them,
not seven times only, but seventy times seven.[21] Show
them every instance of kindness whether they repent or
not. Even though they appear farther and farther from it,
pray for them. In this way, you show that you are genuine
children of God who is in heaven. He shows His goodness
by giving blessings on even His stubbornest enemies. He
makes His sun rise on both the good and the evil, and
sends rain on both the just and the unjust. If you love only
those who love you, what reward have you? Even the
sinners do the same.[22] Even those who pretend to have no
religion, and are without God, will love those who love
them. And if you show kindness only to your friends, and
brethren, and kinsmen, you do no more than the sinners.
We are to follow a better pattern than they. In patience,
in long-suffering, in mercy, in goodness of every kind, we
are to be perfect. Even to our bitterest persecutors, we
are to be perfect in kind, though not in degree, as God in
heaven is perfect.[23]
    This is Christianity in its original form, as was
delivered by Jesus. This is his genuine religion. He
presents it to those whose eyes are opened spiritually.

Here we see a picture of God in so far as He is imitable by man. It is a picture drawn by God's own hand. We should not rest until every line of it is written upon our own hearts. We need to watch, and pray, believe, love and strive for mastery of it. Then we can expect that every part of it will appear upon our souls, put there by the finger of God. We are to continue in this until we are as holy as He who has called us to be holy. We are to persevere in the faith of Jesus, until we are as perfect as our Father in heaven is perfect.

6

The Salt of the Earth[1]

"Ye are the salt of the earth: but if the salt have lost his savour, wherewith shall it be salted? It is thenceforth good for nothing, but to be cast out, and to be trodden under foot of men. Ye are the light of the world. A city that is set on an hill cannot be hid. Neither do men light a candle and put it under a bushel, but on a candlestick; and it giveth light unto all that are in the house. Let your light so shine before men, that they may see your good works, and glorify your Father which is in heaven" (Matt. 5:13-16).

The beauty of holiness catches the eye of everyone, everyone of enlightened understanding. This holiness is that of the inward man with a heart which is renewed in the image of God. It displays a meek, humble and loving spirit. His behavior receives the approval of all of these who are capable, in any degree, of discerning spiritual good and evil. From the moment a person begins to emerge out of the darkness which covers the unthinking world, he perceives how desirable it is to be transformed into the likeness of God. This inward religion bears the shape of God visibly impressed upon it. A person must be wholly immersed in flesh and blood, as a natural man, if he can doubt its divine original. Jesus is the express image of God's person. In a secondary sense, He is the brightness of God's glory. Jesus is so tempered and softened that anyone may look to Him and see God and live. In Him is the original source of all excellency and perfection. He has the stamp, the character, the living impression of God's person. He is the fountain of beauty and love.

If religion stopped with Jesus, no one could doubt it. No one could have any objection against pursuing it with the whole strength of their souls. But they say, "Why is religion clogged with other things? Why is it loaded with doing and suffering? These are what dampen the vigor of the spiritual life. These cause the soul to sink down to earth again. Is it not enough to follow after love and charity? Can we not simply soar upon the wings of His love? Is it not enough to worship God who is Spirit, with the spirit of our minds? Why must we encumber ourselves with outward things, or even think of them at all? Is it not better that all our thoughts be centered upon high and heavenly contemplation? Why should we not commune with God only in our hearts, instead of busying ourselves about externals?"

Many good men have spoken in this way. They have advised us to cease from all outward actions. They have directed us to wholly withdraw from the world. They have said we can leave the body behind us, and abstract ourselves from all those things. They have taught us to have no concern at all with outward religion. They have said to work all the virtues in the mind is a far better way. They have believed that it will perfect the soul in a way more acceptable to God.

This is the simplest of all devices with which Satan has

perverted the gospel of Jesus. It is not necessary that any should inform Jesus of this "masterpiece of wisdom" from below. What instruments Satan has found, from time to time, to employ in this, his service! He has pointed this great weapon of hell against some of the most important truths of God. These eminent teachers would deceive, if it were possible, the very elect of God, the men of faith and love. On occasion, they have deceived and led away no small number of them. Men of all ages who have fallen into this snare have hardly escaped with the skin of their teeth.

But was Jesus lacking on His part? Did He not sufficiently guard us against this delusion? Did He not arm us here with armor of proof against Satan, now transformed into the angel of light? Yes, truly Jesus defended, in the clearest and strongest manner, the active, patient religion He prescribes. What can be fuller and plainer than the words He immediately adds to what He said of doing and suffering? "Ye are the salt of the earth: but if the salt have lost his savour, wherewith shall it be salted? It is thenceforth good for nothing, but to be cast out, and to be trodden under foot of men. Ye are the light of the world. A city that is set on an hill cannot be hid. Neither do men light a candle, and put it under a bushel, but on a candlestick; and it giveth light unto all that are in the house. Let your light so shine before men, that they may see your good works, and glorify your Father which is in heaven."

In order to fully explain and enforce these important words, we shall endeavor to show that Christianity is a social religion. To turn it into a solitary religion is to destroy it. Next, that to conceal this religion is impossible, as well as utterly contrary to the purposes of Jesus. Last, we shall answer some objections to Jesus' teachings. Then, we will conclude the whole with practical applications of it.

First, Christianity is essentially a social religion. To turn it into a solitary religion is indeed to destroy it. By Christianity, we mean that method of worshiping God which was revealed to man by Jesus. When we say this is essentially a social religion, we mean that it cannot exist at all without society. We do not mean that it cannot exist as well without society. We mean that it cannot exist at all without living and conversing with other men. To show this, we shall limit our considerations to those which arise from the discourse before us. We propose to show that turning Christianity into a solitary religion is to destroy it.

In no way do we condemn the intermixing of solitude or retirement with society. This is not only allowable, but also expedient. It is necessary, as daily experience shows. Everyone who already is, or desires to be, a real Christian, understands this. It can hardly be that we could spend one entire day in a continued relationship with other people. To do this would cause loss to our soul. It would to some measure grieve the Holy Spirit. We have need daily to retire from the world, at least morning and evening, to converse with God. We need to communicate freely with our Father, who is in secret. Neither can anyone with religious experience condemn longer times of religious retirement. Spiritual retreat for a period is permissible if it does not imply any neglect of that worldly employment in which God has placed us. However, such retirement must not take up all of our time. This would be to destroy, and not advance, true Christianity. The religion described by Jesus in the foregoing Scripture cannot exist without society. It requires our living and conversing with other people. It is apparent from this that several of the most essential branches of Christianity would be lost if we had no relationship with the world.

There is no disposition, for instance, which is more essential to Christianity than meekness. Meekness implies resignation to God with patience in all things. True, it may exist in a desert, a hermit's cell, or in total solitude. Yet meekness also implies mildness, gentleness, and long-suffering. Those qualities cannot possibly exist without contact with other people. So, to turn this into a solitary virtue is to destroy it from the face of the earth.

Another necessary branch of true Christianity is peacemaking, or doing good. There can be no argument that this is equally essential along with the other parts of the religion. The strongest argument for this is that Jesus inserted it into His original plan of the fundamentals of His religion. Therefore, setting this aside distresses Him as much as setting aside mercifulness, purity of heart, or any other branch of His teachings. This is apparently set aside by all those who would call us to practice a solitary religion. How can one claim that a solitary Christian can be a merciful man? There would be no way to take opportunity for doing good to all people. What can be more clear than this? The religion of Jesus cannot possibly exist without society, without our living and conversing with other men.

Others might ask, "But is it not expedient, however, to converse only with good men? Should we not limit our relationships to those whom we know to be meek, merciful, holy of heart, and holy of life? Is it not wise to avoid conversation or relationships with people of the opposite character? Should we not avoid fellowship with men who do not obey, perhaps do not believe, the gospel of Jesus?" The advice Paul wrote to the Christians at Corinth may seem to favor this. He wrote, "I wrote unto you in an epistle not to company with fornicators."[2] It is certainly not advisable to keep company with them who are workers of iniquity. We should not have any particular familiarity or strict friendship with them. To continue in intimacy with any of these is not expedient for a Christian. This will necessarily expose him to many dangers and snares from which he can have no reasonable hope of deliverance.

But Paul does not forbid us to have any contact with those who do not know God. He wrote, "For then, you must go out of the world." He could never advise them to do so, and added, "If any man that is called a brother be a fornicator, or covetous, or an idolater, or a railer, or a drunkard, or an extortioner; with such an one no not to eat."[3] This necessarily implies that we break off all familiarity, all intimacy of acquaintance with him. Then Paul said, on another occasion, "Yet count him not as an enemy, but admonish him as a brother."[4] This plainly shows that we are not to renounce all fellowship with him. So Paul gives no advice to separate wholly even from wicked men. His words teach us quite the contrary.

Much less does Jesus teach us to break off all commerce with the world. Without it, according to his account of Christianity, we cannot be Christians at all. It would be easy to show that some relationship with even the ungodly and unholy is absolutely necessary. This is necessary to complete the full exertion of every temper which he has described as the way to the kingdom. It is indispensable to complete the exercise of poverty of spirit, of mourning, and every other disposition which has a place in the genuine religion of Jesus.

It is necessary to the very existence of several of them. Meekness, for example, instead of demanding an eye for an eye, does not resist evil. It causes us, when hit on the right cheek, to turn the left also. Mercifulness is that quality whereby we love our enemies. We bless them who curse us. We do good to them who hate us. We pray for them who despitefully use us and persecute us. This produces in us that completion of love and all holy tempers which are exercised in suffering for righteousness' sake. Now all of these, it is clear, would not exist if we had no contact with any but real Christians.

Indeed, if we separate ourselves wholly from sinners, how could we possibly answer that character which Jesus requires in His other teachings? "You are the salt of the earth." It is your very nature to season whatever is around you. It is the nature of your faith to spread it to whatever you touch. You diffuse it on every side to all those around you. In relationship to others, you are lowly, serious, and meek. You show that you hunger after righteousness, and love God and man. In doing that, you do good to all, and often suffer evil in return. This is the great reason why God has put you together with other men. It is so that whatever grace you have received from God, you may communicate it to others. Every holy temper and word and work of yours can have an influence on them also. By this means, a check will in some measure be given to the corruption which is in the world. Through you, a small part, at least, may be saved from the general infection of sin, and rendered holy and pure before God.

Then Jesus proceeds to show the desperate state of those who do not share the religion they have received. They cannot possibly fail to share it as long as it remains in their heart. He does this so we may the more diligently labor at all times, with every holy and heavenly temper. "If the salt has lost its savor, how shall it be resalted? It is then good for nothing but to be cast out and trodden under foot of men." Jesus is speaking of those who were once holy and heavenly minded, zealous of doing good works, and now no longer have that spiritual seasoning within them. If a Christian has grown flat, insipid, dead, careless of his own soul and useless to the souls of other men, how will he be restored? Can tasteless salt be restored to its former state? No, it is then good for nothing except to be cast out, even as the mire in the street. There it is overwhelmed with everlasting contempt and trodden under the feet of men. If you had never known Jesus, there might have been hope. If you had never been found to be in Him, this teaching would not apply to you. A parallel teaching enforcing this was recorded by John. "Every branch in me that beareth not fruit he taketh away. . . . He that abideth in me, and I in him, the same bringeth forth much fruit. . . . If a man abide not in me, he is cast forth as a branch, and is withered; and men gather them, and cast them into the fire."5

God indeed pities and is of tender mercy for those who have never known the gospel. However, justice takes place with regard to those who have experienced His graciousness, and have afterward turned back from the holy commandments which were delivered to them. "For it is impossible to restore again to repentance those who have once been enlightened, who have tasted the heavenly gift, and have become partakers of the Holy Spirit, and have tasted the goodness of the word of God and the powers of the age to come, if they then commit apostasy, since they crucify the Son of God on their own account and hold him up to contempt."6 This is not a supposition, but a flat declaration that it is impossible for those in whose hearts God once shone to be renewed again. So that none should misunderstand these important words, some careful observations should be made. First, this Scripture applies only to those who were once enlightened and tasted that heavenly gift, being made partakers of the Holy Spirit. Those who have not experienced these things can be unconcerned with this Scripture. Next, the falling away spoken of here is an absolute and total apostasy. A believer may fall and not fall away. He may fall and rise again. If he should fall even into sin, his case is not desperate, even though it is dreadful. We always have an advocate with the Father, Jesus, the righteous. Jesus is the propitiation for our sins. However, all believers must remain cautious. All should beware of letting his heart be hardened by the deceitfulness of sin. It is too easy to gradually sink lower and lower until there is a complete falling away. When this occurs, the salt has lost its savor. If we sin willfully after we have received the indwelling Holy Spirit, there remains no more sacrifice for sin. All that remains is a certain fearful looking for judgment and fiery indignation.

Others agree that Christians should not separate themselves wholly from mankind. However, they should seek to transmit their faith to others very quietly. They believe it can be conveyed to others in a secret and almost imperceptible manner. Done in this way, scarcely anyone would be able to observe how or when it was done. They point out that salt conveys flavor without visibility or sound. Consequently, they feel they should be able to live in the world and not go out into it with the gospel. They hope to keep their faith to themselves so as not to offend others.

Jesus was well aware of the plausible reasoning which some would do. He gave a full answer to it in the Word of His teaching. Jesus made it plain that it was impossible to conceal His religion. He gave a twofold comparison.

"You are the light of the world; a city on a hill cannot be hid." Christians are the light of the world with regard to both their tempers and actions. Your holiness makes you as conspicuous as the sun in the sky. As you cannot go out of the world, neither can you stay in it without being visible to all mankind. You may not flee from men. While you are among them, it is impossible to hide your lowliness and meekness. You cannot hide your Christian character. You cannot hide your disposition whereby you aspire to be as perfect as God in heaven is perfect. Love cannot be hidden any more than can light. Least of all, it cannot be hidden when it shines forth in action. When you exercise yourself in a labor of love, in any kind of good work, you are observed. Men may as well try to hide a city as to hide a Christian. They may as well attempt to conceal a city set upon a hill as a holy, zealous, active lover of God and man.

It is true, there are men who love darkness rather than light. This is because their deeds are evil. They will take all possible pains to prove the light which is in you is really darkness. They will say evil, all manner of evil, falsely of the good which is in a Christian. They will charge motives which are farthest from a Christian's mind. They will accuse Christians of the very reverse of what they are, and all that they do. Your patient continuance and welldoing, your meekly suffering all things for the Lord's sake, your humble joy in the midst of persecution, your unwearied labor to overcome evil with good, will make you still more visible and conspicuous than you were before.

If we keep the Christian religion from being seen we make it of no effect. Hiding it is as vain as hiding the light, unless we put it out. Sure it is, that a secret, unobserved religion cannot be the religion of Jesus. Whatever religion can be concealed, it is not Christianity. If a Christian could be hid, he could not be compared to a city set upon a hill. He could not be compared to the light of the world, the sun shining from the sky, to be seen by all the world below. Never, therefore, let it enter into the heart of any whom God has renewed by His Holy Spirit to hide His light. Never let him think that he can keep his religion to himself. Such a thought is contrary to the plan of Jesus himself, and is impossible to accomplish.

The reality of this truth is apparent in the words that follow. "Neither do men light a candle to put it under a bushel." Jesus has said that men do not light a candle only to cover and conceal it. Neither does God enlighten any soul with His glorious knowledge and love, to have that soul covered or concealed. It is not to be covered either by prudence, falsely so-called, or shame, or voluntary humility. It is not to be hidden either in a desert or in the world. It is not to be hidden by avoiding men, or while conversing with them. "But they put it on a candlestick, and it gives light to all that are in the house." In the same way, it is the purpose of God that every Christian should be in open view. He is to give light to all around him, by visibly expressing the religion of God as given by Jesus.

In this manner, God has spoken to all the world in all ages. He spoke not only precept, but by example also. He did not leave himself without a witness in every nation where the sound of the true gospel went forth. He has never been without a few who have testified to His truth by their lives, as well as by their words. These have been as lights shining in a dark place. From time to time, they have been the means of enlightening some. Because of this, they have preserved a remnant, a little seed which continued with the Lord for a generation.

They have led a few poor sheep out of the darkness of the world. They have managed to guide the feet of a few into the way of peace.

So we see that both in Scripture and in reason, these things are spoken of clearly and expressly. One might imagine that there would be very little proposed on the other side. At least, we could suppose that contrary arguments would have little appearance of truth. Those who imagine this know little of the wiles of Satan. After all that Scripture and reason have said about being social, open and active Christians, many have been led into hiding their faith from the world. We need all of the wisdom of God to escape this snare. We need all of the power of God in order to escape it.

Because of this, we must have answers to these misleadings. It has been objected that true religion does not lie in outward things. True religion lies in the heart, the inmost soul. True religion is the union of the soul with God, the life of God in the soul of man. Because this is true, some have said that outward religion is worth nothing. They have commented that God "delightest not in burnt offerings."[7] He does not seek outward services, but a pure and holy sacrifice is a sacrifice which He will not despise.

This is most true. The root of true religion lies in the heart. It is in the inmost soul. It is the union of the soul with God, the life of God in the soul of man. But if this root is really in the heart, it must put forth branches. These branches are the many instances of outward obedience, which are of the same nature as is the root. Consequently, they are not only marks or signs, but substantial parts of true religion.

It is also true that bare, outside religion, which has no root in the heart, is worth nothing. God does not delight in outward services, which are not rooted in the heart. He likes these no more than He does the Jewish burnt offerings. A pure and holy heart is a sacrifice with which He is always pleased. But He is also well pleased with all of the outward services which arise from the pure heart. He is pleased with the sacrifice of our prayers, either in public or private. He is pleased with our praises and our thanksgiving. He is pleased with our sacrifice of goods humbly devoted to Him. He is pleased with the total employment of our bodies to His glory. He has particular claim on our whole being. Verifying these claims of God upon our lives, Paul taught that we should present our bodies unto Him as a living sacrifice, holy and acceptable to Him.[8]

A second objection closely related to this is that love is all in all. It is said that love is the fulfilling of the law. Love is the end of every commandment of God. All we do, and all we suffer, if we do not have love, profits us nothing. Therefore, Paul directs us to follow after charity as the more excellent way.[9]

It is true that the love of God and man, arising from complete faith, is the all in all of fulfilling the law, and the end of every commandment of God. It is true, that without this, whatever we do or suffer profits us nothing. It does not follow, however, that love is all in such a sense as to supersede either faith or good works. Love is the fulfilling of the law. It does not release us from the law. Love requires us to obey the law. It is the end of the commandment, as every commandment leads to and centers in it. It is a fact that whatever we do or allow, unless we have love, profits us nothing. But, it is also true that whatever we do or suffer in love, though it were only the suffering of reproach for Jesus, or the giving of a cup of water in His name, that act shall in no way lose its reward.

But does not Paul direct us to follow after love? Does he not term it a more excellent way? He does direct us to follow after love. He does not direct us to follow after love alone. His words are, "Follow after charity and desire spiritual gifts."[10] We should follow after love, and desire to spend and be spent for our brothers. Follow after love, and as you have opportunity, do good to all men.

In this same verse, where Paul terms the way of love as the more excellent way, he points to the desirability of other gifts besides it. He taught that the other gifts were to be desired earnestly. He wrote, "Covet earnestly the best gifts: and yet show I unto you a more excellent way."[11] More excellent than what? More excellent than the gifts of healing, of speaking in tongues, and interpreting tongues, which were mentioned in the preceding verses. However, not a more excellent way than obedience. Paul is not speaking of this. He is not speaking of outward religion at all. So this text does not speak to the present question.

But suppose Paul had been speaking of outward religion, as well as inward religion. Suppose he had been comparing them with each other. Suppose, in that comparison, he had given preference to one over the other. Suppose he had preferred a loving heart more than all outward works of whatever kind. Even so, it would not follow that we are to reject one or the other. No, God has joined them together from the beginning of the world. Let no man divide the two.

Some will ask, "Is this not enough? Ought we not employ our whole strength of mind in doing this? Does not attending to outward things clog the soul? Do they not prevent it from soaring aloft in holy contemplation? Does it not dampen the vigor of our thought? Has it not a natural tendency to encumber and distract the mind? Paul would instruct us to wait upon the Lord without distraction."

It is true that "God is a Spirit: and they that worship him must worship him in spirit and in truth."[12] This is enough. We ought to employ the whole strength of our mind in this worship. But we must ask, what is it to worship God, a Spirit, in spirit and truth? Why, it is to worship Him with our spirit. It is to worship Him in that manner in which none but spirits are capable of doing. It is to believe in Him. It is to know Him as a wise, just, holy being. It is to know that His eyes are too pure to behold iniquity. It is to know that He is merciful, gracious, and long-suffering. He forgives iniquity, transgression and sin. He casts all of our sins behind His back, and accepts us in the beloved Jesus. To worship Him is to also love Him, and delight in Him. It is to desire Him with all of our heart, mind, soul and strength. It is to imitate Him who we love by purifying ourselves even as He is pure. It is obedience to Him whom we love and in whom we believe, by thought, word and deed. Consequently, one branch of worshiping God in spirit and in truth is the keeping of His outward commandments. To glorify Him with our bodies, as well as our spirits, is genuine worship. It is to go through outward works with hearts lifted up to Him. It is to buy and sell, to eat and drink, to His glory. This is the worshiping of God in spirit and in truth, just as is praying to Him in solitude.

So we see that contemplation is only one way of worship. It is only one way of worshiping God in spirit and in truth. Therefore, to give ourselves up entirely to contemplation would be to destroy many branches of spiritual worship. Both branches are equally acceptable to God, and equally profitable to the soul. The great mistake is to suppose that attention to outward things, to which God has called us, may clog the Christian soul. There is no hindrance at all in our always seeing God who is invisible. It does not all dampen the ardor of our thought. It does not encumber or distract the mind. It gives no uneasy or harmful worry if it is all done as unto the Lord. The true Christian has learned that whatever he does in word or deed is to be done in the name of Jesus. This is having one eye of the soul which moves around on outward things, while the other is fixed immovably upon God. Poor recluses need to learn what this means, so they may clearly discern the smallness of their faith.

There is still a great objection to come. Some will say, "We appeal to our experience. Our light did shine; we used outward things for years. Yet, all this profited us nothing. We attended to all of the ordinances of the church, but were no better for it. Indeed, no one else was better for it. We were worse for it, for we believed ourselves to be Christians for doing these good works. We did not know what true Christianity meant."

We can agree with this statement. We can agree that thousands have abused the ordinances of God. They have mistaken the means for the end. They have supposed that the doing of these things, or some outward works, was either the religion of Jesus, or would be accepted in place of it. Now, let the abuse be removed and the use remain. Now, use all outward things, but use them with a constant eye to the renewal of your soul in righteousness and true holiness.

But this is not all, they still affirm. Experience likewise shows, that the trying to do good is but lost labor. What does it avail to feed or clothe men's bodies, if they are just dropping into everlasting fire? And what good can any man do for their souls? If these are changed, God must do it himself. Besides, all men are either good, or at least they desire to be, or they are obstinately evil. Now the good have no need of us. Let them ask help of God, and it will be given of them. And the evil can receive no help from us. And our Lord forbids us to cast our pearls before swine.

The answer to this is obvious. Whether they will be finally saved or lost is irrelevant. We are still expressly commanded to feed the hungry and clothe the naked. If we can, and do not, regardless of what comes of them, we shall go away into the everlasting fire. Though it is God only who changes hearts, He generally does this through men. It is our responsibility to do all that lies in us. We are to act as diligently as if we could change them ourselves. We are then to leave the event to them. God, in answer to their prayers, builds up His children by each other in every good gift. He nourishes and strengthens the whole body by that which every part supplies, so that the eye cannot say to the hand, I have no need of you. No, not even the head to the feet, I have no need of you.

Lastly, how are you assured that the persons before you are dogs or swine? Judge them not until you have tried. How do you know that you will not gain a brother? You may, with God's help, save his soul from death. If he spurns your love and blasphemes the good Word, then it is time enough to give up. Then you can turn him over to God.

Some say, "We have tried. We have labored to reform sinners. What did it avail? On many we could make no impression at all. If some were changed for a little while, then their goodness was but as the morning dew. They were soon as bad, or even worse, than ever. We not only hurt them, but ourselves also. Our lives were harried and discomposed. Sometimes we were filled with anger instead of love. Therefore, we should have kept our religion to ourselves."

It is very possible this statement may also be true. It is possible to have tried to do good and not to have succeeded. It is true that some who seem reformed have relapsed into sin. It is possible that their last stage was worse than their first. Why should this cause wonder? Is the servant above the master? How often did Jesus strive to save sinners who would not listen to Him? How many followed Him for a while, yet turned back, as a dog to its vomit?[13] With all of this, He did not desist from striving to do good. Neither should you, regardless of your success. It is your part to do as you are commanded. The event is in the hand of God. You are not accountable for this. Leave it to Him who orders all things well. "In the morning sow thy seed, and in the evening withhold not thine hand: for thou knowest not whether shall prosper."[14]

And the objection remains that the trial harried and threatened the believer's own soul. Perhaps it did so for a good reason. Perhaps it did so because they thought they were accountable for the event. No man is, nor indeed can be. Perhaps it is because they were off their guard. They were not watchful over their own spirit. But this is no reason for disobeying God. We must continue to try. We must try, but remain more wary than before. We must do good not only seven times, but seventy times seven. We must become wiser by experience. Every time we attempt to do good, it must be with more caution than before. We must be humbled before God, meekly convinced that of ourselves, we can do nothing. We must always be jealous of our own spirit. We must be more gentle and watchful in prayer. Thus we can continue to cast our bread upon the waters, and we shall find it again after many days.[15]

Notwithstanding all of these plausible excuses for hiding it, let your light so shine before men that they may see your good works, and glorify your father who is in heaven. This is the practical application which Jesus himself makes.

"Let your light shine," your lowliness of heart. Your light is your gentleness and meekness of wisdom. It is your serious, weighty concern for all things of eternity. It is your sorrow for the sin and misery of men. It is your earnest desire of universal holiness. It is your yearning for full happiness in God. It is your tender goodwill for all mankind, and fervent love of God. Endeavor to not conceal this light with which God has enlightened your soul. Let it shine before all men. Let it shine before all with whom you are, in the whole tenor of your conversation. Let it shine still more eminently in your actions. Let it show forth in the doing of all possible good to all men. It shines in your suffering for righteousness' sake. Rejoice and be glad, knowing that your reward in heaven shall be great.

Let your light so shine before men so that they shall see your good works. Let a Christian be far from ever designing or desiring to conceal his religion. On the contrary, let it be your desire not to conceal it. Make every effort to put your light on a candlestick rather than under a bushel. You are to give light to all who are in the house. Take heed not to seek your own praise in this. Do not desire any honor for yourself. Let it be your sole aim that all who see your good works may glorify your Father who is in heaven.

Let this be your ultimate end in all things. With this one view, be plain, open and undisguised. Let your love be without dissimulation. Why should you hide your fair, disinterested love? Let there be no guile in your mouth. Let your words be the genuine picture of your heart. Let there be no darkness or reservations in your conversation. Do not disguise any of your behavior. Leave this to those who have other designs in view. Leave it to those who have designs which cannot stand the light.

Be artless and simple to all mankind.

Through this behavior, all may see the grace of God which is in you. It is true that this will harden the hearts of some. However, others will take knowledge that you have been with Jesus. Through your example, they will return themselves to the Lord of their souls, Jesus. This will then glorify your Father who is in heaven.

Make it your one design that all men may glorify God in you. Go on, in His name, and in the power of His might. Do not be ashamed to stand alone. Stand always in the ways of God. Let the light which is in your heart shine in all good works, both in works of piety and works of mercy. And in order to increase your ability of doing good, renounce all superfluities. Cut all unnecessary expense in food, furniture, and apparel. Be a good steward of every gift of God, even of these lowest gifts. Cut off all unnecessary expense of time, and all needless and useless employment of it. Whatever you are led to do, do it with all of your might. In a word, be full of faith and love. Do good, and be willing to suffer evil. In all of this, be steadfast and unmovable. Always abound in the work of the Lord. In this, you know that your labor is not in vain in the Lord.

7

Fulfilling the Law¹

"Think not that I am come to destroy the law, or the prophets: I am not come to destroy, but to fulfil. For verily I say unto you, Till heaven and earth pass, one jot or one tittle shall in no wise pass from the law, till all be fulfilled. Whosoever therefore shall break one of these least commandments, and shall teach men so, he shall be called the least of the kingdom of heaven: but whosoever shall do and teach them, the same shall be called great in the kingdom of heaven. For I say unto you, That except your righteousness shall exceed the righteousness of the scribes and Pharisees, ye shall in no case enter into the kingdom of heaven" (Matt. 5:17-20).

There were multitudes of reproaches and criticisms which fell upon Jesus. He was despised and rejected by men. He could not fail to be accused of being a teacher of novelties. He was called an introducer of a new religion. This occurred because many of the expressions He used were not common among the Jews. Either they did not use them at all, or else not in the same sense. Sometimes His terms were not used in so full and strong a meaning by them. Added to this, the worshiping of God in spirit and truth always appears to be a new religion to those who have known nothing but outside forms of worship. It is rejected by those who have nothing but the form of godliness.

Some hoped that Jesus was abolishing the old religion. They felt that it was possible He was bringing in another one. They imagined that Jesus would show them an easier way to heaven. But Jesus refutes in these words those vain hopes.

So it is important that we understand each of the statements of Jesus in the same order as they lie in this text. Each verse will be used for a distinct heading in the following discussion.

"Think not that I am come to destroy the law, or the prophets: I am not come to destroy, but to fulfil." The ritual or ceremonial law was delivered to Israel by Moses. It contained all of the injunctions and ordinances which related to the old sacrifices and service of the Temple. Jesus did indeed come to destroy, to dissolve, and utterly abolish all those laws. To this fact, all of the apostles witness. Barnabas and Paul vehemently withstood those who taught that Christians ought to keep the law of Moses.[2] Peter termed the insisting on the observance of the ritual law as tempting God and putting a yoke on the disciples. He said that neither their fathers nor they were able to bear that yoke. When all of the apostles, elders and brethren were assembled with one accord, they declared that to command them to keep this law was to subvert their souls.[3] The Holy Spirit had inspired them to lay no such burden upon the new converts.[4] Jesus blotted out, took away and nailed to His cross, the requirement of the written law.[5]

Jesus did not take away the moral law. The ten commandments remained enforced by himself, as well as by the prophets. It was not the intent of His coming to revoke any part of this. This is a law which can never be broken. It stands fast as the faithful witness in heaven. The moral law stands on an entirely different foundation than the ceremonial law. The latter was designed only for a temporary restraint upon a disobedient and stiff-necked people. Contrary to that, the moral law was from the beginning of the world. It was not written on tables of stone, but upon the hearts of all God's creatures. He put it on their hearts when they came out of His hands. Even though these laws once written by the finger of God are now defaced by sin in a great measure, they can never be wholly blotted out. They remain while we have any consciousness of good and evil. Every part of this law must remain in force upon all mankind. It remains in all ages. It does not depend upon either time or place. It does not change by any other circumstances. It is based upon the nature of God and the nature of man, and their unchangeable relationship to each other.

"I have not come to destroy, but to fulfil." Some have believed that Jesus meant He came to fulfill the law by His entire and perfect obedience to it. Doubtless He did in this sense fully complete every part of it. This does not appear to be what He intends here, however. That idea is foreign to the scope of His present discourse. Without question, here His meaning is: I have come to establish it in its fullness, in spite of all of the changes of men. I have come to declare the truth and full importance of every part of it. I will show its length and breadth, and entire extent. I will display every commandment contained in it, and the height and depth and purity and spirituality of all of its branches.

Jesus adequately performed this in the preceding and subsequent parts of the discourse before us. In this, He has not introduced a new religion into the world. It is the same which was in the world from the beginning. It is a religion with a substance which is without question as old as creation. Being as old as man, it proceeded from God at the very time when man was made a living soul. It was a religion witnessed to by both the law and the prophets, in all succeeding generations. Yet it was never so fully explained, nor so fully understood, as it was when Jesus gave His authentic comments on all of the essential elements of it. At that time, Jesus declared it should never be changed. It was to remain in force until the end of the world. There would be no change in the substance of it even if some circumstances of it now relate to man as a fallen creature.

Next was Jesus' solemn promise which denoted both the importance and certainty of what He was speaking. "For truly I say to you, until heaven and earth pass, not one jot nor one tittle shall pass from the law, till it be fulfilled." One jot is literally not one iota, not the most unimportant vowel. One tittle refers to one corner or point of a consonant. This is a proverbial expression. It signifies that no one commandment contained in the moral law, nor the least part of any one, however inconsiderable it might seem, should ever be changed.

Then Jesus affirmed that none should ever pass from the law. Here He used a double negative. It strengthened the sense so as to allow no contradiction. It may be observed that the meaning is merely future, declaring what will be. This statement has the force of the imperative. It orders what shall be. It is a word of authority, expressing the solemn will and power of Him who spoke. It expresses His word as the law of heaven and earth which stands fast for ever and ever.

One jot and one tittle shall not pass until heaven and earth pass. This means, as expressed immediately thereafter, until all things are fulfilled. It would not pass until the consummation of all things. This leaves no room for poor evasion. Some have said that this means no part of it will pass away until all of the law was fulfilled. Claiming it has been fulfilled by Jesus, it therefore must pass because the gospel has been established. This is not so. The word "all" does not mean all of the law, but all things in the universe. The term as used here does not refer to the fulfilling of the law, but the fulfilling of all things in heaven and earth.

Then from all of this we learn there is no contradiction at all between the law and the gospel. There is no need for the law to pass away in order to establish the gospel. Indeed, neither of them supersedes the other. They agree perfectly with each other. The very same words, considered in different respects, are parts both of the law and the gospel. If they are considered as commandments, they are parts of the law. If they are seen as promises, they are parts of the gospel. Thus, "You shall love the Lord with all of your heart," when considered as a commandment, is a branch of the law. When it is regarded as a promise to be fulfilled in the heart of man, it is an essential part of the gospel. The gospel is none other than the command of the law proposed in a way of promise. Accordingly, poverty of spirit, purity of heart, and whatever else is required in the law, are none other than so many great and precious promises.

Therefore, there is the closest connection that can be conceived between the law and the gospel. On the one hand, the law continually makes way for, and points us to, the gospel. On the other hand, the gospel continually leads us to a more exact fulfilling of the law. The law, for instance, requires us to love God and our neighbor. It requires us to be meek, humble, and holy. We feel that we are not adequate to do these things. With men this is impossible. But we see a promise of God, to give us that love and to make us humble, meek and holy. We grab hold of this gospel, of these glad tidings. This is accomplished in us according to our faith. The righteousness of the law is fulfilled in us through faith which is in Jesus.

We need to understand that every command in the Holy Writ is simply a covered promise. God works to give us the grace to accomplish whatever He commands. He declared, "This is the covenant that I will make . . . after those days, saith the Lord; I will put my laws into their mind, and write them in their hearts."[6] Does He then command us to pray without ceasing, to rejoice evermore, to be holy as He is holy? It is enough. He will work in us those very things. It shall be done in us according to His Word.

But if these things are so, who can undertake to change or supersede some commands of God? We are at a loss to think of such changes being made in those commands when they were professed under the particular direction of His Holy Spirit. Jesus has given us an infallible rule, with which to judge all such pretensions. Christianity, as it includes the whole moral law of God, is both injunction and promise. If we will hear Jesus, the law is designed by God to be the last of His dispensations. There is no other to come after this. This is to endure to the consummation of all things. The result is, all new revelations are of Satan and not of God. All pretenses to another and more perfect dispensation fall to the ground. The moral laws of God shall in no way change until heaven and earth pass away.

"Whoever, therefore, shall break one of the least of these

commandments, and shall teach men to do so, he shall be called the least in the kingdom of heaven. But whosoever shall do and teach them, the same shall be called great in the kingdom of heaven." Who, or what, are they that make the preaching of the law a cause of reproach? Do they not see on whom the reproach must fall? Do they not see on whose head it must light at last? Whosoever on this ground despises us, despises Jesus who sent us. No man ever preached the law like Jesus, even when He came not to condemn, but to save the world. While He came purposely to bring life and immortality to life through the gospel, He continued to affirm the law. Can any preach the law more expressly, more rigorously, than Jesus does in these words? Then who is he who shall amend them? Who is he that shall instruct Jesus on how to preach? Who will teach Him a better way of delivering the message which He had received from God?

"Whosoever shall break one of these least commandments," or one of the least of these commandments. These commandments, we may observe, is a term used by Jesus as equivalent with the law. It means both the law and the prophets. They are the same thing. The prophets added nothing to the law. They only declared, explained, or enforced it, as they were moved to do so by the Holy Spirit.

"Whosoever shall break one of these least commandments," especially if it is done willfully, is guilty of breaking them all. He that keeps the whole law, and thus offends in one point, is guilty of all. The wrath of God abides upon him as surely as if he has broken every one. No allowance is made for one exciting lust. There is no reservation for one idol. There is no excuse from refraining from all besides and giving way to one hardy sin. What God demands is an entire obedience. We are to have an eye to all of His commandments. Otherwise, we lose all of the labor we take in keeping some, and our poor souls can be lost forever.

"One of the least," or one of the least of these commandments. Here is another excuse cut off. We cannot deceive God, we only deceive our own souls. So we say, "Is the sin not a little one? Will not the Lord spare me in this thing? Surely He will not be so extreme as to remember this. I do not offend in the greater matters of the law." This is a vain hope. Speaking after the manner of men, we may term these great, and those little commandments. In reality they are not so. If we use propriety of speech, there is no such thing as a little sin. Every sin is a transgression of the holy and perfect law. Each one is an affront to God.

"And shall teach men so." In some sense, whoever openly breaks any commandment teaches others to do the same. Many times example speaks louder than precept. In this sense, it is apparent that every open drunkard is a teacher of drunkenness. Every Sabbath breaker is constantly teaching his neighbor to profane the day of the Lord. But this is not all. An habitual breaker of the law is seldom content to stop there. He generally teaches others to do so too, by word as well as example. This is especially so when he is hard-headed and hates to be reproved. Such a sinner soon begins to be an advocate for sin. He defends what he is resolved not to forsake. He excuses the sin which he will not leave. Therefore, he directly teaches every sin which he commits.

"He shall be called least in the kingdom of heaven." This means, he shall have no part in it. He is a stranger to the kingdom of heaven which is on earth. He has no portion in that inheritance. He has no share in the righteousness, and peace, and joy, in the Holy Spirit. By consequence, he cannot have any part in the glory which is yet to be revealed.

Where do these false teachers appear? Where are these who Jesus chiefly and primarily described in these words? Where are they, who bearing the character of teachers sent by God, nevertheless break His commandments? Where are these who openly teach others to do so, being openly corrupt both in life and doctrine?

These are of several kinds. The first kind are those who live in some kind of willful, habitual sin. If an ordinary sinner teaches by his example, how much a sinful minister does this. He teaches the wrongdoing, even if he does not attempt to defend, excuse, or extenuate his sin. If he does this, he is a murderer indeed. He is the murderer-general of his congregation. He peoples the region of death. He is the choicest instrument of Satan. When he goes out, hell from beneath is moved to meet him at his coming. As he sinks toward the bottomless pit, he drags a multitude after him.

Next to these are the good natured, good sort of men. They live an easy, harmless life. They never trouble themselves with outward sin, or with inward holiness. They are not outstanding one way or another, either for religion or irreligion. They are very regular in public and private matters, but do not pretend to be any more religious than their neighbor. A minister of this kind breaks not one or only a few of the least commandments of God. He breaks all of the great and weighty branches of the law which relate to the power of godliness. He breaks that law which requires us to pass the time of our lives working out our salvation with fear and trembling. He blocks the commandment to have our loins always girt and our lights always burning. He denies the striving, or agonizing to enter at the narrow gate. He teaches this by the whole form of his life, and the general tenor of his preaching. He uniformly tends to soothe those in their pleasing dreams who imagine themselves to be followers of God when they are not. He persuades those who are in his ministry to sleep on and take their rest. It will be no wonder, therefore, if both he and they who follow him wake together in everlasting burning.

But above all of these, in the highest rank of the enemies of Jesus' gospel, are those who openly and explicitly judge the law itself. These are they who speak evil of the law. They teach men to break, to dissolve, to loose and to untie the obligation of it. They do this to the whole law. They limit it not only to one, whether the least or the greatest, but all of the commandments at a stroke. They teach, without any cover, that Jesus abolished the law. They say there is but one duty. They teach that we are required only to believe. They teach that all commandments are unfit for our times. Far from any demand of the law, no man is obliged now to go one step in it, they say. He is not required to give away one cent, to eat or omit one morsel of food.

This is indeed carrying matters with a high hand. It is withstanding Jesus to His face. It is telling Him that He did not understand how to deliver the message with which He was sent. "Father, forgive them, for they know not what they do."[7]

There are surprising circumstances which accompany this strong delusion. The most surprising of all is that those who follow it really believe they are right in overthrowing His law. They believe they are magnifying His office while they are destroying His doctrine. They honor Him just as Judas did when he said, "Hail, master!" and kissed Him. And Jesus may as justly say to every one of them, "Would you betray me with a kiss?"[8] It is no other than betraying Him with a kiss, to talk of His blood and take away His crown. It is betrayal to make light of any part of His law, under the pretense of advancing His gospel. No one can escape this charge if he preaches faith, but in any manner overcomes the requirement of obedience. He who so preaches Jesus annuls and weakens the least of the commandments of God.

It is impossible to have too high a regard for faith. We must all declare, "By grace, you are saved by faith." The Christian understands that he is not saved by works, lest any man might boast of his works.[9] We must loudly declare to every penitent sinner, "Believe in the Lord Jesus Christ and you shall be saved."[10] At the same time, we must take care to define this faith. We believe in no faith but that which works by love. We have not experienced saving faith until we are also delivered from the power, as well as the guilt, of sin. We have a deep meaning when we say, "Believe and you shall be saved." We do not mean, "Believe and you shall step from sin to heaven without any holiness coming between." Neither do we believe that faith supplies a substitute for holiness. We believe, "Believe, and you shall become holy. Believe in Jesus and you shall have peace and power put together. You shall be given power from Him in whom you believe to trample sin under your feet. You shall have power to love the Lord God with all of your heart. You shall have power to serve Him with all of your strength. You shall have power and patience to continue in welldoing. You shall have power to seek for glory, honor, and immortality through Him. You shall both do, and teach, all the commandments of God. You will hold to even the least, as well as the greatest, of those. You will teach these commandments by your life, as well as by your word. Then, you may be called great in the kingdom of heaven.

Any other way of teaching a way to the kingdom of heaven is, in truth, the way to destruction. Faith without power is not faith. It will not bring a man peace at the last. Jesus affirms this. He said, "I say to you, unless your righteousness exceeds the righteousness of the scribes and the Pharisees, you shall in no way enter into the kingdom of heaven."

The scribes, mentioned so often in the New Testament, were some of the most constant and vehement opposers of Jesus' teachings. These were not secretaries, or men employed for writing only. The term might lead us to believe that. Neither were they lawyers in our common sense of the word. Their employment had no relation at all to that of a lawyer among us, even though scribe is rendered as lawyer in some translations. They were men conversant with the laws of God, and not with the laws of men. Those laws were their study. It was their proper and peculiar business to read and expound the law and the prophets. They did this particularly in the synagogues. They were the ordinary, stated preachers among the Jews. If we are to maintain a sense of the original word, we might render it, the divines. These were the men who made divinity their profession. They were generally men of letters. They were the most educated men in the Jewish nation.

The Pharisees were a very ancient sect, or body of men among the Jews. Originally their name came from the Hebrew word which signifies to separate or divide. This was not to indicate they made any formal separation from, or division in, the national church. They were distinguished only from others by greater strictness of life. They had a more religious exactness of behavior. They were zealous of the law in the minutest details. They tithed even on herbs: mint, anise and cummin. Because of this, they were held in honor by all of the people. They were generally esteemed to be the holiest of all men in the land.

Many of the scribes were also of the sect of the Pharisees. Thus, Paul himself, who was educated for a scribe, declared himself to also be a Pharisee, and the son of a Pharisee.[11] Before King Agrippa, he said, "After the most straitest sect of our religion I lived a Pharisee."[12] The whole body of scribes generally respected, and acted in concert with the Pharisees. Therefore, we find Jesus frequently coupling them together in His teaching. In this place they seemed to be mentioned together as the most eminent professors of religion. The scribes were counted to be the wisest, and the Pharisees the holiest of men.

It is easy to determine what the righteousness of the scribes and Pharisees really was. Jesus has preserved an authentic account of one of the Pharisees. He gave us this account himself. It is clear and full in describing the self-righteousness of the Pharisees. He cannot be supposed to have omitted any part of it. The Pharisee indeed went up to the Temple to pray. There he was so intent upon his own virtues that he forgot the purpose for which he came. Actually, he does not really pray at all. He only tells God how wise and good he has been.

"God, I thank you that I am not like other men are: extortioners, unjust, adulterers, even as this publican. I fast twice a week; I give tithes of all that I possess."

His self-proclaimed righteousness, therefore, consisted of three parts. First, he was different from other men. He was not an extortioner nor unjust nor an adulterer. Second, he fasted twice a week. And third, he gave tithes of all which he possessed. He was not as other men are. That is no small point. Not every man can say that.

It is as if he had said, "I do not allow myself to be carried away by that great torrent which is custom. I do not live by custom, but by reason. I do not follow the examples of other men, but only the Word of God. I am not an extortioner, not unjust, not an adulterer. However common these sins are, even among those who are called the people of God, I am not subject to them. I am not as this publican. I am not guilty of any open or presumptuous sin. I am not an outward sinner. I am a fair, honest man of blameless life and conversation."[13]

"I fast twice a week." There is more implied in this than we may at first perceive. All of the stricter Pharisees observed a weekly fast. They fasted every Monday and Thursday. On Monday they fasted in memory of Moses receiving on that day the two tablets of stone written by God. On Thursday they fasted in memory of his casting them out of his hand when he saw the people dancing around the golden calf. On those days, they took no food until three in the afternoon. That was the hour at which they began to offer up the evening sacrifice in the Temple. Until three, it was their custom to remain in the Temple. They remained in some part of it so they might be ready to assist in all of the sacrifices and to join in all the public prayers. In the time between this, they were accustomed to pray and search the Scriptures. They continually read the Law and the Prophets, and meditated upon their readings. This much is implied in the statement, "I fast twice a week." This is the second part of the righteousness of the Pharisee.

"I give tithes of all that I possess." This the Pharisee did with utmost exactness. They would not omit the most inconsiderable thing from their tithe. They even tithed their herbs. They would not keep back the least part of what they believed properly belonged to God. They gave a full tenth of their whole earnings every year. In addition, they gave a tenth of their increase, whatever it was.

The stricter Pharisees were not content in giving only one tenth. They gave the first tenth to the priests and Levites, and gave another tenth to God through the poor. They gave this tenth as alms, as they were accustomed to give in tithes. They computed this amount with the utmost exactness. They dared not keep back any part. They felt that they must fully render to God the things which were God's. They accounted the almsgiving to properly belong to God. So, upon the whole, they gave away from year to year an entire fifth of all they possessed.

This was the righteousness of the scribes and the Pharisees. It was a righteousness which went far beyond the conception which many have been accustomed to understand concerning it. Perhaps some will say, "It was all false and feigned. They were all a company of hypocrites." Some of them doubtless were. Some could have been men who really had no religion at all, no fear of God, or no desire to please Him. It is possible that some had no interest or concern for the honor that comes of God, but only for the praise of men. Jesus sharply condemned and reproved those on many occasions. But we cannot suppose, because many Pharisees were hypocrites, therefore all were so. Hypocrisy is by no means necessarily the character of a Pharisee. It is not the distinguishing mark of that sect. Rather, it is this, according to Jesus' account. "They trusted in themselves that they were religious, and despised others."[14] This is their genuine mark. But a Pharisee of this kind cannot be a hypocrite. He must be, in the common sense, sincere. Otherwise, he could not believe in himself that he was righteous. The man who was here commending himself to

God unquestionably thought that he was righteous. Consequently, he was not a hypocrite. He was not conscious of being insincere. He spoke to God just what he thought. He thought he was a great deal better than other men.

The example of Paul, were there no other, is sufficient to put this out of all question. As a Christian, he said of himself, "Herein do I exercise myself, to have always a conscience void of offence toward God, and toward men."[15] He said the same of himself concerning the time when he was a Pharisee. Of that time, he said, "Men and brethren, I have lived in all good conscience before God until this day."[16] He was therefore sincere when he was a Pharisee, as well as when he was a Christian. He was no more a hypocrite when he persecuted the church than when he preached the faith which he had once persecuted. So let this, then, be added to the righteousness of the scribes and the Pharisees. They had a sincere belief that they were righteous and doing God's service in all things.

And yet, Jesus said, "Unless your righteousness shall exceed the righteousness of the scribes and Pharisees, you shall in no case enter into the kingdom of heaven." This is a solemn declaration. It is one which all Christians should seriously and deeply consider. But, before we inquire how our righteousness may exceed theirs, let us decide whether we come up to it at present.

First, a Pharisee was not as other men are. In externals, he was singularly good. Are we so? Do we dare to be different at all? Do we not rather swim with the stream? Do we not many times dispense with religion and reason altogether, because we do not want to look peculiar? Are we not often more afraid of being out of fashion than being out of the will of God? Have we the courage to stem the tide, to run counter to the world? Are we willing to obey God, rather than man? If not, the Pharisee leaves us behind at the very first step.

Let us look at this closer. Can we use his first plea with God? He said, "I do no harm. I live in no outward sin. I do nothing for which my own heart condemns me." Are you sure that you live in that manner? Do you avoid practices for which your own heart condemns you? If you are not an adulterer, not unchaste, either in word or deed, are you not unjust? The great measure of justice, as well as mercy, is "do unto others as you would have them do unto you."[17] Do you walk by this rule? Do you never do unto any what you would not have them do unto you? Are you not grossly unjust? Are you not an extortioner? Do you never make a gain from anyone's ignorance or necessity either in buying or selling? Suppose you were engaged in some sale. Do you demand and receive no more than the value of what you sell? Do you demand and receive no more from the ignorant than from the knowledgable? Do you charge the same to a little child as to that of an experienced purchaser? If you don't, why doesn't your heart condemn you? Such acts are barefaced extortion. Notice who demands more for their goods and services than the usual price when one is in a pressing need for them. When one must have those goods or services without delay, how does the one who furnishes them react? If the price is raised, that is flat extortion. Indeed, in so doing, that person does not come up to the righteousness of a Pharisee.

Second, a Pharisee used all the means of grace. He fasted often and much. He also attended to all of the sacrifices. He was constant in public and private prayer. He was continual in reading and hearing the Scripture. Do you go as far as this? Do you fast much and often? Twice a week? At least once on all Fridays in the year? Do you fast twice a year? I am afraid some of us cannot admit even to this. Do you neglect no opportunity of attending and taking the Christian communion? How many are they who call themselves Christians, and yet utterly disregard it. They do not eat of that bread or drink of that cup for months. Some omit it for years altogether. Do you, every day, either hear or read the Scriptures and meditate upon them? Do you join in prayer with others daily, if you have the opportunity? If not daily, whenever you can, particularly on the regular day of worship? Do you strive to make opportunities for worship? Are you glad when someone says to you, "Let us go to church"? Are you zealous of, and diligent in, private prayer? Do you allow no day to pass without it? Rather, are not some Christians far from spending several hours a day in prayer? Do you think that one hour is enough, if not too much? Do you spend an hour a day, or in a week, in praying to God in secret? Do you spend an hour in a month? Have you spent one hour altogether in private prayer since you were born? Ah, poor Christian! Shall not the Pharisee rise up in his judgment against you and condemn you? His righteousness is as far above most Christians as heaven is above the earth.

Third, the Pharisee paid tithes and gave alms of all he owned. He did this in an ample manner. He was a man who did much good. Do we come up to him here? Which of us is as abundant as he was in his good works? Which of us gives a fifth of all of his belongings, both of the principal and the increase? Who of us, out of one hundred dollars a year, gives twenty to God and the poor? Who out of fifty gives ten? When, therefore, shall our righteousness equal at least the righteousness of the scribes and the Pharisees? When shall our giving, the using of the means of grace, and the avoiding of evil while doing good, measure up to them?

Even if our righteousness equals that of the scribes and the Pharisees, it does not help us. "For truly I say to you, unless your righteousness shall exceed the righteousness of the scribes and Pharisees, you shall in no way enter into the kingdom of heaven." But how can it exceed theirs? Where does the righteousness of a Christian exceed that of a scribe or Pharisee?

Christian righteousness exceeds theirs, first, in its extent. Most of the Pharisees, though they were righteously exact in many things, were not in all. The traditions of their elders emboldened them to dispense with other matters of equal importance. Thus, they were extremely exact in keeping the sabbath. They would not even rub an ear of corn on that day. But, they made little of the third commandment. They had little concern about swearing, either false or light. So, their righteousness was partial. As opposed to this, the righteousness of a real Christian is universal. He does not observe one, or only parts of the law of God, and neglect the rest. He keeps all of God's commandments. He loves them all. He values them above gold or precious stones.

Possibly, some of the scribes and Pharisees attempted to keep all of the commandments. Consequently, they would have been blameless regarding the righteousness of the law, according to the letter of it. But, still the righteousness of a true Christian exceeds all of this righteousness of a scribe or Pharisee. A true Christian will fill the spirit as well as the letter of the law. He fulfills it by inward as well as outward obedience. There is no comparison in the inward spirituality of the two. This is the whole point which Jesus has so largely proved in the whole theme of His discourse. Their righteousness was external only. Proper Christian righteousness is in the inner man. The Pharisee cleansed the outside of the cup and the platter. The Christian is clean within. The Pharisee labored to present God with a good life. The Christian wishes to come to God with a holy heart. The one shook off the leaves, and perhaps the fruit of sin. The other lays an ax to the very root of sin. The Christian is not content with the outer forms of godliness no matter how exact they be. He also seeks life with the Holy Spirit, where the power of God, or salvation, is felt in the inmost soul.

Therefore, the acts of doing good, doing no harm, and attending the ordinances of God, are all external. On the contrary, poverty of spirit, mourning, meekness, hungering and thirsting after righteousness, the love of our neighbor, and purity of heart, are all internal. Even peacemaking, doing good, and suffering for righteousness' sake stand entitled to the blessings attached to them. Each of these imply inward dispositions, as they spring from, exercise and confirm those qualities. So, the righteousness of the scribes and Pharisees was external only. Thus it may be said, in some sense, that the righteousness of a Christian is internal only. All of his actions and sufferings are nothing in themselves. They are evaluated by God only by the inner dispositions from which they spring.

Everyone who bears the holy and venerable name of a Christian should first see that his righteousness does not fall short of the righteousness of the scribes and Pharisees. A Christian is not to be as other men are. He is to dare to stand alone if necessary. He is to be an example which is singularly good. He cannot follow the multitude, for that is always to do evil. Custom and fashion cannot be his god. His God is religion and reason. The practice of others has nothing to do with him. He knows that every man must give an account of himself to God. Indeed, he attempts to save the souls of others, if possible. However, he knows that he is required to save at least one, his own. He avoids walking in the broad paths of death, as many do. Because it is broad, and walked by many, he knows its true nature.

Is the way which you walk a broad, well-frequented, fashionable way? This infallibly leads to destruction. Do not be damned for the company you keep. Cease from evil. Fly from sin as from the face of a serpent. At least, do no harm. "He that commits sin is of the devil."[18] Do not be found among those. Concerning outward sins, surely the grace of God is now sufficient for you. Exercise yourself to have a conscience void of offense toward God and toward men.

Second, do not let your righteousness fall short of theirs regarding the ordinances of God. Deal faithfully with your own soul. Fast as often as your strength will permit. Omit no public or private opportunity of pouring out your soul in prayer. Neglect no opportunity of partaking in the communion of the body and blood of Jesus. Be diligent in searching the Scriptures. Read as much as you can, and meditate on those readings day and night. Rejoice to take every opportunity of hearing the Word of God preached. In using all of the means of grace, live up to the righteousness of the scribes and Pharisees, at least until you can exceed it.

Third, do not fall short of a Pharisee in doing good. Give alms of all you possess. Is any hungry? Feed him. Is he thirsty? Give him drink. Is he naked? Cover him with clothing. If you have wealth, do not limit your beneficence to a small proportion of it. Be merciful to the utmost of your power. This is what the Pharisee did.

But do not rest here. Let your righteousness exceed the

righteousness of the scribes and Pharisees. Do not be content to keep the whole law, never offending at even one point. Hold fast to all of God's commandments. Abhor all false ways and false faith. Do all the things that God has commanded, and do that with all of your might. You can do all things through Jesus who strengthens you.[19] Remember, without Him you can do nothing.

Above all, let your righteousness exceed theirs in the purity and spirituality of it. What is the strictest form of religion in you? Is it most perfect outer righteousness? Go higher and deeper than all of this. Let your religion be the religion of the heart. Be poor in spirit. Be little, humble, and base in your own eyes. Be amazed and humbled that the love of God is given you in Christ Jesus, your Lord.

Be serious. Let the whole stream of your thoughts, works, and words, flow from the deepest conviction that you stand on the edge of the great gulf. You and all other men are just ready to drop in. You will drop in either to everlasting glory, or everlasting burning.

Be meek. Let your soul be filled with mildness, gentleness, patience, and long-suffering toward all men. At the same time, let all which is in you be athirst for God. Long for the living God. Long to wake up in his likeness and be satisfied with it. Be a lover of God and of all mankind. In this spirit, do and suffer all things. Thus, you will exceed the righteousness of the scribes and Pharisees. You will then be called great in the kingdom of heaven.

8

When You Pray[1]

"Take heed that ye do not your alms before men, to be seen of them: otherwise ye have no reward of your Father which is in heaven. Therefore when thou doest thine alms, do not sound a trumpet before thee, as the hypocrites do in the synagogues and the streets, that they may have glory of men. Verily, I say unto you, They have their reward. But when thou doest alms, let not thy left hand know what thy right hand doeth: That thine alms may be in secret: and thy Father which seeth in secret himself shall reward thee openly. And when thou prayest, thou shalt not be as the hypocrites are: for they love to pray standing in the synagogues and in the corners of the streets, that they may be seen of men. Verily, I say unto you, They have their reward. But thou, when thou prayest, enter into thy closet, and when thou hast shut thy door, pray to thy Father which is in secret; and thy Father which seeth in secret shall reward thee openly. But when ye pray, use not vain repetitions as the heathens do: for they think that they shall be heard for their much speaking. Be not ye therefore like unto them: for your

Father knoweth what things ye have need of before ye ask him. After this manner therefore pray ye: Our Father which art in heaven, Hallowed be thy name. Thy kingdom come. Thy will be done in earth, as it is in heaven. Give us this day our daily bread. And forgive us our debts, as we forgive our debtors. And lead us not into temptation, but deliver us from evil: For thine is the kingdom and the power, and the glory for ever. Amen.

"For if ye forgive men their trespasses, your heavenly Father will also forgive you: But if ye forgive not men their trespasses, neither will your Father forgive your trespasses" (Matt. 6:1-15).

The various parts of inward religion have been described in the preceding chapter. Jesus shows us those dispositions of soul and mind which constitute real Christianity. He describes the inward tempers contained in that holiness, without which no man may see God. Those tempers flow from a living faith in God through Jesus. They are intrinsically and essentially good and acceptable to God. In this chapter of Matthew, Jesus moves ahead. Here He shows how all of our actions, even those that are indifferent in their own nature, may be made holy, good, and acceptable to God. This is done by pure and holy intentions. Whatever is done without this, Jesus declares, is of no value to God. Therefore, any outward works consecrated to God by pure intentions are in God's sight of great worth.

Jesus then moves forward to show this necessity of purity of intention in religious actions. In doing this, He discusses works of piety, works of charity, and of mercy. Of the latter sort, he particularly names charitable giving. This was discussed under the heading of almsgiving. Other kinds of good works are prayer and fasting. The directions Jesus gave for each of these are to apply equally

to every work. There is no distinction between either
works of charity or of mercy.

We can observe in detail what He said with regard to
works of mercy. "Take heed that you do not give your
alms before men, to be seen by them. Otherwise, you will
have no reward from your Father who is in heaven." The
giving of alms is the only work of charity included in this
teaching. However, every work of charity is included.
Everything which we give, speak, or do, by which our
neighbor may be helped, is an act of mercy. Merciful acts
are those through which another man may receive a
charitable act, either for his body or for his soul. Mercy is
the feeding of the hungry. It is the clothing of the naked.
It is the entertaining or assisting of the stranger. Mercy is
that charitable act of visiting those who are sick or in
prison. Mercy comforts the afflicted. It instructs the
ignorant. It reproves the wicked, while exhorting and
encouraging the welldoer. If there are any other works of
mercy, they are equally included under this direction of
Jesus.

"Take heed that you do not give your alms before men,
to be seen by them." In this teaching, Jesus does not
forbid us only to do good which can be seen by others. This
circumstance alone, that others see what we do, does not
make the action either good or bad. The intention of doing
good works before men, in order to be seen of them, is
what Jesus forbids. If this is our full intention, we are
running contrary to His wishes. However, in some cases
this may be a part of our intention. We may design that
some of our actions should be seen, and yet be also
acceptable to God. We may intend that our light shine
before men. We may desire this when our conscience
bears us witness in the Holy Spirit that our real end is that

of glorifying our Father who is in heaven.

We must always take care that we do not do the least thing with a view to our own glory. We must take care that the praise of men has no place in any of our works of mercy. If we seek our own glory, if we have any desire to gain honor from men in it, whatever is done is not done unto the Lord. He does not accept it. "You have no reward of your Father who is in heaven" for this.

"Therefore when you give your alms, do not sound a trumpet before you as the hypocrites do in the synagogue and in the streets so they may have praise of men." The word synagogue here does not mean a place of worship. It means any public place, such as a marketplace or an exchange. It was a common thing, among the Jews who were wealthy, particularly among the Pharisees, to do what Jesus taught against. When they gave alms, they had a trumpet sounded before them in the most public part of the city. They pretended the reason for this was to call the poor together to receive it. However, their real purpose was that they might receive the praise of men. Do not be like them. Do not cause a trumpet to be blown before you. Use no ostentation in doing good. Aim at the honor which comes from God only. Those who seek the praise of men have their reward. They shall have no praise of God for their show.

"But when you give alms, do not let your left hand know what your right hand does." This is a proverbial expression. It means, whatever you do, do it in as secret a manner as is consistent with doing it at all. It must not be left undone. Omit no opportunity of doing good, whether secretly or openly. Do it in the most effective manner. Another exception to this rule can be made. If you believe that making public your good may excite others to do more good, then you need not conceal it. Under those circumstances, you may let your light appear and shine to all that are in the house. But, unless the glory of God and the good of mankind require you to do otherwise, act in as private and unobserved a manner as the circumstances will allow. See that your alms are given in secret. Then, your Father, who sees in secret, shall reward you openly. Perhaps some in this world will learn of your acts of charity and mercy. However, God will infallibly know of them. They will be known in the world to come, before the great assembly of all men and angels. They are recorded in heaven.

From the works of charity and mercy, Jesus proceeds to those which are termed works of piety. "When you pray, you shall not be as the hypocrites are. They love to pray standing in the streets and in the synagogues so that they may be seen by men." You shall not be as the hypocrites are. Hypocrisy, or insincerity, is the first thing we are to guard against in prayer. Beware that you do not pray what you do not mean. Prayer is the lifting up of the heart to God. All works of prayer, without this, are mere hypocrisy. Whenever you attempt to pray, see that your one purpose is to communicate with God. Desire only to lift up your heart to Him. Be motivated to pour out your soul before Him. Do not be like the hypocrites who love to stand in public to be seen in their prayers. They prayed in the synagogues, the exchange, the marketplace, and in the corners of the street, and wherever most of the people were in order to be seen by them. That was their sole design. That was their motive and their end. That was the purpose of the prayers which they repeated. "Truly, I say to you, they have had their reward." They could expect nothing from God who is in heaven.

But it is not only the having an eye to the praise of men which cuts us off from rewards from heaven. It is not only that which leaves us no room to expect the blessing of God on our works of piety or mercy. Purity of intention is equally destroyed by an eye toward any earthly reward whatever. To do any of these things, with any hope of gain or interest, makes these acts less acceptable to God. The desire for gain falls in the same category as the desire for praise. Neither prayer, worship, nor giving to the poor can be done with any intention of receiving a reward. We can have no purpose other than that of promoting the glory of God, and the happiness of men for God's sake. Any temporal view, any motive on this side of eternity, other than that of promoting the glory of God, is an abomination unto Him. The action should be aimed at the promoting of His glory and the happiness of men for His sake. It does not matter how these acts may appear to men, but only how they appear to God.

"When you pray, enter into your closet, and when you have shut the door, pray to your Father who is in secret." There is a time when you are to pray openly to glorify God. You are to pray and praise Him in church congregations and services. But when you desire to make your complete and particular requests known to God, it should be in private. Whether it be in the evening, morning, or noontime, enter into your closet and shut the door. Use all of the privacy you can. If you do not have a private hideaway, a "closet," do not leave your prayers undone. Pray whether you have any privacy or not. Pray to God, if possible, when no one sees you but Him. If not possible, pray none the less. Thus pray to your Father who is in secret. Pour out all of your heart before Him. Your Father God who sees in secret shall reward you openly.

"But when you pray, do not use vain repetitions as the heathens do," even while praying in secret. Do not use innumerable words without any meaning. Do not say the same thing over and over again. Do not think the results of your prayers depend upon the length of them. That was the belief of the heathens. They thought they would be heard for the continual speaking of their prayer.

The thing taught against here is not simply the length, any more than the shortness, of our prayers. Jesus taught against length without meaning. He objected to the using of vain repetition. He did not object to all repetition, for He himself prayed three times, repeating the same words. The vain repetition which the heathen used was the reciting of the names of their gods over and over. Some Christians do the same thing. They pray a string of prayers, without ever feeling what they speak.

According to Jesus, we should never think we will be heard for this much speaking. We should not imagine that God measures prayers by their length. He is not best pleased with those which contain the most words. He does not respond, necessarily, to those which sound the longest in His ears. There are many instances of superstition and folly which promote such prayer techniques. These are followed by some Christians, as well as some heathens. This is expected of them on whom the light of the gospel has never shined. Christians should know to avoid it.

"Therefore, do not be like them." You who have tasted the grace of God through Jesus are different. You should be thoroughly content that God knows what you need even before you ask Him. The end of your praying is not to inform God, as though He did not know what you want. Prayer is to inform yourself. It is to think the sense of your wants more deeply in your heart. It is to give you a sense of your continual dependence upon Him. It is to affirm in your mind that He only is able to supply your needs. It is not so much to move God, who is always more ready to give than you are to ask, as it is to move yourself. It is to make you willing and ready to receive the good things He has prepared for you.

After having taught the true nature and ends of prayer, Jesus taught an example of it. In this place, He gave us that divine pattern of prayer. It serves as the model and standard of all of our prayers. "After this manner therefore pray." The account in Luke records, "He said unto them, When ye pray, say. . . ."[2]

There are other observations we may make concerning this divine prayer. First, it contains all which we can reasonably or innocently pray to receive. There is nothing which we have need to ask of God, or which we can ask without offending Him, which is not included in it. All of these things are included either directly or indirectly in this comprehensive form. In it we ask for whatever is for the glory of God. We seek whatever is necessary and profitable, not only for ourselves, but for every creature in heaven and earth. This is all that we can innocently and reasonably desire. Indeed, our prayers are the true test of our desires. Nothing is fit to have a place in our desires which is not fit to have a place in our prayers. What we may not pray for, neither should we desire. Also, this prayer contains all of our duty to God and man. Whatever things are pure and holy, whatever God requires of men are in it. Whatever is acceptable in His sight and whatever it is with which we may profit our neighbor, are expressed or implied in it.

This prayer contains three parts. These are the preface, the petitions and the doxology or conclusion. The preface is "Our Father, who art in heaven." It lays a general foundation for prayer. It tells us what we must first know of God before we can pray in confidence of being heard. Likewise, it points out to us all those tempers with which we are to approach God. It tells us which of those are essentially required, if we desire either our prayers or our lives to be acceptable to Him.

"Our Father." If He is our Father, then He is good and loving to all of His children. Here is the first and great reason for prayer. God is willing to bless! Let us ask for a blessing. "Our Father"—our Creator. He is the author of our being. It is He who raised us from the dust and breathed into us the breath of life. By Him, we became living souls. Since He made us, we can ask of Him. He will not withhold any good thing from the work of His own hands. Therefore, let us ask of Him. "Our Father"—our preserver. Day by day, He sustains the life which He has given to us. Through His continuing love, we now, and at every moment, receive life, breath, and all things. Knowing this, we can come boldly before Him. We will obtain mercy and find grace in the time of our needs. Above all, He is the Father of Jesus, and all that believe in Him. Through Him, we are justified, forgiven freely by His grace, through the redemption that is in Jesus. Through Jesus, God has blotted out all of our sins, and healed all of our infirmities. Through Him, God has received us as His own children by adoption and grace. Because we are His children, He has sent forth the Holy Spirit of His Son into our hearts. We now know Him as Father. We cry out, "Abba, Father."[3] It is God who has begotten us again incorruptibly through a new creation in Jesus. Therefore, we know that He hears us always, and we can pray to Him without ceasing. We pray because we love. We love Him because He first loved us.[4]

"Our Father." Not mine only, we who now pray unto Him, but ours, in the most extensive manner. He is the God and Father of all spirits inhabiting flesh. He is the Father of both angels and men. Even the heathens acknowledge Him to be so. He is the Father of the universe. He is the Father of all the families both in heaven and in earth. Therefore, with Him there is no discrimination between persons. He loves all that He has made. He is loving of every man, and has mercy over all of His works.[5] His delight is in them who fear Him, and put their trust in His mercy. It is in them who trust Him through Jesus, knowing that they are accepted in Him. But if He so loved us, we are to so love one another.[6] We are to love all mankind. We are to do this because God so loved the world that He gave His only begotten Son even to die the death, that we might not perish but have everlasting life.[7]

"Which art in heaven." God is high and lifted up, over all, blessed forever. He sits on the circle of the heavens. He beholds all things in heaven and on earth. His eye pervades the whole sphere of created being and of uncreated night. He knows all of His works, and all the works of every creature. He has known these, not only from the beginning of the world, but from all eternity, from everlasting to everlasting. It is He who causes angels and men to cry out in wonder and amazement. "O the depth of the riches both of the wisdom and knowledge of God!"[8]

"Which art in heaven," the Lord and ruler of all, superintending and disposing all things. The King of kings, Lord of lords, the blessed and only God. He is strong and surrounded with power, doing what pleases Him. He is the Almighty. Whatever He wills, He has the power to do. "In heaven"—eminently there. Heaven is His throne. It is the place where His honor dwells. But He is not only there. He fills the entire expanse of heaven and earth. He is throughout space. "Heaven and earth are full of thy glory. Glory be to thee, O Lord most high."[9]

Therefore, we should serve God with all rejoicing. We should give Him all reverence. We should think, speak, and act as continually under His eye. We are always in His immediate presence. We are in the immediate presence of God, the Lord and King.

"Hallowed be thy name." This is the first of six petitions with which the prayer itself is composed. The name of God, is God himself. That is the nature of God, in so far as it can be discovered by man. It means therefore, together with His existence, all His attributes and perfection. It includes His eternity, particularly that which is dignified by His incommunicable name, Yahweh. As the Apostle John translated it, "the Alpha and the Omega, the beginning and the end, he which is and which was, and which is to come."[10] His fullness of being is denoted by His other name, "I Am that I Am."[11] He is omnipresent and omnipotent. He is indeed the only agent of the material world. All matter is essentially dull and inactive. It is moved only by the mind and the power of God. He is the spring of action in every creature, visible and invisible. Nothing could either act or exist without the continual influx and agency of His almighty power. His wisdom is clearly deduced from the things which we see. From it comes the good order of the universe.

He is trinity in unity and unity in trinity. This is discovered to us in the very first line of His written word, which literally translated means "the Gods created." It is a plural noun joined with a singular verb. He is essential purity and holiness. Above all, God is love, which is the very brightness of His glory.

In praying that God, or His name, may be hallowed or glorified, we pray that He may be known. We pray that all intelligent beings may know Him as He is. We pray that all creatures capable of knowing Him may give Him His due honor, fear, and love. We pray that this may be done in heaven above as well as in earth beneath. We pray that this may be done by both men and angels. For that end, He has made us capable of knowing and loving Him for all eternity.

"Thy kingdom come." This has a close connection with the preceding petition. In order that the name of God be hallowed, His kingdom must come. We pray that His kingdom, the kingdom of Jesus may come. This kingdom comes through a particular person when he repents and believes the gospel. Then he is taught of God, not only to know himself, but to know Jesus and His crucifixion. Then comes life eternal. That is to know the only true God and Jesus whom He has sent. So then the kingdom of God begins below. It is then set up in the believer's heart. The Lord God omnipotent then reigns when He is known through Jesus. He takes unto himself His mighty power and subdues all things unto himself. He goes into the soul, conquering and to conquer, until He has put all things under His feet. He works in the soul, until every thought is brought into captivity and obedience to Jesus.[12] We are praying for the time when God will give Jesus to all of the nonbelievers for their inheritance. We pray for the day when the uttermost parts of the earth will again come under His dominion and possession. We pray for the day when all kingdoms will bow before Him and all nations shall do Him service. We pray for the day when the mountain of the Lord's house, His church, shall be established everywhere. We pray for that day when the fullness of the Gentiles shall come in and all Israel shall be saved.[13] In that day it shall be seen that God is King. He will appear to every soul on earth as King of kings and Lord of lords. It is proper for those who love Him and seek this reappearing, to pray that He would hasten the time.

Everyone should pray that His kingdom, the kingdom of grace, would come quickly and swallow up the kingdoms of earth. Their prayer is that all mankind, receiving Him for their King, truly believing in His name, may be filled with righteousness, peace, joy, holiness, and happiness. After receiving that, they may be removed to His heavenly kingdom, there to reign with Him for eternity.

For this also we pray in these words, "Thy kingdom come." We pray for the coming of His everlasting kingdom. We pray for the kingdom of glory in heaven, which is the continuation and perfection of the kingdom of grace on earth. Consequently, this, as well as the preceding petition of the prayer, is offered up for all creation. This is a prayer by all those who are interested in this grand event, the final renovation of all things. It is a prayer for that time when God will put an end to all misery, sin, infirmity, and death. Then He will take all things into His own hands, and set up the kingdom which will endure throughout all ages.

"Thy will be done on earth as it is in heaven." This is the necessary and immediate result wherever the kingdom of God does come. It occurs wherever God dwells in the soul by faith, and Jesus reigns in the heart by love.

It is probable that many, perhaps most men, upon their inspection of these words, imagine that they are only an expression, or petition of resignation. They might appear to be a readiness to suffer the will of God, whatever it may be, concerning us. This is unquestionably a divine and excellent goal. Such a temperament is a precious gift from God. But this is not what we pray for in this petition, at least it is not the chief and primary aim of it. We pray, not so much for a passive, but for an active conformity to the will of God. This is what we mean when we say, "Thy will be done on earth as it is in heaven."

How is God's will done by the angels of God in heaven, those who continually circle His throne rejoicing? They do it willingly. They love His commandments. They gladly listen to His words. It is their food to do His will. It is their highest glory and joy. They do it continually. There is no interruption in their willing service. They do not rest either day or night. They employ every moment in fulfilling His commands, in executing His designs, and in performing the counsel of His will.

And, they do this perfectly. No sin, no defect, belongs to angelic minds. It is true, "The stars are not pure in his sight."[14] In His sight, in comparison to Him, the very angels are not pure. But this does not imply that they are not pure in themselves. Doubtless they are. They are without spot, and are blameless. They are altogether devoted to God's will. Again, they do all of the will of God as He wills it. They do it in the manner which pleases Him and in no other manner. They do this only because it is His will. They do it for that purpose and for no other reason.

Therefore, we mean this when we pray that the will of God may be done on earth as it is in heaven. We petition that all of the inhabitants of earth, the entire race of mankind, may begin to do the will of God who is in heaven as willingly as the holy angels. We pray that all of us may do it continually, even as they do, without any interruption of this willing service. We pray that this will may be done perfectly. We pray that the God of peace, through the blood of the New Covenant, may make them perfect in every good work to do His will. We seek to have His grace work in them all which is well pleasing in His sight.

In other words, we pray that we and all others may do the whole will of God in everything. We pray for nothing else, not the least thing, but what is in the holy and acceptable will of God. We pray that we may do the whole will of God as He wills. We pray that all mankind will behave in a manner that pleases Him. Lastly, we pray that we may do it because it is His will. We pray that this may be the sole reason and ground, the whole and only motive, of whatever we think, speak, or do.

"Give us this day our daily bread." In the three former petitions we have been praying for all mankind. We come now more particularly to desire a supply for our own needs. We are not directed even here to confine our prayer altogether to ourselves. This and each of the following petitions may be used for the whole body of believers, as well as ourselves.

By "bread" we may understand all the things we need, whether for our souls or our bodies. These are the things pertaining to life and godliness. We understand it to include not simply outward bread or food. Jesus termed that the meat which perishes.[15] The term also includes, and even much more, the spiritual bread and grace of God which is the food that endures for everlasting life. It was the opinion of many early church leaders, that we are here to understand the sacramental bread also. In the beginning, that was received daily by the whole church. It was highly regarded, until the love of many grew cold. In the early church, the communion bread was the great channel whereby the grace of His Holy Spirit was conveyed into the souls of all Christians.

"Our daily bread." The word we render as "daily" has been differently explained by different commentators. The most plain and natural sense of it seems to be one which is retained in almost all translations, ancient and modern. It means whatever is necessary for this day, and also for each day as it appears.

"Give us." We claim nothing by our own right. All

things are given to us of God's free mercy. We do not deserve even the air we breathe, the earth that bears for us, or the sun that shines upon us. All we ever deserved, we confess, is hell. But God loves us freely! Therefore, we ask Him to give. We ask for that which we can no more procure for ourselves than we can merit from Him.

We are not to suppose that either the goodness or the power of God is a reason for us to stand idle. It is His will that we should use all diligence in all things. We should employ our utmost endeavors in all things, as much as if our success were the natural effect of our own wisdom and strength. Then, as though we had done nothing, we are to depend upon Him as the giver of every good and perfect gift.

"This day." Here we are instructed to take no thought for tomorrow. To enforce this, our wise Creator has divided life into small portions of time. Each is clearly separated from the other. This is so we might look upon every day as a fresh gift from God. Each is another life which we may devote to His glory. Every evening may be seen as the close of that life. Beyond, we are able to see nothing but eternity.

"And forgive us our trespasses as we forgive those who trespass against us." Nothing but sin can hinder the bounty of good which flows from God to every one of His creatures. Because of this, this petition naturally follows the former one. All hindrances are to be removed so we may more clearly trust in the God of love for everything which is good.

"Our trespasses." This word properly signifies our debts. Thus, our sins are frequently represented by the Scripture to be debts. Every sin lays us under a fresh debt to God, to whom we already owe more than we can repay. What then can we say to Him if He asks, "Pay me what you owe."[16] We are utterly insolvent. We have nothing to pay. We have wasted all of our fortune. Therefore, if He deals with us according to the rigor of His law, and exacts what He justly could, He could command us to be bound hand and foot and delivered over.

Indeed, we are already bound hand and foot by our own sins. These, with regard to ourselves, bind us as chains of iron and fetters of brass. They are as wounds all over our bodies. They are diseases which waste our blood and spirit. Those sins bring us to the very edge of our grave. Considered as they are here, with regard to God, they are debts which are immense and numberless. Therefore, seeing we have nothing to pay, we can only cry to Him that He would frankly forgive us all of them.

The word translated "forgive," implies either to forgive a debt or to unloose a chain. If we accept the former translation, the latter follows of course. When our debts are forgiven, the chains fall off our hands. As soon as we receive forgiveness of our sins through the free grace of God in Jesus, we likewise receive a place among those who have been sanctified by faith. Sin loses its power, it has no dominion over those who are under grace and in favor of God. As there is no condemnation to them that are in Jesus,[17] they are freed from sin as well as from guilt. The righteousness of the law is fulfilled in them, and they walk not after the flesh, but after the Spirit.[18]

"As we forgive them that trespass against us." In these words Jesus clearly declares both the condition and the manner and degree in which we can expect to be forgiven by God. All of our trespasses and sins are forgiven us if we forgive, and as we forgive, others. This is a most important point. Jesus does not want it to slip from our thought at any time. To prevent that, He not only inserts it in the body of the prayer, but presently repeats it twice again. He says, "If you forgive men their trespasses, your heavenly Father will also forgive you, but if you do not forgive men their trespasses, neither will your Father forgive your trespasses." Next we notice that God forgives us as we forgive others. Taints of malice, bitterness, unkindness and anger can remain in us. We are cut off from our own forgiveness to the degree these remain in our hearts. We must clearly forgive all men their trespasses from the heart in order to receive God's clear and full forgiveness. He may show us some degree of mercy without this. However, without our own complete forgiveness, we do not allow Him to blot out our sins and forgive all of our iniquities.

What kind of prayer are we offering to God when we utter these words, if we have not clearly forgiven our neighbor His trespasses? We are indeed coming before God in open defiance. We are daring Him to do His worst. "Forgive us our trespasses as we forgive those who trespass against us." That is, in the clearest terms, "Do not forgive us at all. We desire no favor in your hands. We pray that you will keep our sins remembered and that your wrath may abide on us." Can you seriously offer such a prayer to God? If so, how is it that He has not yet cast you into hell? Tempt Him no longer! Now, even now, see His grace to forgive as you would be forgiven. Have the same compassion on your fellow-man as God has had on you. As He has forgiven and pitied you, forgive and pity those who trespass against you.

"And lead us not into temptation, but deliver us from evil." The word translated "temptation" means trial of any kind. The English word "temptation" was formerly used in an indifferent sense. Now it is usually understood to be a solicitation to sin. James uses the word in both of these senses. He uses it in the former sense when he says, "Blessed is the man that endureth temptation: for when he is tried, he shall receive the crown of life."[19] Next, he immediately uses the word in the latter sense. "Let no man say when he is tempted, I am tempted of God; for God cannot be tempted with evil, neither tempteth he any man. But every man is tempted when he is drawn away of his own lust," or desire. He is tempted when he is drawn away from God, in whom he alone is safe. When that occurs, when he is enticed, he is caught as a fish is caught with bait. Then it is that he actually enters into temptation. Temptation comes after he is drawn away and enticed. Then temptation covers him as a cloud. It overspreads his whole soul. Then he shall hardly escape out of the snare. Therefore, when we pray this, we are asking God to not allow him to be led into it.

"But deliver us from evil." Actually, this is to be rendered as, "deliver us from the evil one." The translation should unquestionably be, "the evil one." The evil one is Satan, emphatically the so-called prince and god of this world, who works with might and power in those who are disobedient to God. All of those who are the children of God by faith are delivered out of his hands. He may fight against them. In fact, he will fight against them. But he will not conquer unless they betray their own soul. He may torment them for a time, but he cannot destroy them. God is on their side. God will not fail in the end to avenge His own elected children, who cry to Him day and night. This prayer is then, "Lord, when we are tempted, do not allow us to enter into that temptation. Make a way for us to escape, so that Satan, the wicked one, cannot touch us."

The conclusion of Jesus' prayer, commonly called the doxology, is a solemn thanksgiving. It is a concise acknowledgment of the attributes and works of God. "For thine is the kingdom"—the sovereign right of all things that are, or ever were created. Your kingdom is an everlasting kingdom, and your dominion endures throughout all ages. "The power"—the executive power whereby God governs all things in His kingdom, and whereby He does what pleases Him in all places in His kingdom. "And the glory"—is the praise which is due from every creature for His power and the mightiness of His kingdom. He receives glory for all of His wondrous works which He has worked from the beginning and shall do to the end, forever and forever.

9

Fasting for Grace[1]

"Moreover when ye fast, be not as the hypocrites, of a sad countenance: for they disfigure their faces, that they may appear unto men to fast. Verily I say unto you, They have their reward. But thou, when thou fastest, anoint thine head, and wash thy face; That thou appear not unto men to fast, but unto thy Father which is in secret: and thy Father, which seeth in secret, shall reward thee openly" (Matt. 6:16-18).

It has been the endeavor of Satan, from the beginning of the world, to put asunder what God has joined together. His purpose is to separate inward from outward religion. He chooses to make one seem to be contrary to the other. He has met with a great deal of success with those who have been ignorant of his purpose.

Men of all ages have been zealous for God. With some of these, their zeal did not correspond with their knowledge. They have been strictly attached to the righteousness of the law. They placed great emphasis on the performance of outward duty. In the meantime, however, they disregarded the necessity of inward righteousness, the righteousness which is in God by faith. Many others have gone to the opposite extreme. They disregarded all outward duties. Some of them went so far as to speak evil of the law. They judged the law in so far as it enjoins the performance of outward duties.

It is by this very work of Satan that faith and works so often have been made to seem contrary to each other. Many who have great feeling for God have, for a time, fallen into the snare on either side. Some have magnified faith to the utter exclusion of good works. They have properly understood our salvation, knowing that man is justified only by the redemption that is in Jesus. However, they forgot the necessary fruit of that redemption. They acted as though good works, the necessary fruit of that faith, had no place in the religion of Jesus. Others were eager to avoid this dangerous mistake. The result was they ran too far in the other direction. They either maintained that good works were the cause of, or at least necessary to, salvation. The result is they spoke of them as if they were all in all, the whole religion of Jesus.

The end of religion has been set at variance with the means to it in the same manner. Some well-meaning men have seemed to place all religion in prayers, in church, communion, attending sermons, and reading books of piety. They neglected the love of God and their neighbor. This very thing has been confirmed in the neglect, if not contempt, of the ordinances of God. They were so completely abused, they were used to undermine and overthrow the very end for which they were established.

But, of all of the means of grace, fasting has been the most misunderstood. There is scarcely any other matter concerning religion in which man has run into greater extremes. Some have exalted this beyond all Scripture and reason. Others have utterly disregarded it. It was as if they were revenging themselves by undervaluing it as much as others have overvalued it. Some have spoken of it as if it were all in all. If it were not the end itself, it seemed to them to be infallibly connected with it. Others said it was just nothing, a fruitless labor, which had no relation at all to grace. Now it is certain that the truth lies between them both. Fasting is not all in all. Neither is fasting worth nothing. It is not the end, but the precious means to it. It is a means which God himself has ordained. It is the means through which, if it is properly used, God will surely give us His blessing.

In order to set this matter in the clearest light, we shall discuss four areas of fasting. First, what is the nature of fasting and what are the several sorts and degrees of it? Second, what are the reasons, grounds and ends of it? Third, how the most plausible objections against it may be answered. Fourth, in what manner fasting should be performed.

First, it is important to understand the nature of fasting, along with its several sorts and degrees. As to the nature of it, all the writers in the Bible take the word "fast" in one single sense. To them it means not to eat. Fasting is to abstain from food. That is so clear that it would be a labor lost to quote the words of David, Nehemiah, Isaiah, and the other prophets of the Old Testament regarding this word. All of them, as well as Jesus, and His apostles, agreed that to fast is to not eat for a period of time.

In olden times, some other circumstances were usually joined to fasting which had no necessary connection with it. Some added to this the neglect of their apparel. While fasting they laid aside ornaments which they usually wore. They put on the appearance of mourning. They sprinkled ashes on their heads, or wore sackcloth next to their skin. We find little mention made in the New Testament of any of these additional circumstances. It does not appear that any importance was put upon them by the Christians of the earliest ages. Some penitents might voluntarily use them as outward signs of inward humiliation. The apostles, and Christian contemporaries with them, did not beat or tear upon their own flesh. Such practices as these were followed by the priests and worshipers of that false god, Baal. The gods of the heathens were but devils. Such behavior was doubtless acceptable to their devil-god. Their priests often cried aloud, and cut themselves until the blood gushed out from them.[2] Such behavior is not pleasing to Jesus, who came not to destroy men's lives, but to save them.[3] This kind of behavior is not becoming of His followers.

As to the degrees or measures of fasting, we have instances of some who fasted several days. Moses, Elijah, and Jesus were endued with supernatural strength for that purpose. It is recorded that they fasted without interruption for forty days and forty nights.[4] However, the time of fasting most frequently mentioned in Scripture is for one day. It was from morning until evening. This was the fast most commonly observed by the first Christians. Besides these, they also had their half-fasts. These were observed on the fourth and sixth days of the week—Wednesday and Friday, throughout the year. On these days, they took no food until three in the afternoon. That was the time when they returned from the public church service.

Closely related to this is what the modern church seems to mean by the term abstinence. This is used when one cannot fast entirely because of sickness or bodily weakness. This is the eating of little. It is the abstaining in part from food. It is the taking of a smaller quantity of food than usual. There seems to be no scriptural instance of this. However, it cannot be condemned in the sense that the Scripture does not condemn it. It may have a use to receive a blessing from God.

The lowest kind of fasting, if it can be called that, is the abstaining from pleasant foods. We have several instances of this in Scripture. Daniel and his brethren did this. They wished to refrain from defiling themselves with the portion of the king's meat and wine. They requested and obtained permission to eat only vegetables and drink only water.[5] The mistaken imitation of this might spring from the ancient custom of abstaining from meat and wine during such times as were set apart for fasting and abstinence. This misunderstanding could have arisen from another supposition. It might have been assumed that because these were the most pleasant foods, it was proper to use what was least pleasing at times of solemn approach to God.

In the Jewish church there were some stated fasts. One was the fast of the seventh month, appointed by God himself. That fast was to be observed by all Israel under the severest penalty. The Jews were directed to it by God speaking through Moses. "On the tenth day of this seventh month there shall be a day of atonement . . . ye shall afflict your souls . . . to make an atonement for you before the Lord your God. For whatsoever soul it be that shall not be afflicted in that same day, he shall be cut off from among his people."[6] In later ages, several other stated fasts were added to this. Mention is made by Zechariah of the fast, not only in the seventh, but also in the fourth, fifth and tenth months.[7]

In the ancient Christian church there were also stated fasts. These were both annual and weekly. One annual sort was that before Easter. It was observed for forty-eight hours by some. Others extended it for a whole week. Many fasted for two weeks. Those engaging in those fasts took no food until the evening of each day.

The fourth and sixth day fasts were observed by Christians everywhere. Epiphanius wrote that it was observed in the whole habitable earth.[8] The annual fasts in the historical church are: the forty days of Lent, the Ember days at the four seasons, the Rogation days, and the Vigils or Eves of several solemn festivals, the weekly, all Fridays in the year, except Christmas Day.

Besides these which are fixed in every Christian nation, there have always been occasional fasts. Those are fasts which are appointed from time to time, when the particular circumstances and occasions of each require fasts. So the Bible reports that when "the children of Moab, and the children of Ammon . . . came against Jehoshaphat to battle. . . . Jehoshaphat feared, and set himself to seek the Lord, and proclaimed a fast throughout all Judah."[9] Also, "In the fifth year of Jehoiakim the son of Josiah . . . in the ninth month . . . [when they were afraid of the king of Babylon, the princes of Judah] proclaimed a fast before the Lord to all the people in Jerusalem."[10]

In our times, there are many who are careful in their ways, and desire to walk humbly and closely with God. In the same manner, they will find frequent occasion for private fasting. Thus, they afflict their souls before God who is in secret. It is to this kind of fasting that these directions are given, and chiefly and primarily refer.

We are to proceed next to investigate the ground, the reason, and the ends of fasting.

Men who are under strong emotions of the mind forget to eat. Those who are affected with any strong passion, such as sorrow or fear, are often swallowed up by them. On those occasions they have no interest in food. They do not take what is even necessary to sustain their bodies. Much less do they have any interest in a variety, or in any delicacies. They are consumed with thoughts quite different than food. Thus, Saul could say, "I am sore distressed; for the Philistines make war against me, and God is departed from me." It is then recorded, "He had eaten no bread all the day, nor all the night."[11] Thus, those who were on ship with Paul during the storm "continued fasting, having taken nothing," no regular meal for fourteen days altogether.[12] The same occurred with David, and all of the men who were with him. They heard that the people had fled from the battle and many had been killed. It was reported that Saul and his son Jonathan were dead also. So they "mourned, and wept, and fasted until even, for Saul, and Jonathan . . . and for the house of Israel."[13]

Many times those whose minds are deeply engaged are impatient with any interruption. They loathe the necessity of eating. It diverts their thoughts from what they desire to receive their full attention. So Saul, on the occasion earlier mentioned, would not eat until his servants compelled him to do so.

Here then is the natural ground of fasting. Included here are those who are under deep affliction, overwhelmed with sorrow for their sins. Also included are those in strong apprehension of the present wrath of God. Those, without any rule and without knowing or considering whether it was a command of God or not, would forget to eat. They would abstain not only from pleasant, but even from necessary food. They would be like Paul after he was led into Damascus, who, "was three days without sight, and neither did eat nor drink."[14]

When storms of living arise, when a horrible dread is overwhelming, those who have been long without God detest eating. Food is unpleasant and irksome to them. They would be impatient to have anything interrupt a ceaseless cry of, "Lord, save us: we perish."[15]

This is strongly expressed by the Church of England in the Homily of Fasting. "When men feel in themselves the heavy burden of sin, see damnation to be the reward of it, and behold, with the eye of their mind, the horror of hell, they tremble, they quake, and are inwardly touched with sorrowfulness of heart, and cannot but accuse themselves, and open their grief unto Almighty God, and call to him for mercy. This being done seriously, their mind is so occupied [taken up] partly with sorrow and heaviness, partly with an earnest desire to be delivered from this danger of hell and damnation, that all desire of meat and drink is laid apart, and loathsomeness of all worldly things and pleasure comes in its place. So that nothing then likes them more than to weep, to lament, to mourn, and both with words and behavior of body to show themselves weary of life."

There is still another reason or ground for fasting. Many of those who have a fear of God are deeply aware of how often they have sinned against Him. Included in their sins against Him is the abuse of the normal use of food and drink. They know how much they have sinned by excessive eating. They are aware of how all along they have transgressed the laws of God with regard to temperance and sobriety. They are aware that they have indulged their sensual appetites, even to the impairing of their bodily health. This indulgence has been of no small harm to their souls. Through their acts, they have continually fed and increased that sprightly folly, that airiness of mind, that levity of temper, that gay inattention to things of the deepest spiritual concern. They have continued in a giddiness and carelessness of spirit, which if it were no other than brokenness of soul, stupefies all of their noblest faculties no less than excessive alcohol would do. To remove that effect, therefore, they remove the cause. They keep at a distance from all excess. They abstain, as far as it is possible, from what has almost plunged them into everlasting separation from God. They often wholly refrain, while always taking care to be sparing and temperate in all things.

Likewise, they well remember how excesses increased not only carelessness and levity of spirit, but also foolish and unholy desires. With these came unclean and vile affections. That such is experienced is beyond all doubt. Even a genteel, regular sensuality is continually sensualizing the soul. It tempts it to sink into a level with the beasts that perish without eternal life. It cannot be expressed what a desire, and delicacy, of food have on the mind as well as the body. Those desires make it ripe for every pleasure of sense, as soon as opportunity for them arises. Therefore, on this ground alone, every wise man will restrain himself. In this matter he refrains his soul and keeps it low. He weans it more and more from all of those indulgences in inferior appetites. He knows they naturally tend to chain it to the earth, and to pollute as well as debase it. Here then is another perpetual reason for fasting. It is to remove the food of lust and sensuality. Its purpose is to withdraw the incentives of foolish and harmful desires, of vile and vain affections.

We need not omit another reason for fasting which some good men have emphasized. However, not much stress should be laid on it. Namely, some punish themselves for having abused the good gifts of God. This self-punishment consists of sometimes wholly refraining from those gifts. In this, they exercise a kind of holy revenge upon themselves for their past folly and ingratitude. This is a self-punishment for turning the thing which should have been for their health into an occasion for their falling. David had this in mind when he said, "I wept and chastened my soul with fasting." They believe Paul meant it when he said, "What revenge" godly sorrow occasioned in the Corinthians.[16]

An even more important reason for fasting is that it is a particular help to prayer. It is a particular help when we set apart larger portions of time for private prayer. Especially in those times, God is often pleased to lift up the souls of those so engaged above all the things on earth. It is on those occasions that sometimes He will lift them up, so to speak, into the third heaven. It is chiefly, then, here a help to prayer. It has frequently been found a means in the hand of God of confirming and increasing virtue and chastity. This grace is not limited to one virtue or one chastity only, as some have imagined, without any ground from Scripture, reason or experience. It also adds to seriousness of spirit, earnestness, sensibility, and tenderness of conscience. It enhances deadness to the world, and consequently the love of God, and every heavenly and holy affection.

One should not assume that there is any natural or necessary connection between fasting, and the blessings God conveys through it. He will have mercy as He will have mercy. He will convey whatever seems to Him good, by whatever means He is pleased to appoint. He has, in all ages, appointed this to be a means of averting His wrath. From time to time, through it we obtain His blessing.

The fast is a powerful means of averting the wrath of God. We may learn this from a remarkable instance of Ahab. Ahab sold himself into works of wickedness like a slave bought with money. Yet, he rent his clothes and put on sackcloth, and fasted. When he did so, God said to Elijah, "Seest thou how Ahab humbleth himself before me? because he humbleth himself before me, I will not bring the evil in his days."[17]

To avert the wrath of God, Daniel sought God with fasting, and sackcloth, and ashes. This appears to be the whole theme of his prayer. It is particularly apparent in the solemn conclusion of it. "O Lord, according to all thy righteousness . . . let thine anger and thy fury be turned away from . . . thy holy mountain. . . . Hear the prayer of thy servant . . . and cause thy face to shine upon thy sanctuary that is desolate . . . O Lord, hear; O Lord, forgive; O Lord, hearken and do; defer not for thine own sake."[18]

It is not only from the people of God that we learn of fasting. From the heathen, we learn that God's anger is moved from those who seek Him by fasting and prayer. When Jonah had declared, "Forty days, and Nineveh shall be overthrown," the people of Nineveh proclaimed a fast and put on sackcloth. Even the king of Nineveh arose from his throne, laid his robe aside and covered himself with sackcloth and sat in ashes. He proclaimed a fast throughout Nineveh. He published an announcement, "Let neither man nor beast, herd nor flock, taste any thing, let them not feed, nor drink water." It was not as if the animals had sinned or could repent. It was thought that by their example, all men might be admonished, knowing that for their sin the anger of God was hanging over all creatures. The king reasoned that who could tell but what God might turn His anger away so that they would not perish. The labor of the people was not in vain. The fierce anger of God was turned away from them. "God saw their works . . . and God repented of the evil, that he had said he would do unto them; and he did it not."[19]

Fasting is not only used for turning away the wrath of God. It is also a means of obtaining whatever blessings we need. When other tribes were smitten before the Benjamites, all of Israel went up to the Temple, and wept and fasted that day until evening. Then the Lord said, "Go up, for tomorrow I will deliver them into thine hands."[20] On another occasion, Samuel gathered all of Israel together. They were in bondage to the Philistines. They fasted on that day before the Lord. When the Philistines drew near to battle with them, the Lord thundered upon them with a great thunder. They were confused and destroyed before Israel.[21] On another occasion, Ezra proclaimed a fast at the river Ahava. The purpose of the fast was to seek God and his way of direction. He was entreated by all of them.[22] Nehemiah reported that he fasted and prayed before the God of heaven. He petitioned, "Prosper, I pray thee, thy servant this day, and grant him mercy in the sight of this man."[23] God granted him that mercy in the sight of the king.

In the same way, the apostles always joined fasting with prayer when they desired the blessing of God on any important undertaking. Thus we read, "There were in the church that was at Antioch, certain prophets and teachers; . . . As they ministered to the Lord, and fasted, the Holy Ghost said, Separate me Barnabas and Saul for the work where unto I have called them. And when they had fasted and prayed, and laid their hands on them, they sent them away."[24]

It is also reported that both Paul and Barnabas did fast themselves. That account is that, when they "returned again to Lystra, and to Iconium, and Antioch, Confirming the souls of the disciples. . . . And when they had ordained them elders in every church, and had prayed with fasting, they commended them to the Lord."[25]

Jesus expressly taught that blessings could be obtained through the use of fasting, which were not otherwise obtainable. Of an obstinate demon, His disciples asked, "Why could not we cast him out? And Jesus said unto them, Because of your unbelief: for verily I say to you, If ye have faith as a grain of the mustard seed, ye shall say unto this mountain, Remove hence to yonder place; and it shall remove; and nothing shall be impossible unto you. Howbeit this kind goeth not out but by prayer and fasting.[26] So, we see the appointed means of obtaining that faith by which the very devils are subject to us comes through prayer and fasting.

Thus we see that fasting has been, from time to time, taught by God himself through clear and open revelations of His will. We understand the need for fasting not merely by the light of reason, or the natural conscience. We see that the people of God have been, in all stages, directed to use fasting as a means toward spiritual ends. The remarkable instance of this is that of the prophet Joel. His prophecy was a direct instruction from God to fast. "Therefore also now, saith the Lord, turn ye even to me with all your heart and with fasting, and with weeping, and with mourning . . . who knoweth if he will return and repent, and leave a blessing behind him. . . . Blow the trumpet in Zion, sanctify a fast, call a solemn assembly; . . . Then will the Lord be jealous for his land, and pity his people. . . . Behold, I will send you corn, and wine, and oil . . . I will no more make you a reproach among the heathen."[27]

It is not only temporal blessings which God directs His people to expect from fasting. He promises even more to those who would seek Him with fasting, weeping and mourning. At the same time He spoke through Joel, He said, "I will restore to you the years that the locust hath eaten, the cankerworm, and the caterpiller, and the palmerworm." He subjoined, "And ye shall eat in plenty,

and be satisfied, and praise the name of the Lord your
God. . . . Ye shall know that I am in the midst of Israel,
and that I am the Lord your God." Then immediately
follows the great gospel promise, "I will pour out my spirit
upon all flesh; and your sons and daughters shall
prophesy, your old men shall dream dreams, your young
men shall see visions; And also upon the servants and
upon the handmaids in those days I will pour out my
spirit."[28]

We have seen the biblical reasons used to alert those in
the days of old to the zealous and constant attending to the
duty of fasting. Those reasons are of equal force to alert us
in our times. Of all of these reasons, we have a peculiar
one for being in fast often. Namely, it is that Jesus
commanded it. He did not in this place in His sermon
expressly require either fasting, giving of alms or prayer.
His directions show how to fast, pray and give alms.
However, these directions touch us with the same force as
injunctions. In commanding us to do anything in a given
manner, He unquestionably requests us to do that very
thing. It is impossible to perform a thing in a given
manner, if it is not performed at all. Consequently, Jesus
saying, "Give alms, fast, pray," in such a manner, is a
clear command to perform all of those duties. We are
commanded to perform them and to do it in the manner
prescribed, in order to not lose our reward.

There is still a further motive and encouragement to the
performance of fasting. There is a promise which Jesus
has annexed to the use of fasting. "Your Father, who sees
in secret, shall reward you openly."

Here are the plain grounds, reasons, and ends of
fasting. Here is our encouragement to persevere in it. We
are to do so, not withstanding the abundant objections
which men, who feel they are wiser than Jesus, have been

continually raising against it.

We are now to consider the objections to fasting. We may now consider the most plausible of these. First, it has been frequently said, "Let a Christian fast from sin, and not from food. This is what God requires of him." So He does. However, He requires fasting also. Therefore, abstaining from sin ought to be done, and fasting should not be left undone. Few view this argument in its full dimension. When you do so, you will easily judge the strength of it. It argues that if a Christian ought to abstain from sin, then he ought not abstain from food. That a Christian ought to abstain from sin is most true. How does it follow from this that he ought not abstain from food? Let him do both one and the other. By the grace of God, let him always abstain from sin. Then, let him abstain from food, for such reasons and purposes as experience and Scripture plainly show to be answered by fasting.

Others give another objection. "But is it not better to abstain from pride and vanity, from foolish and harmful desires, from peevishness, anger, and discontent, than from food?" Without a doubt, it is. Here again we need to be reminded of Jesus' own words. "These things you ought to have done and not left the other undone." Indeed, fasting is done in order to obtain a state of sinlessness. It is as a means to that great end. We abstain from food with this in view. We seek to have the grace of God conveyed into our souls through this outward means. It is done in conjunction with all of the other channels of grace which He has appointed. We pray and fast that through this grace, we may be enabled to abstain from every passion and temper which is not pleasing in His sight. We refrain from food, that being endued with power from God, we may be able to refrain from sin. So this argument proves just the contrary to what one might imagine. It proves that we ought to fast. For if we ought to abstain from evil tempers and desires, then we ought to abstain from food. These little instances of self-denial are the way which God has chosen to bestow upon us that great salvation.

There is still a third objection to fasting. It is an objection through personal experience. Some say, "We do not find it so in our experience. We have fasted much and often. What did it avail? We were not a bit better. We found no blessing in it. Rather, we have found it a hindrance rather than a help. Instead of preventing anger, for instance, or fretfulness, it has resulted in increasing them to such a point that we could neither bear ourselves nor anyone else." This may very possibly be the case. It is possible to either fast or pray in such a manner as to make you worse than before. Some means of doing these things can make you more unhappy and more unholy. Yet the fault does not lie in the means itself. The fault lies in the manner of using the means. Use the means, but change your manner. Do what God commands as He commands it. If you do this, doubtless His promises shall not fail. Then His blessings will no longer be withheld. When you fast in secret, "He that sees in secret shall reward you openly."

The fourth objection is that fasting is mere superstition. Some say, "But is it not mere superstition to imagine that God regards such little things?" If you say it is, you condemn generations of God's children. Will you say that those who came before you were all weak, superstitious men? Can you be so brazen as to affirm this of Moses, Joshua, Samuel, David, Jehoshaphat, Ezra, Nehemiah, and all of the prophets? Do you even accuse Jesus of this? It is certain that Jesus and all of His servants did believe that fasting is no small thing. Jesus has a high regard of it. It is plain that the apostles were of the same judgment after they were filled with the Holy Spirit and all wisdom. When they had received the unction of God, teaching them all things, they still proved themselves the ministers of God by fasting. They did this by fasting, as well as by the armor of righteousness on the right hand and on the left. They would not attempt anything for the glory of God without solemn fasting as well as prayer.

A fifth objection has to do with the means of fasting. Some have asked, "But if fasting is of so great importance, and always attended with blessings, is it not best to fast always? Why do it only now and then? Why not stay in a continual fast? Why not use as much abstinence at all times as our bodily strength will bear?" Do not let this argument discourage you. By all means, exercise as much self-denial at all times as your bodily strength will bear. Use all means to use as little and as plain food as you can. By the blessing of God, this may lead to several of the great ends mentioned before. It may be a considerable help, not only to chastity, but also to heavenly mindedness. It may lead to the weaning of your affections from earthly things, while directing them on heavenly things. But this is not scriptural fasting. It is never termed fasting in all of the Bible. In some measure, it answers some of the ends of fasting. However, it is still another thing. Practice it if you choose. Do not believe it to be commanded by God as a means of averting His judgment and obtaining His blessings.

Continually use as much abstinence as you please. Abstinence in this sense is no other than Christian temperance. This abstinence is never to interfere with your observing the solemn times of your fasting and prayer. For instance, your habitual abstinence, or temperance, should not prevent your fasting in secret. If you are suddenly overwhelmed with a great sorrow, remorse, horrible fear or dismay, fasting is in order. Such a situation of mind would almost require you to fast. You would loathe your daily food. You would barely endure the eating of that which is required for your body. You would not want to eat until the grace of God lifted you up from your pit and set your feet upon the rock of His salvation, and ordered your direction. The same would be the case if you were in agony of desire, vehemently wrestling for God's blessing. You would need no direction to fast. You would willingly do so until you obtained the request from God.

If you had been at Nineveh, your temperance or abstinence would not have excluded you from the national fast. You would have been as much concerned as any other not to taste food on that day. Neither would mere abstinence, or the observing of a continual fast, excuse any Israelite from fasting on the Day of Atonement. There are no exceptions to that solemn decree.

Lastly, if you had been at Antioch at the sending forth of Barnabas and Saul, you would have joined the fast of the church in their behalf. You would have not possibly imagined that temperance or abstinence would have been sufficient cause for not joining in it. If you had, doubtless you would have soon been cut off from the Christian community. You would have been cast out from among them for having brought confusion into the church of God.

Now we need to look at the manner in which we are to fast. We must fast in a manner to make it acceptable to the Lord. First, it should be done unto the Lord. Our eyes should be singly fixed upon Him. Our intention should be this and this alone. The purpose is to glorify our Father who is in heaven. It is to express our sorrow and shame for

our many transgressions of His holy law. It is to wait for
an increase of His purifying grace to draw our affections
to heavenly things. It is to add seriousness and
earnestness to our prayers. It is to avert the wrath of
God. It is to help us obtain all of the great and precious
promises which He has made to us through Jesus.

Let us beware of mocking God. We must be careful not
to turn our fast, or our prayers, into an abomination unto
Him. To mix them with any temporal view, particularly
the seeking of the praise of men, is to pollute the holy
intention. Jesus particularly guards us against this in the
words of the text. "Moreover, when ye fast, be not, as the
hypocrites, of a sad countenance; for they disfigure their
faces, that they may appear unto men to fast. Verily, I say
unto you, They have their reward. But thou, when thou
fastest, anoint thine head, and wash thy face; That thou
appear not unto men to fast, but unto thy Father which is
in secret: and thy Father which seeth in secret, shalt
reward thee openly." Many of the Pharisees, called the
people of God, took on sour and affectedly sad
expressions, twisting their looks into a peculiar form. Not
only did they use unnatural distortions, but they also
covered themselves with dust and ashes. Their chief
purpose, if not their only purpose, was only the affection
and praise of men. During a fast, we are to do as we are
accustomed to do at other times. The admiration of men
should be no part of our intention. If they discover our fast
accidentally, it does not matter. You are neither better
nor worse for their discovery. You must always
remember that it is God in heaven who is to be impressed
by the fast, rather than men on earth.

Even if we desire only the recognition of God in our fast,
we must beware of a second temptation. We must beware
of imagining that we deserve anything from God by our

fasting. We cannot be warned of this too often. Such would be a desire to establish our own righteousness by works. It would be an attempt to procure salvation by debt and not by grace. That temptation is deeply rooted in all of our hearts. Fasting is only a way which God has directed in which we wait for His unmerited mercy. It is a place for waiting. The mercy we receive is without deserving of our own. He has promised to freely give us His blessing.

We are not to imagine the performing of the bare, outward act will receive any blessing from God. "Is it such a fast that I have chosen? a day for a man to afflict his soul? is it to bow down his head as a bulrush, and to spread sackcloth and ashes under him?"[29] Are these outward acts, however strictly performed, all that is meant by a man "afflicting his soul"? Surely not. If it is only a mere external service to him, it is all but lost labor. Such a performance may possibly afflict the body. As to the soul, it profits nothing.

It is possible to afflict the body too much through fasting. We can become unfit for the usual works of our calling. This is to be guarded against with all diligence. We ought to preserve our health as a good gift from God; therefore care is to be taken whenever we fast. We are to proportion the fast to our strength. As we are not to offer God murder for sacrifice, we are not to destroy our bodies to help our souls. Even when we have weakness of body, we may avoid that extreme and fast. If we cannot wholly abstain from food, we can at least abstain from pleasant food. Then we will not seek God's face in vain. "Behold, in the day of your fast ye find pleasure," says the Lord.[30]

Let us take care to afflict our souls as well as our bodies. Let every time of fasting be a season of exercising those holy affections which are implied in a broken and a contrite heart. Let it be a time of devout mourning and of godly sorrow for sin. Let there be a sorrow as that of the Corinthians. Concerning those, Paul said, "I rejoice, not that ye were made sorry, but that ye sorrowed to repentance: for ye were made sorry after a godly manner, that ye might receive damage by us in nothing. For godly sorrow worketh repentance to salvation not to be repented of."[31] This sorrow is according to God, a precious gift of the Holy Spirit. It lifts the soul up to Him from whom it flows. We are to let our sorrowing of this godly sort work in us the same inward and outward repentance. It is to cause in us an entire change of heart, renewed after the image of God, in righteousness and true holiness. It calls also for a change of life, until we are as holy as God is holy, in all manner of our conversation and thought. It is to work in us the same carefulness which is to be found in God. We are to be without spot and blameless. This is the same clearing of ourselves by our lives rather than by our words, by our abstaining from all appearance of evil. It gives us the same indignation, and vehement abhorrence of every sin. It works in us the same fear of our own deceitful hearts. It produces the same desire to be in all things conformed to the holy and acceptable will of God. It provides the same zeal for whatever may be a means of His glory in our growth in our knowledge of Jesus. And it gives the same revenge against Satan and all of his works, and against all filthiness of both flesh and spirit.

We are to always join fervent prayer with our fasting. We are to pour out our whole soul confessing our sins with all of their aggravations. We are to humble ourselves under His mighty hand, laying open before Him all of our needs. We show Him all of our guiltiness and helplessness. This is a time for increasing our prayers, both in behalf of ourselves and our brethren. It is a time to bewail the sins of all of the people. It is a time to cry aloud for the church that God may build up and cause His face to shine upon. Thus, we may observe that the men of God in ancient times always joined prayer and fasting together. This also was true of the apostles in all of the instances cited above. Jesus himself joined them in this understanding in the discourse which is before us.

It remains only, in order to observe a fast which is acceptable to the Lord, that we add our alms to it. Works of mercy, according to our power, both to the bodies and to the souls of men well pleases God. Thus, the angel declared to Cornelius, praying and fasting in his house, "Thy prayers and thine alms are come up for a memorial before God."[32]

God himself expressly declared, "Is not this the fast that I have chosen? to loose the bands of wickedness, to undo the heavy burdens, and to let the oppressed go free, and that ye break every yoke? Is it not to deal thy bread to the hungry, and that thou bring the poor that are cast out to thy house? when thou seest the naked, that thou cover him; and that thou hide not thyself from thine own flesh? Then shall thy light break forth as the morning, and thine health shall spring forth speedily: and thy righteousness shall go before thee; the glory of the Lord shall be thy reward. Then shalt thou call, and the Lord shall answer; thou shalt cry, and he shall say, Here I am. And if thou draw out thy soul to the hungry, and satisfy the afflicted soul; then shall thy light rise in obscurity, and thy darkness be as the noonday. And the Lord shall guide thee continually, and satisfy thy soul in drought, and make fat thy bones: and thou shalt be like a watered garden, and like a spring of water, whose waters fail not."[33]

10

Purity of Intention[1]

"Lay not up for yourselves treasures upon earth, where moth and rust doth corrupt, and where thieves break through and steal! But lay up for yourselves treasures in heaven, where neither moth nor rust doth corrupt, and where thieves do not break through nor steal. For where your treasure is, there will your heart be also. The light of the body is the eye: if therefore thine eye be single, thy whole body shall be full of light. But if thine eye be evil, thy whole body shall be full of darkness. If therefore the light that is in thee be darkness, how great is that darkness!" (Matt. 6:19-23).

In this text, Jesus now proceeds to name the actions of common life. He shows that the same purity of intention is as indispensably required in our ordinary business as it is in our religious actions.

Without question, the same purity of intention which makes our religious actions acceptable must also make our labor or employment a proper offering to God. A man may pursue his business so that he raises himself to a state of importance in the eyes of the world. If he is no longer serving God in his employment, he has no claim to any reward from God. It is the same as he who gives alms so he may be seen, or prays that he may be heard by men. Vain and earthly intentions are no more allowable in our jobs than in our alms and devotions. Those bad intentions then mix with our good works and religious actions. They have the same evil nature when they enter into the common business of our employment. If it were allowable to pursue these intentions in our worldly jobs, it would be allowable to pursue them in our religious life. But, as our prayers and gifts are not an acceptable service to God when they proceed from impure intentions, so our common employment cannot be a service to Him unless it is performed with the same piety of heart.

Jesus declared this in the liveliest manner. In strong and comprehensive words, He explained, enforced and enlarged on this throughout the whole chapter which is at hand. "The light of the body is the eye. If your eye be single, your whole body will be full of light. But if your eye be evil, your whole body shall be full of darkness." The eye is the intention. What the eye is to the body, the intention is to the soul. As the eye guides all of the motions of the body, intentions guide the motions of the soul. This eye of the soul is then said to be single when it looks only at one thing. When we have no other purpose but to know God, and Jesus whom He has sent—to know Him with proper affections—we have a single eye. Pure intention is to love Him as He loved us. It is to please God in all things. It is to serve Him as we love Him, with all of our heart, mind, soul and strength. It is to enjoy God in all things, and above all things, in time and in eternity.

"If your eye be single," thus fixed on God, "your whole body shall be full of light." The whole body—all that is guided by the intention, as the body is by the eye. This is all you are, all you do, all your desires, tempers, and affections. It includes all of your thoughts, words, and actions. The whole of these "shall be full of light." They shall be full of true, divine knowledge. This is the first thing we may understand by light. "In thy light shall we see light."[2] "God, who commanded the light to shine out of darkness, hath shined in our hearts."[3] He shall enlighten the eyes of your understanding with the knowledge of God. His Holy Spirit shall reveal the deep things of God to you. Inspiration of the Holy Spirit shall give you understanding, and cause you to know wisdom. The anointing which you receive from Him, "shall abide in you and teach you all things."[4] How our experience does confirm this! We can lose this light even after God has opened the eyes of our understanding. If we seek or desire anything else than God, how soon is our foolish heart darkened again. Then clouds again rest upon our souls. Doubts and fears again overwhelm us. We are tossed to and fro, not knowing what to do. We do not know what path we should follow. But when we desire nothing but God, clouds and doubts vanish away. We, who were sometimes in darkness, are now light in the Lord. The night now shines as the day. We find, "The path of the just is as the shining light."[5] God shows us the paths which we should follow. He makes plain the way before our faces.

The second thing which we may understand by light is holiness. While you seek God in all things, you shall find Him in all things. The fountain of His holiness continually fills us with His own likeness, justice, mercy and truth. If you look to Jesus and Him alone, you shall be filled with the mind that He had. Your soul shall be renewed day by day, in the image of Him who created it. If the eye of your mind is not moved from God, seeking nothing else in heaven or earth, you will endure in seeking Him who is invisible. Then, as you behold the glory of the Lord, you shall be transformed into the same image, from glory to glory, by His Holy Spirit.[6]

It is a matter of daily experience that by grace we are thus saved by faith.[7] It is by faith that the eye of the mind is opened. Through it, we see the light of the glorious love of God. As long as our eye is steadily fixed upon God as revealed in Jesus, reconciling the world to Him, we are more and more filled with the love of God and man. We increase in meekness, gentleness, long-suffering, and all the fruits of holiness. These come to us through the revelation which is in Jesus, to the glory of God the Father.

Third, the light which fills him who has a single eye implies happiness as well as holiness. Surely, "light is sweet, and a pleasant thing it is for the eyes to behold the sun."[8] It is much sweeter to see the sun of righteousness continually shining upon the soul. And if there be any consolation in Jesus, any comfort of love, any peace that passes all understanding, any rejoicing in the hope of the glory of God, it all belongs to him whose eye is single. Thus, his whole body is full of light. He walks in the light as God walks in the light. He rejoices evermore, praying without ceasing, and in everything giving thanks. He enjoys whatever is the will of God concerning him, as is revealed to him through Jesus.

"But, if your eye is evil, your whole body shall be full of darkness." "If your eye be evil." We see there is nothing between a single and an evil eye. If the eye is not single, then it is evil. Our intentions, in whatever we do, must be singly to God. If we seek anything else, then our minds and consciences are defiled.

Our eye then is evil, if, in anything we do, we aim at any end other than God. If we have any view but to know and to love God, our intentions are evil. We must seek singularly to serve and please Him in all things. We should have only one purpose, to enjoy God and be happy in Him both now and forever.

If your eye is not singly fixed upon God, "your whole body shall be full of darkness." The veil shall remain on your heart. Your mind shall be more and more blinded by the god of this world. Satan seeks to block the light of the glorious gospel of Jesus from shining on you. You will then be full of ignorance and error regarding the things of God. Without this light, you are unable to receive or discern them. And even if you have some desire to serve God, you will be full of uncertainty as to the manner of serving Him. You will find doubt and difficulties on every side, and will be unable to find any way to escape those doubts.

If you seek any of the things of the earth, your eye is not single. You then shall be full of ungodliness and unrighteousness. Your desires, tempers and affections will then be all out of course. They become dark, vile and vain. Your conversation will be as evil as your heart. It will not be seasoned with salt, or capable of ministering grace to your hearers. You will be seen as idle, unprofitable, corrupt and grievous to the Holy Spirit.

Then both destruction and unhappiness are in your ways. Then you will have lost the way of peace. There is no peace, no settled solid peace, for those who do not know God. There is no true or lasting contentment for any who do not seek Him with a whole heart. While you aim at any other thing that perishes, all that comes is vanity. It is not only vanity, but also vexation of spirit. Both the pursuit and the enjoyment of those worldly things is vanity. You walk indeed in a vain shadow and disquiet yourself in vain. You walk in darkness that may be felt. You sleep on, but receive no rest. The dreams of life can give pain. You know that. They cannot give peace. There is no rest in this world or in the world to come. Rest lies only in God, the center of spirits.

"If the light which is in you is darkness, how great is that darkness!" Good intention will enlighten the whole soul. It will fill it with knowledge, love and peace. It does this so long as it is single, as long as it aims at God alone. Darkness is to aim at anything besides God. Those intentions, consequently, cover the soul with darkness instead of light. They yield ignorance, error, sin, and misery. Oh, how great is that darkness. It is the very smoke which ascends out of the bottomless pit. It is the essential night which reigns in the lowest deep, in the land of the shadow of death.

Therefore, "lay not up for yourselves treasures on earth, where moth and rust corrupt, and where thieves break through to steal." If you do, it is plain your eye is evil. It is not singly fixed on God.

Do Christians observe this commandment which they profess to have received from God through Jesus? Not at all. Not in any degree. No more than if such a command had never been given to them. Even the good Christians, as they are accounted by others as well as themselves, pay no manner of attention to it. It might as well be still hidden in its original Greek, for any notice they take of it. In what Christian city do you find one man in five hundred who has the least concern about laying up just as much wealth as he can? Where is he who will not increase his goods just as far as he is able? There are, indeed, those who will not do this unjustly. There are many who will not rob or steal. There are some who will not gain wealth through his neighbor's ignorance or necessity. But that is quite another point. Even those do not object to the act, but only to the manner of doing it. They do not object to the laying up of treasures on earth. They object only to the laying up of them dishonestly. They are not startled at disobeying Jesus, but only at a breach of heathen morality. So even these honest men do no more obey this command than a highway robber or a housebreaker. Indeed, they never plan to obey it. From their youth up, it never entered into their thoughts. They were bred by their Christian parents, teachers, and friends, without any instructions at all concerning it. If they received any instruction at all, it was this, to break it as soon and as much as they could, and to continue breaking it to their life's end.

There is no instance of spiritual infatuation with the world which is more amazing than this. Most of these men read, or hear the Bible read, often. They have read or heard these words a hundred times, and yet never suspected that they themselves were convicted by them. Oh, that God would speak to these self-deceivers with His own mighty voice. May He wake them out of this snare of the devil, and allow these scales to fall from their eyes.

You may wonder what it is to lay up treasures on earth. It is necessary to examine this thoroughly. First, let us observe what is not forbidden in this commandment. Then we may clearly see what is forbidden by it.

We are not forbidden to provide things which are honest in the sight of men. We are not forbidden to earn funds with which to pay our just debts when they are demanded of us. Far from it. We are taught by God to owe no man anything.[9] This is no more than a plain law of common justice. Jesus came not to destroy but to fulfill the law of justice. Second, Jesus does not forbid the providing for ourselves such things as are necessary for the body. We are to receive sufficient, plain, wholesome food to eat. We are to obtain clean clothes to wear. It is our duty to provide these things and not to be a burden to anyone else.

We are not forbidden to provide for our families. This is also our duty. Even the principles of heathen morality require this. Every man ought to provide the plain necessities of life for all of his family. He teaches them a capacity for providing these for themselves by his own example. Thus, when he is dead and gone, they will provide for themselves.

Here I am talking about the plain necessities of life. I am not talking about delicacies, or excesses. It is no man's duty to furnish them, through diligent labor, to his family, any more than to himself. No one is entitled to the means either of luxury or idleness. But if any man does not provide for his own children, he has practically denied the faith, and is worse than an infidel or heathen.[10]

Lastly, Jesus does not forbid us to lay up what is necessary for the carrying out of our worldly business. We may, from time to time, lay up the necessary money to pursue our business in the measure and degree as is necessary. In doing this, the foregoing purposes must be satisfied. First, we are to owe no man anything. Second, we are to enable ourselves to receive the necessities of life. Third, we are to furnish those of our own family with those necessities, and with the means of procuring them while we live.

Now we may clearly see, unless we are unwilling to see it, what is forbidden here. It is the intention of obtaining more wealth than will answer the foregoing purposes. It is the laboring after a larger measure of wealth, a larger increase of money, than these ends require. The laying up of any more than that is what here is expressly and absolutely forbidden. If the words have any meaning at all, it must be this. They are capable of no other meaning. Consequently, he who has adequate food, clothing and shelter for his family, adequate capital for his business, and no debts, answers these reasonable purposes. Let no one who is already in these circumstances seek a still larger portion on earth. He who does, lives in open habitual denial of Jesus. Doing so, he has practically denied the faith.

Hear this, all of you who still live in the world and love the world. You may be highly esteemed by man. You are an abomination in the sight of God. How long shall your souls cleave to the dust of riches? How long will you load yourselves with thick clay? When will you awake and see that many open, speculative heathens are nearer the kingdom of heaven than you? When will you be persuaded to choose the better part which will not be taken away from you? When will you strive to lay up treasures in heaven, renouncing, dreading, and abhoring all others? If you aim at the laying up of treasures on earth, you are simply wasting your time and spending your strength for that which is not bread. What is the gain if you succeed? You have murdered your own soul. You have extinguished the last spark of spiritual life in it. Indeed, in the midst of life and plenty, you are in death. You are a living man, but a dead Christian. "For where your treasure is, there will your heart be also." Your heart is sunk into the dust of the world. Your soul cleaves to the ground. Your affections are set, not on things above, but on things of the earth. Your affections are set upon poor things that may poison, but cannot satisfy, an everlasting spirit made for God. Your love, your joy, your desires, are all placed upon the things which perish in the using. You have thrown away the treasure in heaven. God and His Spirit are lost. You have gained riches and separated from Him.

Oh, how hard it is for those who have gained riches to

enter into the kingdom of heaven.[11] Jesus' disciples were astonished at His teaching this. Far from retracting it, He repeated the same important truth in stronger terms than before. "It is easier for a camel to go through the eye of a needle, than for a rich man to enter into the kingdom of God." How hard it is for them, whose every word is applauded by others, not to be wise in their own eyes. How hard it is for them not to think of themselves better than the poor, common, base, uneducated herd of men. How hard it is not to seek happiness in riches, or in things dependent upon riches. How hard it is to avoid gratifying the desires of the flesh, the desires of the eye, or the pride of life. Oh, how can the rich escape the damnation of hell? Only through God are such things possible.

And if you do not succeed, what is the fruit of your effort? What do you gain by the laying up of treasures on earth? They that want to be rich, that desire and endeavor after it, whether they succeed or not, fall into temptation and a snare. This endeavor is a trap of the devil. It leads to many foolish and harmful lusts—desires with which reason has nothing to do. These desires do not properly belong to rational and immortal beings. They belong only to the brute beasts which have no understanding. They drown men in destruction and perdition, in present and eternal misery. We see melancholy proofs of this if we will but open our eyes and look around. We see men, who desiring and resolving to be rich, covet after money, the love of which is the root of all evil.[12] In so doing, they have already pierced themselves through with many sorrows. They are anticipating the hell to which they are going.

This is not to be affirmed absolutely for all of the rich. A man may possibly be rich without any fault of his own, by the grace of God preventing his own choice. The danger is for those who desire or seek to be rich. Riches, as dangerous as they are, do not always drown men in destruction and perdition. It is the desire for riches which does that. Those who calmly desire, and deliberately seek to obtain riches, whether they do or not in fact gain the world, do infallibly lose their souls. These are selling Jesus, who washed them with His blood, for a few pieces of money. These enter into a covenant with death and hell. Their covenant shall stand. They are daily making themselves ready to partake of their inheritance with the devil and his angels.

Who shall warn this generation of vipers to flee from the wrath to come? Not those who lie at the gate of the rich or cringe at their feet. Not those who desire to be fed with the crumbs that fall from their table. Not those who court their favor or fear their frown. None of those who mind earthly things will sound this warning.

Is there a Christian on earth, a man who has overcome the world, who desires nothing but God? Is there one who fears none but he who is able to destroy both body and soul in hell? If so, O man of God, speak up and spare not. Lift up your voice like a trumpet. Cry aloud and show these honorable sinners the desperate condition in which they stand. It may be that one in a thousand of them will have ears to hear. Then he can arise and shake himself from the dust. He may break loose from those chains that bind him to the earth and at length come to lay up his treasures in heaven.

What if one of these should be awakened by the mighty power of God? What if he should ask, "What must I do to be saved?" The answer, according to the Word of God, is clear, full, and express. God does not say to these, "Sell all you have." Indeed, He who sees the hearts of men, saw it necessary to say that in one particular case only. He said that of the rich young ruler. He never laid it down as a general rule for all rich men, in all succeeding generations.

God's general instruction is, first, do not be high-minded. God does not see as a man sees. He does not esteem us for our riches, grandeur or equipage. He does not value any of our qualifications or accomplishments which are directly or indirectly the result of our wealth. He is not interested in those things which can be bought or procured by money. All of these things are with him worthless. Let them be so with you also. Beware that you do not think yourself to be one bit wiser or better because of your possessions. Weigh yourself on another scale. Estimate yourself only by the measure of faith and love which God has given you. If you have more of the knowledge and love of God than another, you are on this account better. On no other account are you any wiser, better, more valuable or more honorable, than he who is your servant. If you do not have this spiritual treasure, you are foolish and contemptible. If you are not more humble than the lowest servant under your roof, you are less than the beggar laid at your gate.

Second, "do not trust in uncertain riches." Do not trust in them for health. Do not trust in them for happiness. Do not trust in them for help. You are miserably mistaken if you look for help in money. Money is no more able to set you above the world than to set you above the devil. Know that both the world and Satan laugh at all such preparation against them. Money will avail little in the day of trouble, even if it remains in that trying hour. But it is not certain that it will remain. How often does wealth take wings and fly away? But if not, what support will it afford you even in the ordinary troubles of life? The desire of your eye, the wife of your youth, your only son, or the friend who is as close as your own heart, can be taken away in one quick stroke. Will your money reanimate the dead? Can it call back a late inhabitant of this world? Will it secure you from sickness, disease, or pain? Do those afflictions visit the poor only? No. The poor seem to have less sickness than the rich. The poor rarely are visited by these unwelcome guests. If these visitations come at all, they are more easily driven away from the poor than from the affluent. And during the time that the body is chastened with pain, how does money help? Let the ancient poet, Horace, answer.

"When a man is under the bondage of desire or fear, his house and his property give him just as much pleasure as pictures to one with sore eyes, or poultices to a sufferer of gout, or the music of the lyre to a sufferer of ear-ache."[13]

But there is at hand a greater trouble than all of these. Man must die. We must sink into the dust. We must return to the ground from which we were taken, to mix with the common clay. The body is to go into the earth as it was, while the spirit returns to God who gave it. The time of this draws near. The years slide away with a swift, though silent, pace. Perhaps your time is far spent. The noon of life is past, and the evening shadows begin to rest upon you. You feel in yourself sure approaching decay. The springs of life wear away. Now, what help is there in riches? Do they sweeten death? Do they endear that solemn hour? Quite the reverse. "O Death, how bitter is the remembrance of thee to a man that liveth at rest in his possessions!"[14] How unacceptable to the pursuer of wealth is that awful sentence, "This night thy soul shall be required of thee."[15]

Will wealth prevent the unwelcome stroke, or protract that dreadful hour? Can wealth deliver the soul so it will not see death? Can it restore the years that are gone? Can it add to our appointed time a month, a day, an hour, a moment? Will the good things of this world, chosen over spiritual things, follow one over the great gulf? Not so. Naked you came into this world; naked you must return. Surely these truths are too plain to be observed because they are too plain to be denied. No man that is to die could possibly trust in uncertain riches for help.

Likewise, wealth cannot be trusted to bring happiness. Here also wealth will be found to be deceitful on the scales. Every reasonable man may understand this from what has already been observed. Thousands of dollars, or the advantages or pleasures purchased by those dollars, cannot prevent our being miserable. Thus, it evidently follows, money cannot make us happy. Indeed, experience here is so full, strong and undeniable, that it makes all other arguments unnecessary. We simply appeal to facts. Are the rich and great the only happy people? Is each of them more or less happy in the proportion to his wealth? Are they happy at all? It can almost be said that of all men, they are the most miserable. Rich man, for once speak the truth from your heart. You are consumed with a desire for more wealth, and have a fear that you will lose what you have. Speak both for yourselves and for your brethren.

Surely then, to trust in wealth for happiness is the greatest folly of all men on earth. Are you not convinced of this? Is it still possible you should expect to find happiness in money, or all that it can purchase? What? Can money, eating and drinking, property and servants, glittering apparel, diversions and pleasures make you happy? They can just as soon make you immortal.

These things are all dead show. Disregard them. Trust in the living God. You will be safe under the shadow of the Almighty God. His faithfulness and truth shall be your shield and buckler. He is a present help in time of trouble.

He is a help that can never fail. Then you may say, if all of your other friends die, "The Lord lives, and blessed be my strong helper." He will remember you when you lie sick in your bed. He will remember you when there is no help from men. He will be with you when all of the wealth of the world can give you no support. His consolation will sweeten your pain and cause you to clap your hands in the flame. And when your house on earth is almost shaken down, when it is about ready to drop into the dust, He will be with you. He will teach you to say, "O death, where is your sting? O grave, where is thy victory? Thanks be to God which giveth us the victory through our Lord Jesus Christ."[16]

Trust in God for happiness as well as help. All of the springs of happiness are in Him. Trust in Him who gives us all things to enjoy richly. He, of His own free and rich mercy holds them out to us, as in His own hand. Receiving them as His gifts, and as pledges of His love, we may enjoy all that we possess. It is His love which gives a relish to all which we taste. His love puts life and sweetness into all things. He transfuses the joys that are at His own right hand into all He bestows on His thankful children. Those children, having fellowship with the Father and His Son, enjoy Him in all and above all.

Third, do not seek to increase in wealth. "Do not lay up for yourself treasures on earth."[11] This is a flat, positive command. It is fully as clear as, "You shall not commit adultery." Then how is it possible for a rich man to grow richer, without denying Jesus? How can any man, who already has the necessities of life, gain or aim for more, and remain guiltless? If, in spite of this teaching, you continue to do this, why do you call yourself a Christian? You do not obey Jesus. You do not plan to do it. Why do you name yourself by His name? "Why do you call me

Lord, Lord," says Jesus himself, "and do not do the things which I say?"

You may ask, "What must we do with our excess wealth, if we must not store it up? Must we throw it away?" I answer, if you threw it into the sea, if you were to cast it into a fire, it would be better bestowed than it is now. You cannot find a poorer manner of laying up wealth than for your posterity. Of all possible methods of throwing away money, this is the very worst. It is the most opposite to the gospel of Jesus, and the most pernicious to your own soul.

William Law wrote, "If we waste our money, we are not only guilty of wasting a talent which God has given us, but we do ourselves this farther harm, we turn this useful talent into a powerful means of corrupting ourselves; so far as it is spent wrong, so far as it is spent in the support of some wrong temper, in gratifying some vain and unreasonable desires, which as Christians we are obliged to renounce.

"As wit and fine parts cannot be only trifled away, but expose those that have them to greater follies; so money cannot be only trifled away, but, if it is not used according to reason and religion, will make people live a more silly and extravagant life than they would have without it: if, therefore, you do not spend your money in doing good to others, you must spend it to the harm of yourself. You act like one that refuses the cordial to a sick friend, which he cannot drink himself without inflaming his blood. For this is the case of superfluous money: if you give it to those who want it, it is a cordial. If you spend it upon yourself, in something that you do not want, it only inflames and disorders your mind.

"In using riches where they have no real use, nor we any real want, we only use them to our great harm, in creating unreasonable desires, in nourishing ill tempers, in indulging foolish passions, and supporting a vain turn of mind. For high eating and drinking, fine clothes and fine houses, estates and equipage, gay pleasures and diversions, do all of them naturally hurt and disorder our heart. They are the food and nourishment of all the folly and weakness of our nature. They are all of them the support of something that ought not be supported. They are contrary to that sobriety and piety of heart which relishes divine things. They are so many weights upon our mind, that make us less able and less inclined to raise our thoughts and affections to things above.

"So that money thus spent is not merely wasted or lost, but it is spent to bad purposes and miserable effects; to the corruption and disorder of our hearts; to the making of us unable to follow the sublime doctrines of the gospel. It is but like keeping from the poor, to buy poison for ourselves."[17]

Equally inexcusable is the storing up of unneeded wealth for any purpose.

"If a man had hands, and eyes, and feet, that he could give to those who wanted them; if he should lock them off in a chest instead of giving them to his brethren that were blind and lame, should we not justly reckon him an inhuman wretch? If he should rather choose to amuse himself with hoarding them up, than entitle himself to an eternal reward, by giving them to those who wanted eyes and hands, might we not justly reckon him mad?

"Now, money has very much the same nature as eyes and feet. If therefore, we lock it up in chests, while the poor and distressed want it for their necessary uses, we are not far from the cruelty of him who chooses rather to hoard up the hands and eyes, than to give them to those that want them. If we choose to lay it up, rather than to

204 / *The Nature of the Kingdom*

entitle ourselves to an eternal reward by disposing of our money well, we are guilty of this madness that rather chooses to lock up eyes and hands, than to make himself forever blessed by giving them to those that want them."[18]

Is this not another reason why rich men shall hardly enter into the kingdom of heaven? The vast majority of them are under a curse. They are under the peculiar curse of God. In the general thrust of their lives, they are robbing God. They are continually embezzling and wasting God's goods. By that very means, they corrupt their own souls. Also, they are robbing the poor, the hungry, and the naked. By their acts, they wrong the widow and the fatherless. This makes them accountable for all of the wants, afflictions, and distresses which they do not remove. The blood of those who perish for want of what the rich hoard, or store up needlessly, cries out from the earth. Oh, what account will one give to God, who is ready to judge both the quick and the dead?

The true way of using what you do not need yourself may be learned from these words of Jesus. They are the counterpart of what went before. "Store up for yourself treasures in heaven, where neither moths nor rust corrupt, and where thieves do not break in and steal." Put out whatever you can spare on better security than this world can offer. Store up your treasures in the bank of heaven. God will restore them in that day of your need. "He that hath pity upon the poor lendeth unto the Lord; and that which he hath given will he pay him again."[19] Such giving to the poor is the same as giving it unto God's account. In addition, we owe Him not only this, but also ourselves besides.

Give to the poor with a single eye. Give to them with an upright heart and write, "So much given to God."

"Inasmuch as ye have done it unto one of the least of these my brethren, ye have done it unto me."[20]

This is the requirement of a faithful and a wise steward. Sell nothing that is your master's unless some peculiar circumstance should require it. Do not desire or endeavor to increase the wealth, any more than to squander it away in vanity. Employ it wholly to those wise and reasonable purposes for which God has lodged it in your hands. The wise steward, after having provided for his own household, makes himself friends with all that remains. Whenever his earthly tabernacle is dissolved, he will be welcomed into paradise, into the house of God, eternal in the heavens.

Therefore, you who are rich in this world, having authority for it from Jesus, are to be habitually doing good. You are to live in a course of doing good works. You are to be merciful as your Father in heaven is merciful. He does good without ceasing. How far should you be merciful? According to your power, with all of the ability which God has given you. Make this be your measure of doing good. Do not measure it with any beggarly custom of the world. Be rich in good works. As you have much, give much. "Freely ye have received, freely give."[21] It is the same as laying up treasure in heaven. Be ready to distribute to everyone according to his needs. Disperse abroad, give to the poor, deal your bread to the hungry. Cover the naked, entertain the stranger, carry or send relief to them who are in prison. Heal the sick, not only by miracles, but through the blessing of God with your financial support. Let the blessing of him who was ready to die, through some extreme want, come through you. Defend the oppressed, plead the cause of the fatherless, and make the widow's heart sing for joy.

Be a part of the holy fellowship with the early

Christians. They said that nothing they had was their own, and they held all things in common.[22] Be a good and faithful steward of God and the poor.

You differ from the poor in two circumstances only. First, your wants are supplied. Next, you receive the blessedness from giving that portion of your goods which you did not need. Thus, lay up for yourself a good foundation. Lay it up not in the world which now is, but in the world to come for eternal life. That foundation and all of the blessings of God, are in Jesus, His righteousness and what He has done and suffered for us. No other foundation can any man lay. Through His merits, whatever we do in His name is a foundation for a good reward. Every man shall receive his own reward, according to his own labors. Therefore, do not labor for wealth that perishes, but for that which endures for everlasting life. Therefore, whatever you find to do, do it with all of your might.

Be patient in your continual welldoing. Seek God's glory, honor and immortality. Be constant and zealous in the performance of all good works. Wait for that happy hour when the Lord shall say, "I was hungry and you gave me meat. I was thirsty and you gave me drink. I was a stranger and you took me in. I was naked and you clothed me. I was sick and you visited me. I was in prison and you came to me. . . . Come, you blessed of my father. Receive the kingdom prepared for you from the foundation of the world."

11

Single-mindedness[1]

"No man can serve two masters: for either he will hate the one, and love the other; or else he will hold to the one, and despise the other. Ye cannot love God and mammon.

"Therefore I say unto you, Take no thought for your life, what ye shall eat, or what ye shall drink; nor yet for your body, and what ye shall put on. Is not the life more than meat, and the body than raiment? Behold the fowls of the air: for they sow not, neither do they reap, nor gather into barns; yet your heavenly Father feedeth them. Are ye not much better than they? Which of you by taking thought can add one cubit unto his stature? And why take ye thought for raiment? Consider the lilies of the field, how they grow; they toil not, neither do they spin: And yet I say unto you, That even Solomon in all his glory was not arrayed like one of these. Wherefore, if God so clothe the grass of the field, which to day is, and to morrow is cast into the oven, shall he not much more clothe you, O ye of little faith? Therefore, take no thought, saying, What shall we eat? or, What shall we drink? or, Wherewithal shall we be clothed? (For after all these things do the Gentiles seek:) for your heavenly Father knoweth that ye have need of all these things. But seek ye first the kingdom of God, and his righteousness; and all these things shall be added unto you.

"Take therefore, no thought for the morrow; for the morrow shall take thought for the things of itself. Sufficient unto the day is the evil thereof" (Matt. 6:24-34).

After the king of Assyria captured Israel and led it into captivity, he repopulated Samaria with heathens from other lands. It is written that they feared the Lord: that is, they performed an outward service to Him. In fearing the Lord, they also served their graven images. It is recorded that both their children and their children's children did as their fathers did, even until the time of the biblical writings.[2]

The practice of most modern Christians closely resembles that of the ancient heathens. They fear the Lord. They perform an outward service to Him, and thereby show they have some fear of God. But at the same time, they serve their own gods. There are those who teach them about God, as there were those who taught the heathen inhabitants of Samaria. They teach the ways of God, but they do not serve Him alone. They do not fear Him enough for this. "Every nation makes gods of their own; every nation in the cities wherein they dwell." These nations fear the Lord. They have not laid aside the outward form of worshiping Him. However, they still serve the graven images of silver and gold. They worship the work of men's hands: money, pleasure, and praise. They divide their service between God and the gods of this world. In this manner, both their children and their children's children do as their fathers did. They continue to do so even today.

Speaking in a loose way, in the common manner of men,

those poor heathens of old were said to fear the Lord. Yet, observe that the Scripture immediately adds, speaking according to the real truth and nature of things, they did not fear the Lord. They did not fear God, nor the law and commandment which He gave to the children of Jacob. They did not fear the God of their covenant, who had charged them saying, "Neither shall ye fear other gods. But the Lord your God ye shall fear; and he shall deliver you out of the hand of all your enemies."[3]

This same judgment is passed by the unerring Spirit of God upon those commonly called Christians. If we speak according to the real truth and nature of things, "they fear not the Lord, neither do they serve Him." They serve other gods even until this day. Now Jesus said, "No man can serve two masters."

How hopeless it is for any man to attempt this. It is hopeless to attempt the serving of two masters. It is easy to foresee the unavoidable consequence of such an attempt. "Either he will hate the one and love the other, or else he will hold to the one and despise the other." The two parts of this sentence are to be understood to be in connection with each other, although separately proposed. The latter part is a consequence of the former part. He will naturally hold to whom he loves. He will cleave to him and perform to him a willing, faithful, and diligent service. And in the meantime, he will despise the master he hates and have little regard for his commands. If he obeys those commands at all, it will be in a slight and careless manner. Therefore, the wise men of this world will agree, "You cannot serve God and mammon."

Mammon was one of the heathen gods. He was supposed to preside over riches. As it is used here, mammon is understood to be the riches themselves. It is silver and gold. In general, mammon is money. By a common figure of speech, mammon is all that may be purchased with money. This includes ease, honor and sensual pleasure.

But what are we to understand by serving God and by serving mammon, according to this teaching? We cannot serve God unless we believe in Him. This is the only true foundation of serving Him. We are to believe in Him according to the revelation in Jesus. We are to believe in God as reconciling the world to himself through Jesus. We are to believe in Him as a loving, pardoning God. This is the first branch of God's service.

To thus believe in God implies a trust in Him. It is a trust with all of our strength. It is recognizing that without Him, we can do nothing. It is knowing that He, at every moment, endues us with power from on high, without which it is impossible to please Him. It is the seeing of God as our help—our only help—in time of trouble. It is the knowing Him as our shield, our defender, and the lifter up of our heads above all of our enemies that are around about us.

It implies to trust in God as our happiness. It is to know that He is the center of our spirits, the only rest of our souls. He is the only good who is adequate to all our capacities, and sufficient to satisfy all of the desires that are in us.

It implies what is closely related to the other, to trust in God as our end. It is to have an eye to Him in all things. It is to use all things only as a means to enjoying Him. It is, in all times, and in all places, to see Him that is invisible. It is to know that He looks upon us well pleased. It is to refer all things to Him through Jesus.

Thus, to believe is the first thing we are to understand by serving God. The second is to love Him. To love God is to love Him as the one God. This is the manner of love which the Scripture describes. It is the manner God himself requires of us. By requiring this, He engages to work it in us. This is loving Him with all of our heart, and with all of our soul, and with all of our mind, and with all of our strength. It is to desire God alone for His own sake. It is to seek nothing else except with reference to Him. It is to rejoice in God and to delight in Him. It is to not only seek, but to find happiness in Him. It is to enjoy Him as the chiefest of ten thousand. Loving God is to rest in Him as our God and our all. In a word, it is to have such a possession of God as makes us always happy.

The third thing we are to understand by serving God is to resemble or imitate Him. One early Christian said, "It is the best worship or service of God, to imitate Him who you worship." We speak here of imitating or resembling God in the spirit of our minds. Here is where the true Christian imitation of God begins. God is Spirit, and they that imitate Him or resemble Him must do it in spirit and in truth.

Now, God is love. Therefore, they who resemble Him in the spirit of their minds are transformed into the same image. They are as merciful as He is merciful. Their soul is all love. They are kind, benevolent, compassionate, and tender-hearted. They not only do good to the gentle, but also to the mean. Like God, they are loving unto every man. Their mercy extends to all of God's works.

Another thing we are to understand about serving God is obeying Him. Included is the glorifying Him with our bodies as well as our spirits. It is the keeping of His outward commandments. It is zealously doing whatever He has commanded. It includes carefully avoiding whatever He has forbidden. Obedience is the performing of all the ordinary actions of life with the single eye and the pure heart. It is the offering of all acts with a holy, fervent love, as sacrifices to God through Jesus Christ.

Now, let us consider what we can understand about serving mammon. First, it implies trusting in riches, in money, or the things purchasable by riches. It is trusting money as our strength, the means by which we shall perform whatever project we have in hand. It is trusting in them as our help by which we look to be comforted in, or delivered from, trouble.

It implies trusting in the world for happiness. It is supposing that a man's life and the comforts of life consist of the abundance of things which he owns. Trusting mammon is looking for rest in things which are seen. It is seeking contentment in outward plenty. It is expecting satisfaction in the things of the world, which can never be found outside of God.

If we do this, we cannot but make the world our goal. It becomes the ultimate end, if not of all, at least of many of our undertakings. Many of our actions and designs are aimed in this direction. In these activities, we aim only at an increase of wealth, at obtaining pleasure or praise. It is believing that happiness is increased by gaining a larger measure of temporal things, without any concern about eternal things.

Serving mammon implies, secondly, loving the world. It is desiring the world for its own sake. It is placing our joy in the things of the world, and setting our hearts on them. It is seeking our happiness in the world. It is resting, with the whole weight of our souls, upon these passing things. Although daily experience shows it cannot support us in happiness, we continue to depend upon it.

To resemble, to be conformed to the world, is the third thing we are to understand by serving mammon. It is not only to have designs, but desires, tempers, affections, suitable to those of the world. It is to be of an earthly, sensual mind, chained down to the things of earth. It is to be self-willed, inordinate lovers of ourselves. It is thinking highly of our own attainments. It is to desire and delight in the praises of men. It is to fear, shun, and abhor criticism. It is to be impatient of reproof, easy to be provoked, and swift to return evil for evil.

To serve mammon is, lastly, to obey the world. It is to outwardly conform to its maxims and customs. It is to walk as other men walk, in the common road, on the broad, smooth, beaten path. It is to be in fashion. It is to follow the multitudes, to do like the rest of our neighbors. That is, it is to do the will of the flesh and the mind. It is to gratify our appetites and inclinations, and to sacrifice to ourselves. It is to aim at our own ease and pleasure, in a general course, both by our words and actions.

Now, what can be more undeniably clear than that we cannot serve both God and mammon? Every man should see that he cannot comfortably serve both. To walk between God and the world is a sure way to be disappointed in both, and to have no rest in one or the other. What an uncomfortable condition is he in, who has the fear, but not the love, of God. How miserable is he who serves Him, but not with all of his heart. He has only the toils and not the joys of religion. He has religion enough to make him miserable, but not enough to make him happy. His religion will not let him enjoy the world. The world will not let him enjoy God. So, by halting between both, he loses both. He has no peace either in God, or the world.

Every man must see that he cannot serve both. No more glaring inconsistency can be conceived. This must continually appear in the whole behavior of him who is endeavoring to obey both of these masters. He is indeed a sinner who goes two ways, striving to serve both God and mammon. He goes one step forward and another step backward. He is continually bearing up with one hand, and pulling down with the other. He loves sin and he hates it. He is always seeking and yet always fleeing from God. He would and he would not. He is not the same man for one whole day. No, not even for an hour altogether. He is a motley mixture of all sorts of contrarieties. He is a heap of contradictions jumbled into one. Be consistent with yourself one way or the other. Turn to the right hand or the left. If mammon is your god, serve him. If the Lord is your God, then serve Him. But never think of serving either at all, unless it is with your whole heart.

Does not every reasonable, thinking man, see that he cannot serve God and mammon? There is the most absolute difference, the most irreconcilable enmity between them. The difference between the most opposite things on earth—fire and water, darkness and light—vanishes into nothing when compared to the difference between God and mammon. In whatever respect you serve the one, you necessarily renounce the other. Do you believe in God as revealed through Jesus? Do you trust in Him as your strength, your help, your shield, and your exceeding great reward? Is He your happiness, your end in all, above all things? Then you cannot trust in riches. It is absolutely certain you could not, so long as you have this faith in God.

Do you thus trust in riches? Then you have denied the faith. You do not trust in the living God. Do you love God? Do you seek and find happiness in Him? Then you cannot love the world or the things of the world. You are crucified to the world and the world crucified to you. Do you love the world? Are your affections set on things on earth? Do you seek your happiness in those things? Then it is impossible that you could love God. The love of the Father is not in you.

Do you resemble God? Are you as merciful as your Father is merciful? Are you transformed by the renewal of your mind into the image of Him who created you? Then you cannot be conformed to the present world. You have renounced all its affections and lusts. Are you conformed to the world? Does your soul still bear the image of the earthly? Then you are not renewed in the spirit of your mind. You do not bear the image of the heavenly.

Do you obey God? Are you zealous to do His will on earth as the angels do it in heaven? Then it is impossible that you could obey mammon. Then you set the world at open defiance. You trample its customs and maxims under foot, and will neither follow nor be led of them. Do you follow the world? Do you live like other men? Do you please men? Do you please yourself? Then you cannot be a servant of God. You are of your master and father, the prince of this world, the devil.

You are called to worship the Lord your God and Him only shall you serve. You shall lay aside all thoughts of obeying two masters, of serving both God and mammon. You shall propose to yourself no end, no help, no happiness but God. You shall seek nothing on earth or heaven but Him. You shall aim at nothing but to know, love and enjoy God. This is all of your business here below. It is the only view you can reasonably have. It is the one design you are to pursue in all things. "Therefore I say unto you, Take no thought for your life, what ye shall eat, or what ye shall drink; nor yet for your body, what ye shall put on." This is a deep and weighty direction. It is important to us to consider it well and to thoroughly understand it.

Jesus does not require that we would be utterly without a thought to the concerns of this life. A giddy, careless temper is far removed from the whole religion of

Jesus. Neither are we to be slothful in business. We are not to be slack and dilatory in it. This, likewise, is contrary to the whole spirit and quality of Jesus' religion. A Christian abhors sloth as much as drunkenness. He flees from idleness as he does from adultery. He knows well that there is one kind of thought and care with which God is well-pleased. A single-minded concern with him is absolutely necessary for the proper performance of those outward duties to which the providence of God has called us.

It is the will of God that every man should labor to eat his own bread. It is God's will that every man should provide for his own, for those of his own household. It is likewise God's will that we should owe no man anything, but to provide things honestly in the sight of all men. This cannot be done without taking some thought, without having some care upon our minds. Often it requires long and serious thought with much earnest care. Consequently, this care to provide for ourselves and family, this thought of how to render to all of these needs, Jesus does not condemn. This is good and acceptable in the sight of God our Savior.

It is God's will that we should take thought concerning whatever we are to do. We are to have a clear understanding of what we are about to do, and to plan our business before we enter upon it. It is right that we should carefully consider what steps we are to take in it. We should prepare all things beforehand, in order to carry on our business in the most effective manner. This care, termed by some the care of the head, is by no means condemned by Jesus.

What Jesus condemns is the anxious care of the heart. It is an anxious, uneasy care that has torment. He condemns any such care as causes hurt either to the body or the soul. What He forbids is that care, which sad experience shows, wastes the body and drinks up the spirit. Sinful care anticipates all of the misery it fears, and comes to torment us before the time. Jesus forbids only that care which poisons the blessings of today by fear of what may be tomorrow. Then we cannot enjoy the present plenty, through apprehension of future want. This care is not only a sore disease, a grievous sickness of the soul, but it is also an offense against God. It is a sin of the deepest dye. It is a high affront to the gracious governor and wise disposer of all things. This anxiety necessarily implies that the great judge of all does not do right. It implies that He does not order things well. It plainly implies that He is lacking, either in wisdom, or in goodness. He would be lacking wisdom if He does not know what things we need. He would be lacking in goodness if He does not provide those things for all who put their trust in Him. Beware, therefore, that you take no thought in this sense. Do not be anxiously careful for anything. Take no uneasy thought. This is a plain, sure rule. Uneasy care is unlawful care. With a single eye to God, do all that lies in you to provide things honestly in the sight of all men. Then give all this up to better hands. Leave the results of the event to God.

"Take no thought for your life, what ye shall eat, or what ye shall drink; nor yet for your body, what ye shall put on. Is not the life more than meat, and the body than raiment?" If God gave you life, the greatest gift, will He not give you food to sustain it? If He has given you your body, how can you doubt but that He will give you clothes to cover it? This is more especially true if you give yourselves to Him and serve Him with your whole heart. Jesus said, therefore, "Behold the fowls of the air: for they sow not, neither do they reap, nor gather into barns." Yet the birds lack nothing. Your heavenly Father feeds them. Are you not much better than they? You that are creatures made in the image of God, are you not of more value in the eyes of God? Are you not of a higher rank in the scale of beings? "Which of you by taking thought, can add one cubit unto his stature?" What do you gain then from this anxious thought? It is in every way fruitless and unavailing.

"And why take ye thought for raiment?" Have you not a daily reproof wherever you look? "Consider the lilies of the field, how they grow; they toil not, neither do they spin: And yet I say unto you, That even Solomon in all his glory was not arrayed like one of these. Wherefore, if God so clothe the grass of the field, which to day is, and to morrow is cast into the oven, shall he not much more clothe you, O ye of little faith?" Yes, you, whom He made to last forever, to be pictures of His own eternity. You are indeed of little faith. Otherwise, you could not doubt His love and care. You could not doubt it for a moment.

"Therefore, take no thought, saying, What shall we eat?" so we do not store up our wealth on earth; or, "What shall we drink?" because we serve God with all our strength and our eye is singly fixed on Him. We do not say, "Wherewithal shall we be clothed?" if we are not conformed to the world, even if we offend those by whom we might be profited. "After all of these things the Gentiles seek," those who do not know God. You are aware that "your heavenly Father knows that you need all of these things." He has pointed out the infallible way of being constantly supplied with them. "Seek first the kingdom of God and his righteousness, and all of these things shall be added unto you."

"Seek first the kingdom of God," before you give any room to any other thought or care. Let your concern be that God, the Father of our Lord Jesus, may reign in your heart. Seek to have Him manifest himself in your soul, and dwell and rule there. Then He may cast down every high thing which exalts itself against the knowledge of God. He will bring into "captivity every thought to the obedience of Christ."[4] Let God have the sole dominion over you. Let Him reign without a rival. Let Him possess all of your heart, and rule alone. Let Him be your one desire, your joy, your love. Then all that is within you may continually cry out, "The Lord God omnipotent reigneth."[5]

Seek the kingdom of God and His righteousness. Righteousness is the fruit of God's reigning in the heart. And what is righteousness but love? It is the love of God and of all mankind flowing from faith in Jesus. It is a love which produces humbleness of mind, meekness, gentleness, long-suffering, patience, and deadness to the world. It gives every right disposition of heart toward God and toward man. By all of these, it produces all holy actions. It produces whatever is lovely or of good report. It produces whatever works of faith and labors of love that are acceptable to God and profitable to man.

"His righteousness." This is all of His righteousness still. It is His own free gift to us, for the sake of Jesus the righteous. It is through Jesus alone that it is purchased for us, and through His work. It is He alone that works it in us, by the inspiration of the Holy Spirit.

Perhaps the proper way of observing this may give light to some other Scriptures which have not always been so clearly understood. One of these is from Paul in his Epistles to the Romans concerning the unbelieving Jews. He said, "They being ignorant of God's righteousness, and going about to establish their own righteousness, have not submitted themselves unto the righteousness of

God."[6] This may be one sense of the word; they were "ignorant of God's righteousness." They were ignorant of the righteousness of Jesus, imputed to every believer, whereby all of his sins are blotted out, and he is reconciled to the favor of God. They were ignorant of that inward righteousness, of that holiness of the heart, which is with the utmost propriety termed, "God's righteousness." That is His own free gift through Jesus, and His own work by His own mighty Spirit. Because they were ignorant of this, they went about to establish their own righteousness. They labored to establish that outside righteousness which might very properly be termed their own. It was not wrought by this Spirit of God, and it was not owned or accepted by Him. They sought to work this in themselves by their own natural strength. And when they had finished, it was unacceptable to God. Yet trusting in their own works, they would not submit themselves to the righteousness of God. They hardened themselves against that faith through which it was alone possible to obtain righteousness. "For Christ is the end of the law for righteousness to every one that believeth."[7] When Jesus said, "It is finished," He put an end to the law of external rites and ceremonies.[8] He did this to bring a better righteousness through His blood. Through this one oblation of himself, once offered, the image of God may come into the inmost soul of everyone who believes.

Closely related to this are the words of Paul in his Epistle to the Philippians. There he wrote, "I count all things but loss . . . that I may win Christ."[9] Paul sought an entrance into His everlasting kingdom, believing in Him. He believed not in his own righteousness, which was of the law, but that which was through faith in Christ, the righteousness of God through faith. "Not having mine own righteousness which is of the law."[10] That is a bare

external righteousness, the outside religion he formerly
had when he hoped to be accepted by God because of it.
Paul was blameless, according to the righteousness of the
law. This was accomplished through his own work. But
that was not the righteousness which was through faith.
It was not holiness of heart, that renewal of the soul in all
of its desires, tempers and affections, which is from God.
That is the work of God, and not the work of man. It comes
by faith. It comes by the faith of Christ, through the
revelation of Jesus in us. It is by faith in His blood
atonement, whereby we alone obtain the remission of our
sins, and the inheritance among those who are sanctified.

Seek first this kingdom of God in your hearts. Seek this
righteousness which is the gift and work of God, the image
of God renewed in your soul. When you do, all these things
shall be added to you. All things necessary for the body, in
a measure as God sees fit for the advancement of His
kingdom, will be given to you. These things shall be
added—they shall be thrown in over above. In seeking the
peace and love of God, you shall find what you more
immediately ask, the kingdom that cannot be moved. You
shall find in your way to His kingdom, all the outward
things that are necessary to you. This care of you God has
taken upon himself. Cast all of your care on Him. He
knows your wants. Whatever is lacking, He will not fail to
supply.

"Therefore, take no thought for tomorrow." Take no
thought of how to lay up treasures on earth, how to
increase in worldly wealth. Take no thought of how to
procure more food than you can eat or more raiment than
you can wear, or more money than is required from day to
day for the reasonable purposes of life. Also, take no
uneasy thought even concerning those things that are
absolutely necessary for life. Do not trouble yourself with

thinking what you shall do at a time which is yet far off. Perhaps that time will never come. Or, if it does, it will be no concern of yours. Perhaps by then, you will have passed through all of the waves and be landed in eternity. All of those distant concerns do not belong to you. You are but a creature of a day. What have you to do with tomorrow, more strictly speaking? Why should you perplex yourself about it when there is no need to do so? God provides you today with what is necessary to sustain the life which He has given you. It is enough. Give yourself over into His hands. If you live another day, He will provide for that also.

Above all, do not make the care of future things a pretense for neglecting your present duties. This is the most fatal way of worrying about tomorrow. How common this is among men. Many do not like to hear this. All are exhorted to keep a conscience void of offence. We preach for them to abstain from what they are convinced is evil. They do not fail to reply, "How then will we live? Must we not take care of ourselves and our family?" And this they imagine to be a sufficient reason for continuing in known willful sin. They say, and perhaps think, they would serve God now, were it not possible that they might lose their income. They would prepare for eternity, but they are afraid of needing the necessities of life. So they serve the devil for a morsel of bread. They rush into hell for the fear of want. They throw away their poor souls, lest they should some time or other fall short of what is necessary for their bodies.

Is it not strange that they who thus take this matter out of God's hands should be so often disappointed in the very things they seek? While they throw away heaven to secure the things of earth, they lose the one but do not gain the other. The jealous God, in the wise course of His providence, frequently allows this. Then those who will not cast their care on God lose the very portion which they have chosen. There is a visible blast on all of their undertakings. Whatever they do does not prosper. They fail in so much that after they have forsaken God for the world, they lose what they sought, as well as what they did not seek. They fall short of the kingdom of God and His righteousness. Then, other things are not added to them either.

There is another way of taking thought for tomorrow which is equally forbidden in these words. It is possible to take thought in a wrong manner, even with regard to spiritual things. It is possible to be so careful about what may be by and by, as to neglect what is now required at our hands. How insensibly do we slide into this if we are not continually alert in prayer. How easily we are carried away, in a kind of waking dream, in projecting distant schemes. How we draw fine scenes in our own imaginations. We think what good we will do when we are in such a place, or when such a time has come. How useful we will be, how plenteous in good works, when we are easier in our circumstances. How earnestly we will serve God, when our hindrances are out of the way.

Perhaps you are now in heaviness of soul. God, as it were, hides His face from you. You see little of the light of His countenance. You cannot taste His redeeming love. In such a temper of mind how natural it is to say, "Oh, how I will praise Him when His countenance shall again be lifted upon my soul. How I will exhort others to praise Him when His love is again shed abroad in my heart. Then I will do many things. I will speak for God in all places. I will not be ashamed of the gospel of Christ. Then I will redeem the time. I will use to the uttermost every talent I have received."

Do not believe yourself. You will not do it then, unless you do it now. He that is faithful in that which is little, of whatever kind it be, will be faithful in that which is much.[11] If you now hide one talent in the earth, you will then hide five. That is, you will hide them if ever they are given, but there is small reason to expect they ever will be. Indeed, unto him that has, who uses what he has, shall be given and he shall have more abundantly. But from him who has not, he who does not use the grace which he has already received, that shall be taken away.[12]

And take no thought for the temptations of tomorrow. This is also a dangerous snare. Do not think, "When such a temptation comes, what shall I do? How shall I stand up to it? I feel I have no power to resist. I am not able to conquer that enemy." Most true. You do not now have the power which you do not now need. You are not able at this time to conquer that enemy. At this time, he does not assault you. With the grace you now have, you could not withstand the temptations which you do not have. But when the temptations come, the grace will come. In greater trials you will have greater strength. When sufferings abound, the consolations of God will abound in the same proportion. So, in every situation, the grace of God will be sufficient for you. He does not allow you to be tempted today above what you are able to bear. In every temptation He will make a way to escape. As your days are, so your strength shall be.

Therefore, let tomorrow take thought for the things of itself. That is, when tomorrow comes, then think about it. Live today. Let it be your earnest concern to improve the present hour. This is your own, and it is your all. The past is as nothing, as though it had never been. The future is nothing to you. It is not yours. Perhaps it never will be. There is no way to depend upon what is yet to come. You do not know what a day may bring forth. Therefore, live today. Do not lose an hour. Use this moment, for it is all you have. Who knows the things which have been before him or which shall be after him? The generations that were from the beginning of the world, where are they now? They are gone away, forgotten. They once were. They lived their day. Then they were shaken off the earth as leaves off the tree. They mouldered away in the common dust. Another and another race succeeded. Then they followed the generation of their forefathers and shall never more see daylight. Now it is your turn on earth. Rejoice, O young man, in the days of your youth. Enjoy the very now by enjoying Him whose years do not fail. Now, let your eye be singly fixed upon Him in whom there is no variableness. Now, give Him your heart. Now, put yourself on Him. Now, be as holy as He is holy. Now, lay hold of the blessed opportunity of doing His acceptable and perfect will. Now, rejoice to suffer the loss of all things so you may win the prize of Jesus.

Gladly accept today whatever He permits this day to come upon you. Look not at the problems of tomorrow. "Sufficient unto the day is the evil thereof." Evil it is, speaking after the manner of men, whether it be reproach, or want, or pain or sickness. But, in the language of God, all is a blessing. It is a precious balm prepared by the wisdom of God and variously dispensed among His children, according to the various needs of their souls. And He gives in one day sufficient for that day, proportioned to the need and strength of the person. If you snatch today what belongs to tomorrow, if you add this to what is given to you already, it will be more than you can bear. This is the way not to heal, but to destroy your own soul. Therefore, take just as much as He gives you today. Today, do and accept His will. Today, give up yourself, your body, soul and spirit to God, through Jesus. Desire nothing but that God may be glorified in all that you are, all you do, and all that you suffer. Seek nothing but to know God and His Son Jesus, through the eternal Holy Spirit. Pursue nothing other than to love Him, to serve Him, and to enjoy Him at this hour and all eternity.

12

Receiving God's Gifts[1]

"Judge not that ye be not judged. For with what judgment ye judge, ye shall be judged: and with what measure ye mete, it shall be measured to you again. And why beholdest thou the mote that is in thy brother's eye, but considerest not the beam that is in thine own eye? Or how wilt thou say to thy brother, Let me pull out the mote out of thine eye; and, behold, a beam is in thine own eye? Thou hypocrite, first cast out the beam out of thine own eye; and then shalt thou see clearly to cast out the mote out of thy brother's eye.

"Give not that which is holy unto the dogs, neither cast ye your pearls before swine, lest they trample them under their feet, and turn again and rend you.

"Ask, and it shall be given you; seek, and ye shall find; knock, and it shall be opened unto you: For every one that asketh receiveth; and he that seeketh findeth; and to him that knocketh it shall be opened. Or what man is there of you, whom if his son ask bread, will he give him a stone? Or if he ask a fish, will he give him a serpent? If ye then, being evil, know how to give good gifts unto your children, how much more shall your Father which is in heaven give good things to them that ask him? Therefore all things whatsoever ye would that men should do to you, do ye even so to them: for this is the law and the prophets" (Matt. 7:1-12).

At this point, Jesus has finished His main purpose. He had delivered the total of true religion and carefully guarded against changes by men which would make the Word of God worthless. Then He had laid down the rules regarding right intentions which we are to preserve in all of our outward actions. Next in the sermon, He proceeds to the main hindrances of that religion. Then He concluded the sermon with applications of the religion.

In the fifth chapter of Matthew, Jesus fully described inward religion and its various branches. There He laid before us the disposition of souls which constitute real Christianity. He taught of the tempers contained in that holiness, without which no man shall see the Lord. He described the affections which flow from a living faith in God, through His revelation. He showed that only these are intrinsically good and acceptable to God.

In Matthew, the sixth chapter, He showed how all of our actions, even those that are indifferent in their own nature, may be made holy, good and acceptable to God by a pure and holy intention. Whatever is done without that intention, He declared, is of no value to God. However, whatever outward works are consecrated to God with holy intentions are of great value in His sight.

In the first parts of chapter seven, He points out the most common and fatal hindrances to holiness. In the latter part of the chapter, Jesus exhorts us to break through all, and secure that prize of our high calling.

The first hindrance He cautions us against is judging. "Judge not, that you be not judged." Do not judge others, so you will not be judged by God. Do not bring His vengeance on your head on this account. "For with what judgment you judge, you shall be judged, and with what measure you give, it shall be measured to you again." This is a plain and equitable rule. Through it, God permits you to determine for yourselves the manner in which He shall deal with you. By your own actions you determine which judgment you will receive from Him.

This caution is necessary for every person. There is no time, station or place in life in which it is not important. Until we are made perfect in love, the temptations and occasions for judging are never lacking. The temptations to it are innumerable. Many are so artfully disguised that we fall into the sin before we suspect any danger. Unlimited damage is produced by it. The damage always comes to him who judges another. By his wounding of his own soul, he exposes himself to the righteous judgment of God. Frequently, those who are judged are weakened and hindered in their own search for God. Sometimes they are completely turned away, and caused to draw back even to their final perdition. When this root of bitterness turns up, many are defiled by it. Christianity is often spoken evil of for this reason. Its worthy name is blasphemed because of the practice.

However, it does not appear that Jesus gave this caution only, or chiefly, for Christians. Rather, He gave it for all of the people in the world. He gave it for men who do not know God. The godless cannot help but hear of those who follow after Christianity. They observe those who strive to be humble, serious, gentle, merciful, and pure in heart. They see those who earnestly desire such measures of these holy attitudes which they have not yet attained. While they wait for this holy mind, they do good to all men and patiently suffer evil. Whoever goes this far cannot be hidden, any more than a city set on a hill.

Why do those who see these good works not glorify God who is in heaven for them? What excuse do they give for not following in the steps of the true Christian? Why will they not imitate their example, and become followers of them as they are also of Jesus?

In order to provide an excuse for themselves, they condemn those whom they ought to imitate. They spend their time in finding out their neighbors' faults, instead of correcting their own. They are so concerned about others going astray, that they never come into the faith at all. They never advance. They never go beyond a poor, dead form of godliness, without the power of the Holy Spirit.

Jesus spoke especially to those. "Why do you see the speck that is in your brother's eye?" Why do you see the infirmities, the mistakes, the imprudence, and the weakness of the children of God? Why do you do this without considering the beam that is in your own eye? Do you not see your own condemning impenitence? You ignore your satanic pride, your perverse self-will, and your idolatrous love of the world. These are in you and they make your whole life an abomination to God. Above all, you are dancing your way to hell with supine carelessness and indifference. And how then can you say to your brother, "Let me pull the speck out of your eye?" With what authority, with what decency or modesty can you do this? You would criticize him for his zeal for God, self-denial, and great disengagement from worldly cares and employments. You would correct him for the desire to be in prayer or hearing the words of God day and night.

Behold, a beam is in your own eye. It is not a speck like one of those. You hypocrite. You pretend to care for others, but have no care for your own soul. You make a show of zeal for the cause of God, when in truth you neither love nor fear Him. First get the beam out of your own eye. Next, cast out the beam of impenitence. Know yourself. See and feel yourself to be a sinner. See your wickedness. Feel that you are altogether corrupt and abominable, and that the wrath of God abides upon you. Cast out the beam of pride. Abhor yourself. Sink down and become little and base in your own eyes. Cast out the beam of self-will. Learn what it means, "If any man will come after me, let him deny himself."[2] Deny yourself, and take up your cross daily. Let your whole soul cry out, "I came down from heaven." So you did, you never-dying spirit, whether you know it or not. You came not to do your own will, but the will of God who sent you. Rid yourself of the love of the world. Be crucified to the world and the world crucified to you. Just use the world, but enjoy God. Seek all of your happiness in Him.

Above all, cast out that great beam of supine carelessness and indifference. Deeply consider the one thing which is necessary, the one thing which you scarcely ever think about. Know and feel that you are a poor, guilty sinner, quivering at the edge of eternity. Are you a sinner born to die, a leaf driven before the wind? Are you a vapor ready to vanish away, just appearing, and then scattering into the air to be seen no more? Understand this. When you do, you shall see clearly how to cast the beam out of your own eye. Then, if you have leisure time from the concerns of your own life, you shall know how to correct your brother also.

What is the proper meaning of this instruction, "Judge not?" What is the judging which Jesus forbids? It is not the same as evil speaking, although it is frequently joined with it. Evil speaking is the relating of anything that is evil concerning an absent person. Judging may indifferently refer either to the absent or the present. It does not necessarily imply speaking at all. It can be only the thinking evil of another. Jesus does not condemn all kinds of evil speaking of others in this injunction. If you see one commit robbery or murder, or hear him curse the name of God, you cannot refrain from thinking ill of him. This is not evil judging. There is no sin in this, nor anything contrary to Christian affection.

The thinking of another in a manner which is contrary to love is that judging which Jesus condemns here. This may be of various types. First, we may think another to blame when he is not. We blame at least in our own mind, for things which he is not guilty. We may blame him for words he never spoke, or actions he has never done. We may think his manner of acting was wrong, although in reality it was not. Judging can occur when the manner of acting was not wrong. We can believe the act was wrong, although in reality it was not. And where nothing is justly blamed, we can suppose his intention was not good. We can condemn him on that ground. We are in judgment of him at the same time God sees his heart to be filled with good intentions and godly sincerity.

Falsely condemning the innocent is not the only way of judging. Judging can be the condemning the guilty in a higher degree than he deserves. This species of judging is also an offence against justice and mercy. Only the strongest and tenderest affections can keep us from it. Without them, we readily suppose a person who is known to be in fault, to be more in fault than he really is. We undervalue whatever good is found in him. We cannot be easily convinced to believe anything good can remain in him whom we have found guilty.

All of this shows a complete lack of that love which thinks no evil. That love never draws an unjust or unkind conclusion from any premises whatever. Love will not infer from a person's once falling into an act of open sin, that he usually sins. It will not believe that he is habitually guilty of sin. And if he was habitually guilty at one time, love does not conclude that he is still so. Much less will it conclude that he is now guilty of this, therefore, he is guilty of other sins also. These evil reasonings all pertain to that sinful judging which Jesus guards us against. We must have the greatest concern in avoiding these if we love either God or our own souls.

But suppose we do not condemn the innocent. Suppose we do not condemn the guilty any further than they deserve. Still, we may not be altogether clear of this snare of judging. There is a third part of sinful judging, which is the condemning any person when there is not sufficient evidence. Even if the facts which we suppose to be true are true, that does not acquit us. We ought not to have supposed, but proved the guilty. Until the guilt is proved, we ought to have formed no judgment. We are not excused, even if the facts admit to ever so strong a proof, unless that proof is produced before we judge. Until we compare the evidence on both sides, we cannot judge. We can never be excused, if we pass a full sentence before the accused has spoken for himself.

Even a Jew might teach us this mere lesson of justice, abstracted from mercy and brotherly love. Nicodemus said, "Doth our law judge any man before it hear him, and know what he doeth?"[3] Even a heathen could reply, when the chief of the Jewish nation desired to have a judgment against his prisoner. It was the custom of the Romans not to judge any man before the accused could meet his accusers face to face. He had the right to answer for himself concerning the crime with which he was accused.

We could not easily fall into sinful judging if we were to

observe those rules which come to us from the heathen Romans. One wrote of his personal rules concerning the practice of judging. He said, "I am so far from lightly believing every man's evidence, or any man's evidence against another, that I do not easily or immediately believe a man's evidence against himself. I always allow him second thoughts, and many times counsel him to do so."[4] Those who are called Christians should go and do likewise. Otherwise, even the heathen's practice can rise up and condemn us.

So it is that we should rarely condemn or judge one another. This evil would soon be corrected if we were to walk by the clear and express rules which Jesus taught us. Another of these is, "If thy brother shall trespass against thee, go and tell him his fault between thee and him alone." If you hear or believe you have been offended, this is the first step you are to take. "If he will not hear thee, then take with thee one or two more, that in the mouth of two or three witnesses every word may be established." This is the second step. "If he shall neglect to hear them, tell it unto the church."[5] Tell it either to the church leaders or to the whole congregation. You will have done your part. Then think no more of the matter. Turn it all over to God.

Suppose, by the grace of God, you have cast the beam out of your own eye, and clearly now see the speck which is in your brother's eye. Then beware you do not hurt yourself by endeavoring to help him. Still, "give not that which is holy unto dogs." Do not hastily judge that any deserve this title. But, if it does appear that some do, then "do not cast your pearls before swine." Beware of a zeal which is not according to knowledge. These acts can be another hindrance in their way to becoming perfect as their father is perfect. Those who desire this perfection cannot help wanting all others to partake in the same blessing. When we first receive the heavenly gifts, the divine evidence of things unseen, we wonder why all people do not see the things which we see so plainly. We have no doubt at all that we shall be able to open their eyes and explain it to all of them. Hence, we are for preaching to all whom we meet without any delay. We push to see and speak to them whether they want us or not. We often suffer in our own souls through the poor success arising from this intemperate zeal. To prevent this spending in vain, Jesus adds this necessary caution. This caution is necessary to all, but especially so for those who are still warm in their first love through the Holy Spirit. "Give not that which is holy unto the dogs, neither cast ye your pearls before swine, lest they trample them under their feet and turn again and rend you."

"Do not give that which is holy unto the dogs." Be careful in thinking that any deserve this title. Have full and incontestable proof before you do. Have a proof that you can no longer resist. When it is clearly and indisputably proved that one is an unholy and wicked person, an enemy to God and all righteousness and holiness, then do not give him that which is holy. Literally, this is the "holy thing." It is the good news of Jesus.

The holy, the particular doctrines of the gospel, were hidden from the ages and the generations of old. They are now made known to us only by the revelation of Jesus, and the inspiration of His Holy Spirit. These are not to be prostituted before the unholy men, those who do not know even if there is any Holy Spirit. Ministers of the church cannot refrain from speaking the gospel to them in services, where some of them probably will be. Ministers must speak there, whether unholy men will hear or not.

This is not the case with private Christians. They do not bear that responsibility. They are under no obligation to force these great and glorious truths on those who contradict and blaspheme them. They are not required to give this gospel to those who have a rooted enmity against them. They are not to do so. They should spend their time on those who are able to hear and bear it. Do not begin a discourse with those on remission of sins and the gifts of the Holy Spirit. Talk with them in their own way, and upon their own principles, with the rational and honorable, reason of righteousness, temperance and judgment to come. This is the most probable way to get their attention. Reserve higher subjects for those of higher attainments.

"Do not cast your pearls before swine." Be very unwilling to pass this judgment on any man. If the fact of it is plain and undeniable, if it is clear beyond all dispute, then do not cast your pearls before them. A "swine" is one who does not endeavor to disguise himself. Rather, he glories in his shame, making no pretense of purity. He has neither purity of heart nor of life, and works with all uncleanliness and greediness. Do not talk to him of the mysteries of the kingdom. Do not speak of the things which his eye has not seen or his ear heard. Since he has no spiritual senses, it cannot enter into his heart to conceive these things. Do not tell him of the exceedingly great and precious promises which God has given us in the revelation of Jesus. What conception can he have to being made a partaker of the divine nature? He does not even have a desire to escape the corruption that is in the world. He has as much knowledge of these things as a swine has about pearls. He relishes the deep things of God just as much as swine relish a pearl. He who is immersed in the mire of this world, in worldly pleasures, desires, and cares, has no knowledge of the mysteries of the gospel. Do not cast your pearls before those, lest they trample them under their feet. They will utterly despise what they cannot understand, and speak evil of the things which they do not know. It is possible this would not be the only inconvenience which would follow. It would not be strange, if they were according to their nature, to turn and rend you. They are apt to return you evil for good, a cursing for your blessing, and hatred for your goodwill. Such is the enmity of the carnal mind against God, and all of the things of God. Such is the treatment you are to expect from these, if you offer them the unpardonable affront of endeavoring to save their souls from death. They will not forgive you for attempting to pluck them as brands out of the burning.

However, you need not utterly despair even of these who for the present turn and rend you. When all of your arguments and persuasions fail, there is still another remedy left. It is one that is frequently found to be effective, when no other method avails. This is prayer. Therefore, whatever you desire or want, either for others or for your own soul, "Ask, and it shall be given you; seek, and ye shall find; knock and it shall be opened unto you." The neglect of this is the third great hindrance of holiness. We have not because we ask not.[6]

If you would only ask, you could be meek and gentle, and lowly of heart, and full of love to both God and man. All you need to do is to continue in prayer. Therefore, in this case, ask and it shall be given unto you. Ask that you may thoroughly experience, and perfectly practice, the whole religion which Jesus has here so beautifully described. You shall be given that holiness which is in Him, both of heart and all manner of conversation.

Seek in the way He has directed. Search the Scriptures.

Hear the Word. Meditate on the Word. Fast and partake of communion. Surely then you will find that pearl of great price, that faith which overcomes the world. You will receive that peace which the world cannot give and which is the reward of your inheritance.

Knock. Continue in prayer and in every other way of the Lord. Do not be weary or faint of mind. Press on to the mark. Take no denial. Do not let God go until He blesses you. And the door of mercy, of holiness, of heaven, shall be opened to you.

Jesus had compassion for the hardness of our hearts. He knew we were unready to believe the goodness of God. So Jesus had to enlarge upon, repeat and confirm what He had taught. He said, "Every one that asketh, receiveth." None need fall short of the blessing. "And he that seeketh." Everyone that seeks will find the love and the image of God. "And he that knocks." To everyone who knocks, the gate to the kingdom shall be opened. They will receive righteousness. So there is no room to be discouraged. This means that no one will ask, seek, or knock in vain. Remember to always pray, seek, knock and not to faint. Then this promise stands sure. It is as firm as the pillars of heaven. It is even more firm, for heaven and earth shall pass away, but the Word of God shall not pass away.

Jesus sought to cut off every pretense for unbelief. In the following verses, He illustrates even farther what He had said. He appeals to what passes by in our own heart. He said, "What man is there of you, whom if his son ask bread, will he give him a stone?" Will even your natural affection allow you to refuse a reasonable request of one you love? "Or if he ask a fish, will he give him a serpent?" Will he give him something harmful instead of useful? So that even from what you feel and do yourselves, you may receive the firmest assurance of God. You may be assured on the one hand that no ill effects can come from your asking. On the other hand, you may be assured that you will receive a blessing, a full supply for all of your needs. "If ye then, being evil, know how to give good gifts unto your children, how much more shall your Father which is in heaven," who is pure, unmixed, essential goodness, "give good things to them that ask him?" On another occasion Jesus expressed this as, "give the Holy Spirit to them that ask him?"[7] In Him, the Holy Spirit, are included all good things. From Him comes all wisdom, peace, joy, and love. He gives the whole treasures of holiness and happiness. He gives all that God has prepared for those who love Him.

See that you are in charity with all men. Then your prayer may have its full weight with God. Otherwise, it is more likely to bring a curse than a blessing to you. You cannot expect to receive any blessing from God while you have no charity toward your neighbor. Therefore, let this hindrance be removed without delay. Confirm your love toward one another and toward all men. Love them not in a word only, but in deed and in truth. "Therefore all things whatsoever ye would that men should do to you, do ye even so to them: for this is the law and the prophets."[8] That is the royal law. It is the golden rule of mercy as well as justice. Even a heathen emperor had this written over the gate of his palace.[9] It is a rule which many believe to be naturally engraved on the mind of everyone born into the world. This much is certain: it commends itself, as soon as it is heard, to every man's conscience and understanding. No man can knowingly offend against it, without carrying condemnation in his own heart.

"This is the law and the prophets." Jesus' sermon includes all of the essentials which were revealed to mankind by God through His prophets from the time of the world's beginning. They are all summed up in these few words. They are all contained in this short direction. This, properly understood, comprises all of the religion which Jesus came to establish on earth.

This may be understood either in a positive or a negative sense. In the negative sense, the meaning is, "Whatever you would not have men do to you, do not that to them." Here is a plain rule, always ready at hand, always easy to be applied. In all cases relating to your neighbor, make his case your own. Suppose the circumstances were changed. Suppose yourself to be just as he is now. Then beware that you indulge neither temper nor thought, that no word gets out of your lips, that you take no step, which you would have condemned in him upon the reverse of the circumstances. If understood in a direct and positive sense, the meaning is plain. "Whatever you could reasonably desire of him, supposing you were in his circumstances, do that to the uttermost of your power, to every person on earth."

We can apply this in one or two obvious instances. It is clear to every man's conscience that we would not want others to judge us. We would not want anyone to think evil of us, either lightly or without cause. We would not have anyone speak evil of us, or publish our real faults or failings. Apply this to yourself. Do not do unto another what you would not have them do unto you. You, if you apply this, will never again judge your neighbor. You will never causelessly or lightly think evil of anyone. Much less will you speak evil. You will never mention even the real faults of an absent person, unless you are convinced it is absolutely necessary for the good of other souls.

We would have all men love and esteem us. We would have them behave toward us according to justice, mercy and truth. We would have them do all of the good for us that they can without injuring themselves. In all outward things, according to the known rule, their luxury should give way to our conveniences. Their conveniences should give way to our necessities. Their necessities should give way to our extreme needs. Now, let us walk by the same rule. Let us do to all as we would have them do unto us. Let us love and honor all men. Let justice, mercy and truth govern all of our minds and actions. Let our luxuries give way to our neighbor's conveniences. If this is done, who will have any luxuries left? Let our conveniences give way to our neighbor's necessities. Let our necessities give way to his extreme needs.

This is pure and genuine morality. Do this and you shall live. As many as walk by this rule, peace be to them and mercy. They are the Israel of God. Let it be observed, however, none can walk by this rule without God's grace. None can love his neighbor as himself, unless he first loves God. None can love God unless he first believes in Jesus. He cannot love God unless he has the redemption through Jesus and the Holy Spirit bearing witness with his spirit that he is a child of God.

Faith is still the root of all present as well as future salvation. We must say to every sinner, believe in Jesus and you shall be saved. You shall be saved now, that you shall be saved forever. You may be saved on earth, so that you may be saved in heaven. Believe in Him, and your faith will work by love. You will love the Lord God because He has loved you. You will love your neighbor as yourself. Then, it will be your glory to exert and increase this love. You will not only abstain from what is contrary to it, every unkind thought, word, and action, but will show all that kindness to every man which you would have him show to you.

13

The Narrow Gate¹

"Enter ye in at the strait gate: for wide is the gate, and broad is the way, that leadeth to destruction, and many there be which go in thereat: Because strait is the gate, and narrow is the way, which leadeth unto life, and few there be that find it" (Matt. 7:13, 14).

Jesus warned us of the dangers which would easily beset us at our first entrance into real religion. Hindrances would naturally arise within us from the wickedness of our own hearts. Now, Jesus proceeds to apprise us of the hindrances from without. These particularly come from bad example and bad advice. By one or the other of these, many who once ran well have drawn back into sinfulness. Many of those were not novices in the faith. They had made some good progress in righteousness. Therefore, Jesus presses His cautions upon us with all possible earnestness. He repeats again and again, in a variety of expressions, lest by any means we should let it slip by. To effectively guard us against this, He says, "Enter ye in at the strait gate: for wide is the gate and broad is the way that leadeth to destruction, and many there be which go in thereat. Because strait is the gate, and narrow is the way, which leadeth unto life, few there be that find it." To protect us from missing the way, he warned, "Beware of false prophets."[2] We shall at present consider the first part of this warning.

In considering Jesus' description of the two gates, we observe first the inseparable properties of the way to hell. It is a wide gate and a broad way that leads to destruction. Many will go that way. Second, the inseparable properties of the way to heaven are described. That gate is narrow and the way is hard. There are only a few who will find that way. Third, He gives us a serious exhortation based upon the teaching. Enter at the narrow gate.

Sin is the gate of hell, and corruption is the way to destruction. Thus, the wide gate is sin, and the broad way is wickedness. And how wide a gate is that of sin! How broad is the way of wickedness! Compare this to the broadness of the commandments of God. Those commandments extend not only to all of our actions, but to every word that goes out of our mouth, and even every thought that rises in our heart. Sin is equally broad with this commandment. Any breach of the commandment of God is sin. Sin is even a thousand times broader, since there is only one way of keeping the commandment. We do not properly keep it, unless we do it both in act and manner. Notice that there are thousands of ways of breaking every commandment. This shows us that the gate is wide indeed.

Let us consider this a little more in detail. Notice how far the primary sins extend, from which all of the rest come. Observe that carnal mind which is striving against God. It displays pride of heart, self-will, and the love of the world. There are no bounds to these sins. They diffuse themselves through all of our thoughts, and mingle with all of our feelings. They are the leaven which permeates, more or less, the whole mass of our affections. On a close examination of ourselves, we may perceive these roots of bitterness continually springing up. They infect all of our words and taint all of our actions. And how many additional sins they do bring forth in every age and nation. They bring forth enough to cover the whole earth with darkness and cruel living conditions.

Who is able to reckon up their accursed fruit? Who can count all of the sins, whether against God or against our neighbor? We need not appeal to imagination, but only to daily melancholy experience. We need not range over the whole earth to find them. Survey any one nation. Observe any single country, or city, or town. How many are the examples to be seen. You need not even look at those countries which are still overspread with pagan darkness. We need only look to those who name the name of Christ, and profess the light of the Christian gospel. Go no farther than the country in which you live, and the city where you now are. We call ourselves Christians, yes, Christians of the purest sort. We are enlightened, modern, rational Christians. But, alas, who shall carry on the enlightenment of our opinions into our hearts and lives? Is there not a cause? How innumerable are our sins, and how deep is their dye. The grossest acts of every kind abound among us from day to day. Sins of every sort cover the land as the waters cover the sea. They are countless. It is easier to go and count the drops of rain or the sands of the seashore. So it is that wide is the gate and broad is the way that leads to destruction.

And many there will be that go in at that gate. Many will walk in that way. Almost as many go in it as at the gate of death, to sink into the chambers of the grave. It cannot be denied that even in so-called Christian countries, people of every age and sex, of every profession and employment, of every rank and degree, high and low, rich and poor, are walking in the broad way of destruction. The far greater portion of the inhabitants of your city, to this day, live in sin. They live in some palpable, habitual, known transgression of the laws of God which they profess to observe. They engage in some outward transgression, some gross, visible kind of ungodliness or unrighteousness. They perform some open violation of their duty, either to God or to man. These then, none can deny, are all in the way that leads to destruction.

Add to them those who are called Christians, but were never alive to God. They outwardly appear fair to men, but are inwardly full of all uncleanness. They are full of pride, or vanity, anger, or revenge, ambition or covetousness. They are lovers of themselves, lovers of the world, and lovers of pleasure, more than lovers of God. They may be highly regarded by men, but they are an abomination to the Lord. They will greatly increase the number of those going on their way to hell.

Added to all of these is still another group. Some, whatever they be in other respects, have more or less the form of godliness. However, they are ignorant of God's righteousness. They seek to establish their own righteousness for their acceptance by God. The result is they have not submitted themselves to the righteousness which is of God by faith.

Now, join all of these together in one. See how terribly true is Jesus' assertion. Indeed, wide is the gate and broad is the way that leads to destruction. Many there will be who go in it.

This does not only concern the common herd of people.

It is not limited to the poor, base, stupid part of mankind. Men of eminence in the world, men who have much wealth, are not excused from this. On the contrary, many wise men of the world, according to the human methods of judging, are called into the broad way by the world. Many of these are considered mighty in power, in courage, and in riches. Many who are called noble are following the calling of the flesh and the devil. The higher they are raised in fortune and power, the deeper they sink into wickedness. The more blessings they have received from God, the more sins they commit. They use their honor or riches, their education or wisdom, not as a means of working out their salvation. Rather, they use them for excelling in vice, and so insuring their own destruction. The very reason why so many of these go on securely in this way is because it is broad. They do not consider that this is an inseparable property of the way to destruction.

There is also an inseparable property of the way to heaven. That is a narrow way that leads to life. It leads to life everlasting, through a gate so narrow that nothing unclean, nothing unholy, can enter. No sinner can pass through that gate, until he is saved from all of his sins. This is not limited to his outward sins, his evil conversation received by tradition from his fathers. It will not suffice that he has ceased to do evil and learned to do well. He must not only be saved from all sinful actions, but also from all evil and useless discourse. He must be inwardly changed and thoroughly renewed in the spirit of his mind. Otherwise he cannot pass through the gate of life. He cannot enter into glory.

The way of universal holiness is the narrow way that leads to life. Narrow indeed is the way of poverty of spirit. Narrow is the way of holy mourning. Narrow is the way of meekness. Narrow is that way of hungering and thirsting after righteousness. Narrow is the way of mercifulness and of love unfeigned. So is that way of charity of heart, of doing good to all men. Narrow is the way of gladly suffering evil, all manner of evil, for righteousness' sake. "And few there will be that find it." Alas, how few find even the way of bare heathen honesty. How few there are that do nothing to another which they would not have another do unto them. How few that are clear before God from acts either of injustice or unkindness. How few there are that do not offend with their tongues by speaking nothing unkind or untrue. What a small portion of mankind is innocent even of outward transgressions. And how much smaller proportion have their hearts right with God. Few are clean and holy in His sight. Where are they, whom His all searching eye discerns to be truly humble? Where are those who abhor themselves in the presence of God their Savior? How few are deeply and steadily serious, feeling their lack and passing the time of sojourning with holy fear. There are but a few who are truly meek and gentle, who never overcome evil with evil, but overcome evil with good. It is they who are athirst for God and continually panting after a renewal in His likeness. How thinly are they scattered over the earth whose souls are enlarged with love to all mankind. How scarce are those who love God with all their strength, and have given Him their hearts, and desire nothing else in heaven or on earth. How few are those lovers of God and man, who spend their whole strength in doing good to all men. How few are the ones who are ready to suffer all things, even death itself, to save one soul from eternal death.

While so few are found in the way of life, and so many in the way of destruction, there is a great danger lest the torrent of the bad examples should carry us away with them. Even a single example, if it is always in view, is apt to make a great impression upon us. This is especially so when it has nature on its side. Then, it can fall within our own inclinations. How great then, is the force of so many examples which are continually before our eyes. They all conspire, together with our own hearts, to carry us down the stream of nature. How difficult it is to stem the tide and keep ourselves unspotted in the world.

What heightens the difficulty still more is that these examples are not the rude and senseless part of mankind. At least, not these alone who set us an example, and throng the downward way. Often, they are the polite, the well-bred, the gentle, the wise, the men who understand the world. They can be men of knowledge, of deep and various learning, fashionable and eloquent. These are all—nearly all—against us. How difficult it is to stand against these. Their tongues drop manna, and they have learned all of the arts of soft persuasion. They also apply reasoning. They are well versed in all controversies and strife of words. It is, therefore, an easy thing with them to prove that their way is right because it is broad. Only he who will not follow them is wrong. They say our way must be wrong because it is narrow and because there are so few who find it. They will make it clear to a demonstration that evil is good and good is evil. They will show the way of holiness is the way of destruction. They will prove that the way of the world is the only way to heaven.

How can the unlearned and ignorant maintain their cause against such opponents? And yet these are not all with whom they must contend, however unequal they are to the task. There are many mighty, noble and powerful men, as well as wise, in the road that leads to destruction. They have a shorter way of disproving than that of reason and argument. They usually apply not to understanding, but to fear. They threaten any who oppose them. It is a method that seldom fails to have success, even when arguments do not. All men can fear, whether they can reason or not. And all who do not have a firm trust in God, a sure reliance both on His power and love, cannot but succumb to fear. They dare not offend those who have the power of the world in their hands. What wonder, therefore, if the example of these is a law to all those who do not know God.

Many of the rich are also in the broad way. These appeal to the hopes of men, and to all of their foolish desires. This appeal is as strong and effective as when the mighty and the noble appeal to fear. You can hardly hold on in the way to the kingdom unless you are dead to all of the world. Unless you are crucified to the world and the world is crucified to you, unless you desire nothing more than God, the broad way is attractive.

In contrast, how dark, how uncomfortable and how forbidding is the prospect of the opposite side—a narrow gate and a hard way. And only a few will find that gate. Only a few walk in this way. Besides, even those few are not all wise men or men of learning or eloquence. Often, they are not able to reason either strongly or clearly. They cannot propose an argument to any advantage. They do not know how to prove what they profess to believe. They cannot even explain the faith they say they have experienced. Surely such advocates as these will not recommend, but rather discredit, the cause which they espouse.

Added to this is the fact that they are not noble, and not famous men. If they were, you might bear with their folly. They are men of no interest, no authority, and of no fame in the world. They are low in social station. As such, they have no power to hurt anyone. Therefore, there is nothing at all to be feared from them. There is nothing at all to hope for from them. The greatest part of them may say, "Silver and gold have I none."[3] If they do, at least it is only a moderate share. And some of them scarcely have food to eat, or clothes to put on. For this reason, and also because their ways are not like those of other men, they are criticized everywhere. They are despised and have their names cast about as evil. They are variously persecuted and treated as the filth and offscouring of the world. So it is that both your fears, your hopes and all of your desires, all your natural passions, continually incline you to turn into the broad way. Only the guidance which you receive immediately from God will prevent you from doing so.

Therefore, it is that Jesus so earnestly exhorts, "Enter in at the strait gate." Or, as the same exhortation is elsewhere expressed, "Strive to enter in."[4] Strive as if in agony. Many will seek to enter in, according to Jesus. They shall indolently strive, and shall not be able.

It is true that Jesus intimates what may seem to be another reason for this. In the words which immediately follow these, it appears that there is another reason for not being able to enter in. After He said many would not be able, He subjoins, "Once the master of the house is risen up, and hath shut to the door, and ye begin to stand without, and to knock at the door, saying, Lord, Lord, open unto us; and he shall answer and say unto you, I know you not whence ye are. . . . Depart from me, all ye workers of iniquity."[5]

It may appear, upon a quick look at these words, that the delaying to seek, rather than the manner of seeking, was the reason why they were not able to enter in. This, in effect, comes to the same thing. They were commanded to depart because they had been workers of iniquity. They had walked in the broad road. In other words, they had not agonized to enter in at the narrow gate. Probably they did seek before the door was shut, but that was not adequate. They did strive after the door was shut, but it was too late.

Therefore, strive now. Strive in this, your day, to enter in at the narrow gate. In order to do this, settle it in your own heart. Let it ever be uppermost in your thoughts that if you are in the broad way, you are in the way that leads to destruction. If many go with you, as sure as God is true, both they and you are headed toward hell. If you are walking as most men walk, you are walking to the bottomless pit. Are many wise, rich, mighty, or noble, traveling with you in the same way? By this, without looking any farther, you know it does not lead to life. Here is a short, plain, infallible rule, before you enter into particulars. In whatever profession you are engaged, you must be singular or be damned. The way to hell has nothing singular in it. The way to heaven is singularity all over. If you move but one step toward God, you are not as most other men are. But do not let this bother you. It is far better to stand alone than to fall into destruction. Run then, with patience, the race which is set before you. Run the race though your companions in it are but few. It will not always be so. After a little while, you will come to an innumerable company of angels. You will arrive at the general assembly and the church of the first-born. You will meet with the spirits of just men who were made perfect.

Now then, strive to enter at the narrow gate, being penetrated with the deepest sense of the inexpressible danger your soul is in, as long as you are in a broad way. You are in this danger as long as you lack poverty of spirit and all of that inward religion. It is that inward religion and poverty of spirit that the many, the rich and wise, account as madness. Strive to enter in. Be pierced with sorrow and shame for having run so long with the unthinking crowd. Remember how long you utterly neglected, if not despised, that holiness without which no man can see the Lord. Strive as if in an agony of holy fear, lest a promise made to you of entering into His rest is lost. Strive in all of the fervor of desire, with "groanings which cannot be uttered."[6] Strive by prayer without ceasing at all times and in all places. Lift up your heart to God, giving Him no rest, until you wake up in His likeness. Then you know you are satisfied in it.

Strive to enter the narrow gate not only by this agony of soul, of conviction, of sorrow, of shame, of desire, of fear, and of unceasing prayer. Strive to enter in by ordering all of your conversation correctly. Strive by walking with all of your strength in the way of God, the way of innocence, piety, and mercy. Abstain from all appearances of evil. Do all possible good to all men. Deny yourself your own will in all things, and take up your cross daily. Do this so you will be ready to enter into the kingdom of heaven.

14

False Prophets¹

"Beware of false prophets, which come to you in sheep's clothing, but inwardly they are ravening wolves. Ye shall know them by their fruits. Do men gather grapes of thorns, or figs of thistles? Even so every good tree bringeth forth good fruit; but a corrupt tree bringeth forth evil fruit. A good tree cannot bring forth evil fruit, neither can a corrupt tree bring forth good fruit. Every tree that bringeth not forth good fruit is hewn down, and cast into the fire. Wherefore by their fruits ye shall know them" (Matt. 7:15-30).

It is hardly possible to express or conceive the great numbers of people who run into destruction because they could not be persuaded to walk in the narrow way. They would not go in that way even though it was a way to everlasting salvation. We may observe this daily. This is the folly and madness of mankind. Thousands of men still rush on in the way to hell, only because it is the broad way. They walk in it themselves because others do. Because so many will perish, they will add to the number. Such is the amazing influence of example over weak, miserable

255

humans. This vast influence continually increases the inhabitants of the regions of death. It drowns numberless souls in everlasting perdition.

Every man needs to be warned against this. To protect as many as possible against this spreading contagion, God has raised up ministers. He commanded His watchmen to call out and show the people the dangers they were in. For this purpose, He sent prophets in their succeeding generations to point out the narrow way. They exhort all men not to be conformed to this world. But what if the watchmen themselves should fall into the snare themselves, against which they were to warn others? Suppose these prophets began to prophesy deceitfully? Suppose they began to cause people to err from the way? Then, what they pointed out as the way of eternal life could turn out in truth to be the way to eternal death. They would exhort others to walk as they did themselves, in the broad way, and not in the narrow way.

This is not an unheard of, or an uncommon thing. God knows it is not. The instances of this are almost innumerable. We find them in every age and nation. How terrible it is when the ministers of God turn out to be ambassadors for the devil. It is miserable when those who are commissioned to teach the way to heaven to men do in fact teach them the way to hell. These are like the locusts of Egypt. They eat up the residue that escaped and remained after the hail.[2] They devour even the residue of men who have escaped, who were not destroyed by their bad example. It is not without cause that Jesus solemnly cautions us against them. "Beware of false prophets who come to you in sheep's clothing, but inwardly are ravening wolves."

This is a caution of the greatest importance. We need to let it sink effectually into our hearts. So let us inquire,

first, who these false prophets are. Second, let us see
what appearance they put on. Third, let us learn how we
may know what they really are, notwithstanding their
good appearance.

We are first to ask who these false prophets are. It is
necessary to do this with all diligence. These same false
prophets have wrested this Scripture to their own,
though not only their own, destruction. Therefore, we
must cut off all dispute. We must not raise dust by use of
any loose, rhetorical exclamations, which deceive the
hearts of the simple. We must speak rough, plain truths,
which none who have understanding or honesty left can
deny. These truths must have the closest connection with
the whole theme of Jesus' preceding discourse. Too many
have interpreted these words out of context, without any
regard to all that went before. It is as if they bore no
relationship to the sermon in which they stand. Prophets,
as used here, are not those who foretell things to come.
They are those who speak in the name of God. They are
those men who profess to be sent by God to teach others
the way to heaven.

False prophets are those who teach a false way to
heaven. They teach a way which does not lead to it. They
do not teach the true way to heaven. The broad way is
infallibly a false way. Therefore, there is one plain and
sure rule. "They who teach men to walk in a broad way, a
way in which many walk, are false prophets."

Again, the true way to heaven is the narrow way.
Therefore, there is another plain and sure rule. "They
who do not teach men to walk in a narrow way, to be
singular, are false prophets."

We can make a more particular statement about this.
The only true way to heaven is that which was pointed out
in the preceding sermon. Therefore, they are false

prophets who do not teach men to walk in this way of Jesus.

Now, the way to heaven pointed out in the preceding sermon is the way of lowliness, mourning, meekness, and holy desire. It is a way through the love of God and our neighbor, doing good and suffering evil for Jesus' sake. They are, therefore, false prophets who teach any way other than this as the way to heaven.

It does not matter what they call that other way. They may call it faith. They may call it good works, or faith and works. It may be named repentance, or repentance, faith and new obedience. All of these are good works. If, however, under these or any other terms whatever, they teach men any way distinct from Jesus', they are properly false prophets.

Those who speak evil of this good and narrow way fall under even greater condemnation. That condemnation extends to all who teach the directly opposite way. The opposite way is the way of pride, levity, passion, worldly desires and of loving pleasure more than God. It allows unkindness to our neighbor and unconcern for good works. It ignores the suffering of evil and persecution for righteousness' sake.

Some might ask, "Why, whoever did teach this? Or, who does teach it as the way to heaven?" We answer, ten thousand wise and honorable men. Included in these are some from every denomination. These encourage the proud, the trifler, the passionate, the lover of the world, the man of pleasure, the unjust or unkind, the easy, careless, harmless, useless creature, the man who accepts no reproach for righteousness' sake to imagine he is on the way to heaven. These are false prophets in the highest sense of the word. They are traitors to both God and man. They are no other than the first-born of Satan. These are far above the ranks of ordinary cut-throats. They murder the souls of men. They are continually peopling the realms of hell. Whenever they follow the poor souls whom they have led there, "Hell from beneath is moved for thee to meet thee at thy coming."[3]

Do they come showing their true colors? By no means. If it were so, they could not destroy. You could then take alarm and flee for your lives. They put on the opposite appearance. This is the second thing to be considered. "They come to you in sheep's clothing, although inwardly they are ravening wolves."

By coming to you in sheep's clothing, it is meant that they come with an appearance of harmlessness. They come in a mild, inoffensive manner. They carry no mark or token of ill-will. Who can imagine that these quiet creatures would do any hurt to anyone? Perhaps they may not be so zealous in doing good as one might wish. However, there seems no reason to suspect that they have even the desire to do any harm. But this is not all. They come secondly, with an appearance of usefulness. Indeed, to this doing good, they are particularly called. They are set apart for this very thing. They are particularly compassionate in watching over your soul, to train you up to eternal life. That is their main business. It is to go about doing good and healing those who are oppressed by the devil. You have always been accustomed to looking upon them in this light. You see them as messengers of God, sent to bring you a blessing.

Third, they come to you with an appearance of religion. All they do is for conscience's sake. They assure you it is out of zeal for God that they are making God a liar. It is out of pure concern for pure religion that they would destroy it. All they speak is only from the love of truth. Their only fear, they say, is that the truth should suffer. They may

260 / *The Nature of the Kingdom*

also claim a great regard for the church, and a desire to defend her from all of her enemies.

Above all, they come with an appearance of love. They take all of these pains for your own good. They should not trouble themselves about you, but they have a great kindness for you. They make large professions about their good will. They will announce their concern for the danger you are in. They will speak of their earnest desire to preserve you from error. They hope to shield you from being entangled in new and mischievous doctrines. They would be very sorry to see anyone who means as well as you do, to be pushed into any extreme. They would not like to have you perplexed with strange and unintelligible ideas. They do not want you to be deluded into fanaticism. Therefore, they advise you to keep in the middle of the road. They advise you to beware of being overly religious, lest you destroy yourself.

If this is so, how then will we know them? How may we know what they really are, notwithstanding their good appearance? This is the next matter into which we must inquire. Jesus saw how necessary it was for all men to know God's prophets, however disguised. Jesus also knew how most men are unable to deduce a truth through a long train of consequences. Therefore, He gave us a short and plain rule. He gave us a rule easy to be understood by men of the most average capacity. It is a rule which is easy to be applied on all occasions. "You shall know them by their fruits." You may easily apply this rule on all occasions. Through it, you may know if any who speak in the name of God are true or false prophets. It is easy to observe what the fruits of their doctrines are as regards to themselves. Notice the effect it has had upon their own lives. Can you see if they are holy and blameless in all things? Can you tell what effect it has had upon their hearts? Observe the general tenor of their conversation and their tempers. True prophets generally appear to be holy, heavenly and divinely minded. True prophets have the mind in them which was in Jesus. True prophets are meek, lowly, patient, lovers of God and man, and zealous of good works.

You may observe the fruits of their doctrines as they appear in all those who hear and follow them. You may observe this in most, at least, though not in all. The apostles themselves did not convert all who heard them. Followers of true prophets should have a mind that was in Christ, and walk just as He walked. Did any one begin to do this after hearing these prophets teach? Were they inwardly and outwardly wicked until they heard them? If so, it is absolute proof that these are true prophets, teachers sent of God. If this effect does not result, if they do not effectually teach either themselves or others to love and serve God, it is an absolute proof that they are false prophets. God has not sent them.

This is a hard thing, and few can bear it. Jesus was aware of this. Therefore, He proves it by several clear and convincing arguments. "Do men gather grapes from thorns, or figs from thistles?" You should not expect that evil men could bring forth good fruits. You might as well expect that thorns will bring forth grapes or that figs would grow upon thistles. "Every good tree brings forth good fruit; but a corrupt tree brings forth evil fruit." Every true prophet, every teacher sent by God, brings forth good fruit of holiness. A false prophet, a teacher who has not been sent by God, brings forth only sin and wickedness. "A good tree cannot bring forth evil fruit, neither can a corrupt tree bring forth good fruit." A true prophet, a teacher sent from God, does not bring forth good fruit only sometime. He does it always. He does not do this accidentally, but by a kind of necessity. In like manner, a false prophet not sent by God does not bring forth evil fruit accidentally or occasionally. He brings forth evil fruit always out of necessity. "Every tree that does not bring forth good fruit is hewn down and cast into the fire." This will infallibly be the lot of these prophets who do not bring forth good fruit. It is the lot for those who do not save those from sin and do not bring sinners to repentance. Therefore, this stands as an eternal rule, "By their fruits shall you know them."

They who bring the proud, passionate, unmerciful, lovers of the world to be lowly and gentle lovers of God—they are true prophets. They are sent from God, and He therefore confirms their word. On the other hand, they whose hearers remain as unrighteous as before, are not sent by God. The false prophets were false to the ground, without a miracle of grace. They and their hearers together will fall into the bottomless pit. Beware of false prophets. Although they come in sheep's clothing, they are like ravening wolves. They not only destroy and devour the flock, they tear them into pieces. They will not, and cannot, lead into the way of heaven. How could they, when they do not know it themselves. Beware they do not turn you out of the narrow way, and cause you to lose what you have gained.

Perhaps some will ask, "If there is such a danger in hearing them, ought we to listen to them at all?" That is an important question which deserves the deepest consideration. It ought not be answered but on the calmest reflection and deliberate thought. There are many reasons which would support either choice. These readily occur and incline one to say, "Do not listen to them." Yet, what Jesus said concerning false prophets of his own time seems to imply the contrary. "Then spake

Jesus to the multitude, and to his disciples, Saying, The scribes and the Pharisees sit in Moses' seat: All therefore whatsoever they bid you observe, that observe and do; but do not ye after their works: for they say, and do not."[4] The scribes and Pharisees were the ordinary teachers of the church. They were false prophets in the highest sense. Jesus showed this during the whole course of His ministry. He does it in these very words, "They say, and do not." Therefore, by their fruits, His disciples could not but know them. They were in open view to all men. Accordingly, Jesus warns them again and again to beware of those false prophets. And yet, Jesus did not forbid them to hear even those. In effect, He commanded them to do so in these words, "All therefore whatsoever they bid you observe, that observe and do." Unless they heard them, they could not know, or observe, whatever they told them to do. Here then, Jesus gives a plain direction. He gives it to His apostles and all of the multitudes. In some circumstances, it is all right to hear even false prophets who are known and acknowledged to be so.

Perhaps some will say this is a false understanding. They might say that Jesus only directed them to hear the scribes and Pharisees when they read Scripture to the congregation. The truth is that when they read Scripture they generally expounded upon it also. There is no intimation here that they were to hear one but not the other. Contrarily, the very terms are "all things whatsoever they bid you observe," excludes any such limitation.

Again, the administration of the communion sacrament is on occasion under the ministry of false prophets. To direct men not to hear them would be, in effect, to cut them off from the ordinances of God. But we dare not do this. The validity of the ordinance does not depend upon the goodness of him who administers it. It depends upon the faithfulness of Him who ordained it and who will meet us in His appointed ways. Therefore, on this account we cannot say do not hear the false prophets. Even through men who are under a curse themselves God can and does give us His blessing. For the bread broken at communion, we have experimentally known to be communion of the body of Christ. The cup which God blessed, even if by unhallowed lips, was to us the communion of the blood of Christ. Therefore, in any particular case, wait upon God by humble and earnest prayer. Then act according to the best light you have. Act according to what you are persuaded, upon the whole, will be most for your spiritual advantage. Take care that you do not judge rationally. Do not lightly think any to be false prophets. When you have full proof that someone is, see that no anger or contempt has any place in your heart. In the presence and the fear of God, determine for yourself what course you should follow. If by experience you find that hearing them hurts your soul, do not hear them. Quietly refrain, and hear only those who profit your spiritual growth. If, on the other hand, you find it does not hurt your soul, then continue to listen to them. Only take heed as to how you hear. Beware of them and their doctrines. Listen with fear and trembling, lest you might be deceived. Take care that you do not fall, like them, into strong delusion. You can see how continually they mingle truth and lies. It is too easy for you to take in both together. Hear with continual and fervent prayer to Jesus, who alone teaches man wisdom. And see that whatever you hear you judge according to the Scriptures. Do not receive anything untried until it is weighed in the balance of the sanctuary. Do not believe anything they say, unless it is clearly confirmed by plain passages of holy Scripture. Wholly reject whatever differs from Scripture. Ignore whatever is not confirmed by it. In particular, reject with the utmost vehemence, whatever is described as the way of salvation, if it differs in any part from the way Jesus has marked out in the foregoing discourse.

We cannot conclude without pointing a few words to those who are false prophets. O you false prophets! O you dry bones! For once hear the word of the Lord. How long will you mislead in the name of God, claiming that God speaks through you? You claim this when God has not spoken by you. How long will you pervert the right ways of the Lord, substituting darkness for light and light for darkness? How long will you teach the way of death and call it the way of life? How long will you deliver to Satan the souls of those whom you profess to bring to God?

"Woe unto you, scribes and Pharisees, hypocrites! for ye shut up the kingdom of heaven against men; for ye neither go in yourselves, neither suffer ye them that are entering to go in."[5] Those who strive to enter at the narrow gate, you call back into the broad way. Those who have only gone one step in the way of God, you devilishly caution against going too far. Those who just begin to hunger and thirst after righteousness, you warn against being too righteous. Thus, you cause them to stumble at the very threshold. They fall and rise no more. Why do you do this? What profit is there in their blood, when they go down into hell? It is a miserable profit to you. They shall perish in their iniquity, but their blood is on your hands.

Where are your eyes? Where is your understanding? You have deceived others, and you have deceived yourself also. Who required this from you, to teach a way which you never knew yourself? Are you given up to so strong a delusion that you not only teach, but believe your error? Is it possible to believe that God has sent you, and you are His messenger? If the Lord sent you, the work of the Lord would prosper in your hands. As the Lord lives, if you were His messenger, He would confirm your words. But the work of the Lord does not prosper in your hands. You do not bring sinners to repentance. The Lord does not confirm your word, for you save no souls from death.

You cannot possibly evade the force of Jesus' words which are so full, strong, and express. You cannot evade knowing yourself by your fruits. Evil fruits come of evil trees. It cannot be otherwise. Men do not gather grapes from thorns nor figs from thistles. Take this to yourselves, to whomever it belongs. O barren trees, you cumber the ground. "Every good tree brings forth good fruit." There is no exception. From this, understand that you are not a good tree for you do not bring forth good fruit. "But a corrupt tree brings forth evil fruit." This is what you have done from the beginning. Your speaking as the word from God has only confirmed others who heard you in their wrong ways and works of the devil. Take warning of Him in whose name you speak. Be warned before the sentence He has pronounced takes place. "Every tree which does not bring forth good fruit is hewn down and cast into the fire."

Do not harden your hearts. Too long you have shut your eyes against the light. Open them now before it is too late. Open them before you are cast into outer darkness. Do not let any worldly considerations lead you. Eternity is at stake. You have run a race before you were sent. Go no farther. Do not continue to mislead yourselves and those who hear you. You have no fruit of your labors. And why is this? It is because the Lord is not with you. You cannot go into this warfare without Him. Humble yourself before Him. Cry to Him out of the dust so He may quicken your soul. Ask Him to give you the faith that works by love. It is a faith which is lowly, meek, pure, and merciful, zealous of good works, rejoicing in reproach and persecution for righteousness' sake. Then the Spirit of glory and Christ will rest upon you. Then it will show that God has sent you. Then you shall indeed do the work of an evangelist and make full proof of your ministry. Then the Word of God in your mouth will be a hammer that breaks the rocks to pieces. You will then be known by your fruits that you are a prophet of the Lord. It will be shown by the children of God who has sent you. Then having turned many to righteousness, you shall shine as the stars shine, forever and ever.

15

The Chosen and the Unchosen[1]

"Not every one that saith unto me, Lord, Lord, shall enter into the kingdom of heaven; but only he that doeth the will of my Father which is in heaven. Many will say to me, in that day, Lord, Lord, have we not prophesied in thy name? and in thy name have cast out devils? and in thy name done many wonderful works? And then will I profess unto them, I never knew you: depart from me, ye that work iniquity.

"Therefore whosoever heareth these sayings of mine, and doeth them, I will liken him unto a wise man, which built his house upon a rock: And the rain descended, and the floods came, and the winds blew, and beat upon that house; and it fell not: for it was founded upon a rock. And every one that heareth these sayings of mine, and doeth them not, shall be likened unto a foolish man, which built his house upon the sand: And the rain descended, and the floods came, and the winds blew, and beat upon that house; and it fell: and great was the fall of it" (Matt. 7:21-27).

At this point in His sermon, Jesus had declared the

269

whole counsel of God regarding the way to salvation. Also, He had observed the chief hindrances of those who wish to walk in the way of salvation. He now closes the whole sermon with these important words. It is as if He were setting His seal to His prophecy. He is impressing His whole authority on the sermon He has delivered so that it might stand firm through all generations.

Jesus wanted none to ever believe there could be any other way than this. So He said that anyone who heard the sermon and did not follow it was headed for final destruction.

To thoroughly understand Jesus' meaning, we have three things to consider. First, let us consider the case of him who builds his house on sand. Second, we will see the wisdom of him who builds his house on rock. Third, we will conclude the chapter with a practical application.

First is the case of him who builds his house upon the sand. Concerning him, Jesus said, "Not every one that saith unto me, Lord, Lord shall enter into the kingdom of heaven." This is a decree which cannot change. It stands fast forever and ever. It is, therefore, important for us to thoroughly understand these words. Now what are we to understand by that expression, "That says unto me, 'Lord, Lord' "? It undoubtedly means anyone who thinks of going to heaven by any way other than that which Jesus has described. It therefore implies all good words and verbal religion. This is the lowest degree of His meaning. It includes whatever creeds we may rehearse. It includes whatever professions of faith we make, and whatever number of prayers we may repeat. It includes all thanksgiving we read or say to God. We may speak good of His name. We may declare His loving kindness to everyone. We may talk of His mighty acts and tell of His salvation every day. By comparing spiritual things with

Scripture, we may show the meaning of the Scriptures. We may explain the mysteries of His kingdom, which have been hidden from the beginnings of the world. We may speak with the tongues of angels, rather than men, concerning the great mysteries of God. We may proclaim to sinners, "Behold the Lamb of God who takes away the sin of the world!" We may even do this with a measure of the power of God and a demonstration of the Holy Spirit. Through our efforts, men may be saved from death and a multitude of sins. And yet, it is very possible that this is no more than saying "Lord, Lord." It is possible that after we have successfully witnessed to others, still we ourselves may be castaways. We may, by the grace of God, snatch souls from hell and yet drop into it when we have finished. We may bring others to the kingdom of heaven, and yet never enter ourselves.

Second, the saying of "Lord, Lord," may imply the doing of no harm. We may abstain from every presumptuous sin and every kind of outward wickedness. We may refrain from all of those ways of acting or speaking which are forbidden by God. We may be able to say to all of those among whom we live, "Which of you can accuse me of a sin?" We may have a conscience void of external offence toward God or man. We may be clear of all uncleanness, ungodliness and unrighteousness, as to any outward act. This is what Paul meant when he testified concerning himself. He said that touching the righteousness of the law, that is outward righteousness, he was blameless.[2] But yet we are not saved by this. This still is no more than saying, "Lord, Lord." If we go no farther than this, we shall never enter into the kingdom of heaven.

Third, the saying of, "Lord, Lord," may imply what are usually called good works. A man may attend communion and hear many excellent sermons. He may omit no opportunity of partaking in all of the other ordinances of God. He may do good to his neighbor and give bread to the hungry. He may cover the naked with clothes. He may be zealous of good works, and even give all of his goods to feed the poor. He may do all of this with a desire to please God, and a real belief that he does please God. Even with all of this, he still may have no part in the glory which is to be revealed. If any man wonders at this, let him understand that he is a stranger to the whole religion of Jesus. In particular, he does not understand that perfect portraiture of it which Jesus has set before us in this Sermon on the Mount. How far short is all of this of the righteousness and true holiness which Jesus had described in the sermon. How widely distant are good works from that inward kingdom of heaven which is now open in the believing soul. The kingdom is first sown in the heart as a grain of mustard seed. Afterwards it grows and puts forth great branches, on which grow all of the fruits of righteousness, every good temper, and word, and work.

Jesus had clearly declared, frequently, that none who do not have this kingdom of God within them shall enter the kingdom of heaven. Jesus well knew that many would not understand and accept this teaching. Therefore, He confirmed it yet again. He said that many—not a few only, not a rare or uncommon case but many—"shall say to me on that day, 'Lord, Lord.' "

They will say, "We have said many prayers. We have spoken your praise. We have refrained from evil. We have exercised ourselves in doing good. Even more abundantly than this, we have prophesied in your name. In your name we have cast out demons. In your name we have done many wonderful works. We have declared your will to mankind. We have showed sinners the way to peace and glory. And we have done all of this in your name, according to the truth of your gospel. We have done it by your authority, who did confirm the Word with the Holy Spirit sent down from heaven. For in or by your name, by the power of the Word and your Spirit, we have cast out devils from souls long afflicted. And in your name and by your power, which is not our own, we have done many wonderful works, so that even the dead heard the voice of Jesus speaking through us and lived."

"And then will I profess unto them, I never knew you." No, He did not know them even when they were casting out devils in His name. Even then He did not know them as His own. Their hearts were not right toward God. They were not meek or lowly. They were not lovers of God and of all mankind. They were not renewed in the image of God. They were not holy as Jesus is holy.

"Depart from me, ye that work iniquity." Notwithstanding all of this, they were transgressors of Jesus' law. Jesus' law is of holy and perfect love.

To put this beyond all possibility of contradiction, Jesus confirms it by an opposite comparison. He says, "Every one that heareth these sayings of mine, and doeth them not, shall be likened unto a foolish man, which built his house upon the sand: And the rain descended, and the floods came, and winds blew, and beat upon that house; and it fell: and great was the fall of it." This will surely happen, sooner or later, on the soul of every man. There will be floods of outward afflictions or inward temptations. There will be storms of anger, pride, fear or desire. Any who rest in anything short of that religion which Jesus has described, will receive this bitter portion. And greater will their fall be, because they heard those things and did not do them.

Next, we are to look at the wisdom of him who does these things. It is he who builds his house upon a rock. He, indeed, is wise. He does the will of God who is in heaven. He is truly wise whose righteousness exceeds the righteousness of the scribes and Pharisees.[3]

He is poor in spirit, knowing himself even as God knows him. He sees and feels all of his sin and all of his guilt. He knows this until it is washed away by the atoning blood of Jesus. He is conscious of his lost estate, of the wrath of God abiding upon him. He is aware of his utter inability to help himself, until he is filled with peace and joy in the Holy Spirit. Then he is meek and gentle, and patient toward all men. He never returns evil for evil, or railing for railing. On the contrary, he is always blessing, until he overcomes evil with good. His soul is thirsty for nothing on earth but only for God, the living God. He has springs of love for all mankind. He is ready to lay down his life for his enemies. He loves the Lord his God with all of his heart, all of his mind and soul and strength.

He alone shall enter into the kingdom of heaven who is of this spirit. He does good to all men. For this reason he is despised and rejected by all men. He is hated, reproached and persecuted. He rejoices and is glad, knowing in whom he has believed. He is assured that these light, momentary afflictions will work out for him an eternal weight of glory. How truly wise is this man. He knows himself. He is an everlasting spirit which came forth from God. This spirit was sent down into a house of clay, not to do his own will, but the will of God who sent him. He knows the world. It is a place in which he is to pass a few days or years, not as an inhabitant, but as a stranger and sojourner. It is a way station of his way to the everlasting habitations. Accordingly, he uses the world by not abusing it, and in knowing the fashion of it passes away. He knows God. God is his Father and his friend, the parent of all good. God is the center of the spirits and all flesh, the sole happiness of all intelligent beings. He sees, clearer than the light of the noonday sun, that this is the end of man. It is to glorify Him who made him for himself, and to love and to enjoy God forever. With equal clearness, he sees the means to that end, to the enjoyment of that glory. The means to that end is now to know, to love, to imitate God and to believe in Jesus Christ whom He has sent.

He is a wise man, even in God's account, for he builds his house upon a rock. He builds it upon the Rock of ages, the everlasting Rock, the Lord Jesus. Fitly, Jesus is called the Rock of ages. He does not change. He is the same yesterday, today and forever.[4] Those men of God of old, and the Apostle Paul bear witness to this fact. "Thou, Lord, in the beginning, hast laid the foundation of the earth; and the heavens are the works of thine hands. They shall perish; but thou remainest; and they all shall wax old as doth a garment; And as a vesture shalt thou fold them up, and they shall be changed: but thou art the same, and thy years shall not fail."[5]

Therefore, the man who builds upon Him is wise. He lays Jesus as his only foundation. He builds only upon Jesus' blood and righteousness. He attends upon what Jesus has done and suffered for us. On this cornerstone he fixes his faith, and rests the whole weight of his soul upon it. He is taught of God to say, "Lord, I have sinned! I deserve hell; but I am saved freely by your grace, through the redemption that is in Jesus Christ. The life I now live, I live by faith in Him who loved me, and gave himself for me.[6] The life I now live, namely a divine, heavenly life, is a life which is hid with Christ in God. I now live even in the flesh a life of love. It is a life of pure love, both to God and to man. It is a life of holiness and happiness, praising God and doing all things to His glory."

Yet, let not such a person think that he shall never see problems again. Let him not imagine he is now out of reach of temptation. It still remains for God to prove the grace which He has given. He shall be tried as gold in the fire. He shall be tempted no less than those who do not know God. Perhaps he will be tempted even more, for Satan will not fail to try to the uttermost those whom he is not able to destroy. Accordingly, the rain will impetuously descend. It will descend only at such times and in such manner as seems good, not to Satan, but to God, whose kingdom rules over all. The floods or torrents will come. They will lift up their waves and rage horridly. But of them also the Lord who sits above the floodwaters will remain king forever. God will say how far the floods can come. Then He will stop them. He will stay the proud waves of persecution and temptation. The winds will blow and beat upon that house, as though they would tear it from the foundation; however, they cannot prevail. It will not fall. It is founded upon a rock. It is built upon Christ by faith and by love. Therefore, it shall not be cast down. He who builds there shall not fear even though earth is moved and the hills are carried into the middle of the sea. Though the waters of the sea rage and swell, and the mountains shake at the tempest of the same, it still dwells under the defense of God, who is most high and above all. He is safe under the shadow of the Almighty.

It does greatly concern every person to practically apply these things to himself. Every man should diligently examine upon what foundation he is building. Is it on a rock, or on the sand? How deeply you are concerned to inquire, "What is the foundation of my hope? On what do I build my expectations of entering into the kingdom of heaven? Is it not build upon the sand? Is it built upon my orthodox or right opinions, which by a great abuse of words I have called faith? Am I depending upon my having a set of opinions which I suppose to be more rational or scriptural than others have?"

Alas, what madness is this. Surely this is building on the sand, or rather on the froth of the sea. Rather, question what you are doing. Say, "Am I not again building my hope on what is equally unable to support it? Am I trusting upon belonging to a particular denomination, reformed after the true scriptural model, on believing that it is blessed with the purest doctrine and the most original liturgy, depending upon it being the most apostolic form of government?" These are many good reasons for praising God. They are good helps to holiness. However, they are not holiness itself. If they separate us from holiness, they will profit us nothing. They will leave us the more without excuse, and the more exposed to a greater damnation. Therefore, if we build our hope upon this foundation, we are still building on the sand.

We cannot, we dare not, rest here. Upon what next will we build the hope of salvation? Will it be upon innocence? Will it be upon doing no harm, the not wronging of anyone? Well, this plea could be true. We need to be just in all of our dealings and be downright honest men. We need to pay every man his own, and not cheat nor extort. We ought to act fairly with all mankind, and to have a conscience toward God. We are not to live in any known sin. Thus far, all is well. But it is still not the thing. We can go this far, and yet never come to heaven. When all of this harmlessness flows from the right principle, it is the least part of the religion of Jesus. But if it does not flow from a right principle, it has no part in His religion. So, in grounding the hope of salvation on this, we are still building upon the sand.

Can you say that he goes farther even than this? Is added to all of this of doing no harm the attending of the ordinances of God? Is added to this the partaking of communion at all opportunities, and the use of public and private prayer? Is added also fasting, and hearing and searching the Scriptures, and meditation upon them? These things also we all ought to do, from the time we first set our faces toward heaven. Yet these things are nothing standing alone. They are nothing without the weightier matters of the law. Many have forgotten those, at least they do not experience them. These are faith, mercy and the love of God. They include holiness of heart, which is heaven opened in the soul. Therefore, without these, one is still building upon the sand.

Over and above all of this, are we zealous of good works? Do we, as we have time, do good to all men? Do we feed the hungry, and clothe the naked, and visit the fatherless and widowed in their afflictions? Do we visit those who are sick, and relieve them who are in prison? Do we take in strangers? Friends, we must come up higher than this!

Do we prophesy in the name of Jesus? Do we preach the truth as it is in Jesus? And does the influence of His Spirit attend our words and make them the power of God for salvation? Does Jesus enable us to bring sinners from darkness to light, from the power of Satan to God? Then we must go and learn what we have so often taught. "By grace are ye saved through faith."[7] "Not by works of righteousness which we have done, but according to his mercy he saved us."[8] Learn to hang naked upon the cross of Christ, counting all that you have done as worthless. Apply to Him just as in the spirit of the dying thief, as the harlot with her seven devils. Otherwise you are still on the sand, and after saving others you will lose your own soul.

But what does it profit, if a man says he has faith and has not works? Can that faith save him? Oh, no! True faith must have works which produce inward and outward holiness. It must stamp the whole image of God upon the heart and purify as He is pure. Faith which does not produce the whole religion described in the Sermon on the Mount is not the faith of the gospel. It is not the Christian faith, the faith which leads to glory. Beware of this, above all other snares of the devil. Beware of resting on unholy, unsaving faith. If you put your trust on this, you are lost forever. You are building your house upon the sand. Then when the rains come, and the floods come, it will surely fall, and great will be the fall of it.

Now, therefore, build upon the rock. By the grace of God, know yourself. Know and feel that you are by nature a child of wrath, a son of disobedience. Know that you have been heaping sin upon sin ever since you could discern good from evil. Admit yourself guilty for eternal death. Renounce all hope of being able to save yourself. Let it be your hope to be washed in His blood and purified by His Spirit. Be saved by Jesus, who bore all of your sins upon His body on the cross.

If you know He has taken away your sins, so much the more abase yourself before Him. Remain in a continual sense of total dependence upon Him for every good thought, word and work. Know your total inability to any good unless He waters you with grace at every moment.

Now, weep for your sins, and mourn after God, until He turns your heaviness into joy. Then, weep with them who weep. Weep for those who cannot do it for themselves. Mourn for the sins and miseries of mankind. See before your eyes the immense ocean of eternity, without a bottom or shore, which has already swallowed up millions and millions of men. It is still gaping to devour men that yet remain. See here the house of God eternal in the heavens, and there hell, and destruction without a covering. Then from this, learn the importance of every moment which appears and then is gone forever.

Now, add to your seriousness a meekness in your wisdom. Hold an even scale to all of your passions. In particular, be concerned as to your anger, sorrow and fear. Calmly acquiesce to whatever is the will of God. Learn in whatever state you are in to be content. Be mild to the good. Be gentle toward all men. Be especially gentle toward the evil and unthankful. Beware, not only of outward expressions of anger, but of every inward emotion contrary to love, even though it goes no farther than your heart. Be angry at sin as an affront against God. Love the sinner still as Jesus did when He looked around about the Pharisees with anger, and grieved for the hardness of their hearts. He was grieved at the sinners and angry at the sin. Thus, be angry and sin not. Hunger and thirst, not for the meat that perishes, but for that which endures for everlasting life. Trample the world underfoot along with the things of the world. Ignore all of those riches, honors and pleasures. What is the world to you? Let the dead bury the dead, but you follow after the image of God. Beware of quenching that thirst, if it is already excited in your soul, by what is commonly called religion. It is a poor, dull farce, a religion of form, of outside show, which leaves the heart still cleaving to the dust, as earthly and sensual as ever. Let nothing satisfy you but the power of godliness. Seek a religion that is

Spirit and life, the dwelling in God and God in you. Continue to yearn to become an inhabitant of eternity, entering it by the blood sprinkling. Then, you will be sitting in heavenly places with Jesus.

You can do all things through Christ who strengthens you.[9] Therefore, be as merciful as your Father in heaven is merciful. Love your neighbor as yourself. Love friends and enemies the same as you love your own soul. Let your love be long-suffering and patient toward all men. Let it be kind, soft and benign. Let it inspire you with the most amiable sweetness and the most fervent and tender affection. Let it rejoice in the truth wherever that is found. Know that truth which is after godliness. Enjoy whatever brings glory to God, and promotes peace and goodwill among men. In love, cover all things. Speak nothing but good of the dead and the absent. Believe all things which may in any way tend to clear your neighbor's reputation. Hope all things which are in his favor. Endure all things, triumphing over all opposition. True love never fails, either in time or in eternity.

Now, be pure of heart, purified through faith of every unholy affection. Cleanse yourself from all filthiness of flesh and spirit. Seek perfect holiness in the fear of God. Be, through the power of His grace, purified from pride, by poverty of spirit. Be cleansed from anger and from every unkind and turbulent passion, by meekness and mercifulness. Be released from every desire except to please and enjoy God, through hungering and thirsting after righteousness. Now, love the Lord your God with all of your heart and with all of your strength.

In a word, let your religion be the religion of the heart. Let it lie deep in your inmost soul. Be small, average and common in your own sight. Be amazed and humbled by the love of God which is in Jesus. Be serious. Let the

282 / *The Nature of the Kingdom*

whole stream of your thoughts, words, and actions flow from the deepest conviction that you stand on the edge of the great gulf, you and all other men, just ready to drop in. You will drop in either to everlasting glory, or everlasting burning. Let your soul be filled with mildness, gentleness, patience and long-suffering toward all men. Let all that is in you thirst for God, the living God, while longing to wake up in His likeness and to be satisfied with it. Be a lover of God and of all mankind. In this spirit, do and suffer all things. Thus, show your faith by your works. Thus, you will be doing the will of your Father who is in heaven. As you now walk with God on earth, you shall reign with Him in glory.

Footnotes and Scripture References

Chapter 1

1. Wesley, "The Spirit of Bondage and of Adoption," *Forty-four Sermons*, Sermon IX
2. Rom. 8:15.
3. Eph. 5:14.
4. Col. 3:3.
5. Matt. 5:18.
6. Matt. 7:21.
7. Prov. 24:16.
8. 1 John 3:15.
9. Matt. 5:22.
10. Matt. 5:28.
11. Prov. 18:14.
12. Rom. 7:24.
13. Rom. 7:9.
14. Rom. 7:12.
15. Rom. 7:15.
16. Exod. 33:19.
17. Gal. 2:20.
18. 1 John 3:8.
19. Matt. 22:37.

Chapter 2

1. Wesley, "Satan's Devices," *Forty-four Sermons*, Sermon XXXVII.
2. Rom. 14:17.
3. Matt. 22:37.
4. 1 Thess. 5:16-18
5. 1 John 4:17.
6. 1 John 1:7.
7. 2 Cor. 7:1.
8. 1 John 3:3.
9. Matt. 6:10.
10. Col. 3:17.
11. 2 Cor. 6:14.
12. Phil. 3:14.
13. Acts 3:19.
14. 1 Cor. 3:11.
15. Rom. 3:24.
16. Matt. 12:33.
17. Phil. 2:5.
18. Rom. 6:2; 1 Cor. 15:34.
19. Phil. 3:10.
20. Heb. 12:14.
21. Rom. 8:2.
22. 1 Tim. 6:12.
23. Isa. 35:3; Heb. 12:12.
24. 1 John 4:19.
25. 2 Cor. 4:4; Eph. 2:2, 6:12; John 12:31
26. Heb. 10:36.
27. Heb. 3:6.
28. Rom. 8:21.
29. Rev. 2:10; John 1:12.
30. Heb. 12:2.
31. 2 Pet. 2:21.
32. Rom. 3:4.
33. 1 Thess. 5:24.
34. Col. 1:23.
35. Ps. 68:2.
36. Phil. 3:9; Eph. 2:8; Titus 3:5.
37. Rom. 3:24.
38. John 3:16.
39. Phil. 4:6.
40. Rev. 3:11.
41. 2 Tim. 1:6.
42. 1 John 2:1.
43. Gal. 2:20.
44. Job 19:25.

45. Eph. 1:7.
46. Phil. 3:14.
47. Heb. 12:22.
48. Rev. 22:4, 5.
49. Col. 1:12.
50. Rom. 13:11; Heb. 10:37.

51. 2 Cor. 1:3-7.
52. 1 Cor. 12:26.
53. Phil. 3:12.
54. 2 Pet. 1:5-7; 2 Cor. 7:1.
55. 2 Pet. 1:11.

Chapter 3
1. Wesley, "Upon Our Lord's Sermon on the Mount, Discourse I," *Forty-four Sermons*, Sermon XVI.

2. Matt. 4:23.
3. Matt. 4:25.
4. Deut. 18:19.
5. Acts 3:23.
6. Matt. 7:29.

7. 1 Tim. 6:10.
8. Rom. 1:18 ff.
9. Rom. 8:35-39.
10. John 16:19, 20.
11. John 16:21, 22.

Chapter 4
1. Wesley, "Upon Our Lord's Sermon on the Mount, Discourse II," *Forty-four Sermons*, Sermon XVII.

2. Luke 22:42.
3. Matt. 5:21 ff.
4. Mark 3:5.
5. Matt. 5:23, 24.
6. Matt. 5:26.

7. 1 Cor. 13:1-3.
8. Seneca.
9. Exod. 32:31 ff.
10. Rom. 9:3.
11. Acts 15:39.

Chapter 5
1. Wesley, "Upon Our Lord's Sermon on the Mount, Discourse III," *Forty-four Sermons*, Sermon XVIII.

2. Matt. 5:27.
3. Matt. 5:28.
4. Matt. 5:29.
5. Matt. 5:30.
6. Matt. 5:31, 32.
7. Matt. 5:34-37.
8. Matt. 26:63, 64.
9. Heb. 6:17.
10. Rom. 1:9.
11. 2 Cor. 1:23.
12. Phil. 1:8.

13. Heb. 6:16.
14. Gal. 4:29.
15. 2 Tim. 3:12.
16. 1 John 3:13, 14.
17. John 15:18 ff.
18. Luke 12:51.
19. 2 Tim. 2:12.
20. Matt. 5:38, 39.
21. Matt. 18:22.
22. Matt. 5:46.
23. Matt. 5:48.

Chapter 6
1. Wesley, "Upon Our Lord's Sermon on the Mount, Discourse IV," *Forty-four Sermons*, Sermon XIX.

2. 1 Cor. 5:9.
3. 1 Cor. 5:11.
4. 2 Thess. 3:15.
5. John 15:2, 5, 6.
6. Heb. 6:4-6 RSV.
7. Ps. 51:16.
8. Rom. 12:1.

9. 1 Cor. 12:31 ff.
10. 1 Cor. 14:1.
11. 1 Cor. 12:31.
12. John 4:24.
13. Prov. 26:11; 2 Pet. 2:22.
14. Eccles. 11:6.
15. Eccles. 11:1.

Chapter 7
1. Wesley, "Upon Our Lord's Sermon on the Mount, Discourse V," *Forty-four Sermons*, Sermon XV.
2. Acts 15:5.
3. Acts 15:24.
4. Acts 15:28.
5. Col. 2:14.
6. Jer. 31:33; Heb. 8:
7. Luke 23:34.
8. Luke 22:48.
9. Eph. 2:8, 9.
10. Acts 16:31.

11. Acts 23:6.
12. Acts 26:5.
13. Luke 18:10-14.
14. Luke 18:9.
15. Acts 24:16.
16. Acts 23:1.
17. Matt. 7:12.
18. 1 John 3:8.
19. Phil. 4:13.

Chapter 8
1. Wesley, "Upon our Lord's Sermon on the Mount, Discourse VI," *Forty-four Sermons*, Sermon XXI.
2. Luke 11:2.
3. Rom. 8:15; Gal. 4:6.
4. 1 John 4:19.
5. Ps. 145:9.
6. 1 John 4:11.
7. John 3:16.
8. Rom. 11:33.
9. Communion Service, Book of Common Prayer, Church of England.

10. Rev. 1:8; 21:6; 22:13.
11. Exod. 3:14.
12. 2 Cor. 10:5.
13. Rom. 11:25.
14. Job 25:5.
15. John 6:27.
16. Matt. 18:28.
17. Rom. 8:1.
18. Rom. 8:4.
19. James 1:12.

Chapter 9
1. Wesley, "Upon Our Lord's Sermon on the Mount, Discourse VII," *Forty-four Sermons*, Sermon XXII.
2. 1 Kings 18:28.
3. Luke 9:56.
4. Deut. 9:18; 1 Kings 19:8; Matt. 4:2.
5. Dan. 1:8, 12.
6. Lev. 23:27-29.
7. Zech. 8:19.

8. Epiphanius, (ca. 315-403) became the Archbishop of Constantia, capital of Cyprus. He wrote extensively against various heresies. In addition, he is credited with compiling a list of 292 Old Testament Scriptures which were confirmed and completed by the facts of Jesus' life as reported in the Gospels.

9. 2 Chron. 20:1-3.
10. Jer. 36:9.
11. 1 Sam. 28:15, 20.
12. Acts 27:33.
13. 2 Sam. 1:12.
14. Acts 9:9.
15. Matt. 8:25.
16. 2 Cor. 7:11.
17. 1 Kings 21:29.
18. Dan. 9:16-19.
19. Jon. 3:4 ff.
20. Judg. 20:26 ff.
21. 1 Sam. 7:10.
22. Ezra 8:21.
23. Neh. 1:4-11.
24. Acts 13:1-3.
25. Acts 14:23.
26. Matt. 17:19 ff.
27. Joel 2:12-19.
28. Joel 2:25.
29. Isa. 58:5.
30. Isa. 58:3.
31. 2 Cor. 7:9 ff.
32. Acts 10:4 ff.
33. Isa. 58:6 ff.

Chapter 10
1. Wesley, "Upon our Lord's Sermon on the Mount, Discourse VIII," *Forty-four Sermons*, Sermon XXIII.
2. Ps. 36:9.
3. 2 Cor. 4:6.
4. John 14:16-26.
5. Prov. 4:18.
6. 2 Cor. 3:18.
7. Eph. 2:8.
8. Eccles. 11:7.
9. Rom. 13:8.
10. 1 Tim. 5:8.
11. Matt. 19:23 ff.
12. 1 Tim. 6:10.
13. Horace, Epistles 1.2, 52.
14. Ecclesiasticus 41:1.
15. Luke 12:20.
16. 1 Cor. 15:55, 57.
17. William Law, (1686-1761) *A Serious Call to a Devout and Holy Life.* (London: Printed for William Innys, 1729), cli. vi. pp. 82-84.
18. Ibid., p. 81.
19. Prov. 19:17.
20. Matt. 25:40.
21. Matt. 10:8.
22. Acts 2:44; 4:32.

Chapter 11
1. Wesley, "Upon our Lord's Sermon on the Mount, Discourse IX," *Forty-four Sermons*, Sermon XXIV.
2. 2 Kings 17:33 ff.
3. 2 Kings 17:38, 39.
4. 2 Cor. 10:5.
5. Rev. 19:6.
6. Rom. 10:3.
7. Rom. 10:4.
8. John 19:30.
9. Phil. 3:8.
10. Phil. 3:9.
11. Luke 16:10.
12. Matt. 25:29, 30.

Chapter 12
1. Wesley, "Upon our Lord's Sermon on the Mount, Discourse X," *Forty-four Sermons*, Sermon XXV.
2. Luke 9:23.
3. John 7:51.
4. Seneca.
5. Matt. 18:15-17.
6. James 4:2.
7. Luke 11:9-13.
8. Matt. 7:12.
9. Alexander Severus, ca. A.D. 222-235.

Chapter 13
1. Wesley, "Upon Our Lord's Sermon on the Mount, Discourse XI," *Forty-four Sermons*, Sermon XXVI.
2. Matt. 7:15-20.
3. Acts 3:6.
4. Luke 13:24 ff.
5. Luke 18:25 ff.
6. Rom. 8:26.

Chapter 14
1. Wesley, "Upon our Lord's Sermon on the Mount, Discourse XII," *Forty-four Sermons*, Sermon XXVII.
2. Exod. 10:5.
3. Isa. 14:9.
4. Matt. 23:1-3.
5. Matt. 15:14; 23:13.

Chapter 15
1. Wesley, "Upon our Lord's Sermon on the Mount, Discourse XIII," *Forty-four Sermons*, Sermon XXVIII.
2. Phil. 3:6.
3. Matt. 5:20.
4. Heb. 13:8.
5. Heb. 1:10-12.
6. Gal. 2:20.
7. Eph. 2:8-9.
8. Titus 3:5.
9. Phil. 4:13.